For my family and my students

ITALY AND THE ISLAMIC WORLD

ITALY AND THE ISLAMIC WORLD

From Caesar to Mussolini

Ali Humayun Akhtar

EDINBURGH
University Press

Edinburgh University Press is one of the leading university presses in the UK. We publish academic books and journals in our selected subject areas across the humanities and social sciences, combining cutting-edge scholarship with high editorial and production values to produce academic works of lasting importance. For more information visit our website: edinburghuniversitypress.com

© Ali Humayun Akhtar, 2024

Edinburgh University Press Ltd
13 Infirmary Street
Edinburgh EH1 1LT

Typeset in 11/15 EB Garamond by
IDSUK (DataConnection) Ltd, and
printed and bound by CPI Group (UK) Ltd, Croydon, CR0 4YY

A CIP record for this book is available from the British Library

ISBN 978 1 3995 1961 8 (hardback)
ISBN 978 1 3995 1962 5 (paperback)
ISBN 978 1 3995 1963 2 (webready PDF)
ISBN 978 1 3995 1964 9 (epub)

The right of Ali Humayun Akhtar to be identified as author of this work has been asserted in accordance with the Copyright, Designs and Patents Act 1988 and the Copyright and Related Rights Regulations 2003 (SI No. 2498).

CONTENTS

List of Figures   vi
Timeline   ix
Glossary   xiii
Sources   xxv
Preface   xxxi

1   Italians in the East (*Levante*) and the Making of Modern Europe   1
2   After Caesar: The Roman Empire and its Arabian Frontiers   23
3   The Formation of the Papal State during the Early Caliphates   37
4   A New Turn to Carthage (Tunisia) and the Start of the Crusades   52
5   Pisan Trade Hubs from Seville to Crusader Syria   72
6   Genoese Commerce across the Habsburg–Ottoman Mediterranean   96
7   The Venetian Republic Turns Global   122
8   Florentine Commerce and the Renaissance   139
9   Livornans in North Africa during Italian Unification   161
10   Italian Citizens between Rome and the East (*Levante*)   187
11   The Last Levantines (*Gli Levantini*)   203
Epilogue: Memories of the Levant in Exile   219

Notes   221
Acknowledgments   242
Index   244

FIGURES

1.1	Istanbul's Galata Tower	1
1.2	The military naval ensign used by the Italian navy	6
1.3	Alexandria was one of the many places where Italians with recent and more distant connections to the Italian peninsula debated the rise of Mussolini-era fascism	12
2.1	Christian Bedouin in Jordan	23
2.2	Map	27
2.3	Roman Emperor Philip of Aurantis, like imperial empress Julia Domna Augusta of the Severan family, came from the same part of the Roman Empire as Zenobia	30
3.1	During the reign of Justinian and Theodora in the 500s, Constantinople recaptured much of the European and North African territory once held by Rome that fell under the rule of the Goths and Vandals in the late 400s	37
3.2	Map	42
3.3	Map	46
4.1	Map	52
4.2	Monasteries, like San Zeno Abbey in Pisa, were among the key socioreligious institutions in the 1000s that aligned local communes with Rome's papacy	58

4.3	Roger II was the patriarch in a line of polyglot Arabic-speaking Norman kings in Palermo who oversaw a similarly polyglot administrative bureau (Arabic: *diwan*) inherited from the earlier Sicilian emirate	64
5.1	The Cathedral of Pisa, adjacent to the leaning tower, was built partly with funds that came from the spoils of the failed Mahdia campaign	72
5.2	The Arabic-language documents of the Cairo *genizah*, the storeroom of a Cairene synagogue	78
5.3	The *fondaco dei turchi*, a warehouse-inn in Venice for visiting Ottoman subjects	85
6.1	Map	97
6.2	Quinto Cenni's fourteenth-century representation of the Genoese navy captures the Genoese Republic's use of high-sided armed merchant cogs alongside a variety of high-speed oar-powered galleys	104
6.3	The Church of San Antonio di Padova, located on Istiklal Avenue in Istanbul's Pera district	111
7.1	Istanbul's Fener district, one of the city's principal Greek neighborhoods	122
7.2	The Alhambra Decree of Granada	127
7.3	The arrival of Sephardic Jewish exiles throughout the Adriatic and Aegean during the height of Venetian–Ottoman commercial exchange saw Spanish-speaking Jewish communities live alongside older Greek-speaking Romaniote Jewish families	134
8.1	Pope Leo X (r. 1513–1521), born Giovanni di Lorenzo de' Medici	139
8.2	The history of the Duchy of Tuscany and its predecessor, the Republic of Florence, saw the once-dominant city of Pisa become eclipsed by both Florence and the growing Tuscan port of Livorno	149
8.3	Florentine paintings representing biblical scenes incorporate visual cues that accurately depict select aspects of the contemporary Middle East and North Africa in imaginative contexts	155

9.1	Ferdinando de' Medici (r. 1587–1609) was the primary figure associated with the rise of Livorno as an international port that attracted merchants from a variety of backgrounds and imperial associations	161
9.2	The Chiesa della Santissima Annunziata	167
9.3	Travelers to Fez who met local Livornese Jewish communities were struck by how individual members were both multilingual and dressed variously according to both local and European fashions	181
10.1	By 1812, the Napoleonic armies brought the first French Empire to its greatest territorial extent	187
10.2	Yaqub Rafael Sanu	193
10.3	Danielle Frida Hélène Boccara	198
11.1	The heyday of Istanbul's Levantine community was in the final decades of the Ottoman Empire	203
11.2	Yaqub "James" Rafael Sanu, Tommaso Marinetti, and Fausta Cialente	208
11.3	Dalida, born Iolanda Gigliotti, remains Egypt's most famous "Levantine" Italian	214

TIMELINE

476	Odoacer captures Rome
732	Battle of Tours
751	collapse of the Exarchate of Ravenna
756	establishment of an independent Papal State
800	coronation of Frankish King Charlemagne in Rome as *Imperator Romanorum*
843	Frankish empire begins to fracture
921	selection of Mahdia (Tunisia) as the first capital of the Fatimid Empire
961	establishment of Cairo by the Fatimid Empire
1053	Pope Leo IX confirms authority of Bishop Thomas of Carthage across North African dioceses
1054	Catholic–Orthodox schism
1056	Saxon king Heinric (Henry) IV becomes king at the age of six, with his mother Empress Agnes as regent
1063	failed Pisan attempt to capture the Emirate of Sicily
1071	Roger becomes first Norman ruler of Sicily
1075	papacy issues a compilation of twenty-seven statements, known as the *Dictatus Papae*, confirming its authority

1076	Pope excommunicates Saxon king during growing clash between royal and clerical authority
1081	Heinric (Henry) IV invades Rome
1096	Crusaders invade eastern Roman and Muslim-held territories
1063	construction of Cathedral of Pisa begins
1087	invasion of Mahdia (Tunisia) by the papacy, Pisans, Genoese
1088	Frankish Margravine Matilda oversees appointment of Daimbert (Dagobert) as bishop of Pisa
1099	Sicilian Norman King Roger II's first cousin Bohemond enters Jerusalem
1099	Crusader Kingdom of Jerusalem is established
1101	Genoese send squadron of ships in support of Baldwin, Lord of Edessa and King of Jerusalem
1115	Pisan–Catalan joint force captures Ibiza and reaches Denia on the Alicante coast
1116	Pisans lose Ibiza and Balearic territories to the rising Almoravids
1125	Pisan *Majorcan Book of the Deeds of the Illustrious Pisans* is completed
1133	Pisans secure trade agreement with Almoravids
1136	Pisan–Genoese force captures Algerian port of Annaba (Bône)
1137	King Roger II sends Arabic-language letter to Fatimid caliph al-Hafiz confirming relations
1137	King Roger II captures Gerba from the Fatimids
1149	Genoese conclude a trade-oriented ten-year peace agreement with Ibn Mardanish of the Balearics
1150	Pisans secure trade relations with Ibn Mardanish
1154	Pisan ambassador Ranieri Botacci goes to Fatimid Cairo to negotiate a trade deal
1157	Pisans return to Mahdia to secure a trade agreement with rising Almohad caliphate
1161	Genoese secure trade relations with the Almohads based on a likely earlier agreement in 1053

1164	Saladin first arrives in Cairo from the Levant to work for the Fatimid caliphs
1171	Saladin's coup of the Fatimid government in Cairo
1182	Pisan vessels are among the ships that breach Saladin's naval siege of Beirut
1186	expansion of Pisan–Almohad trade relations
1187	Saladin captured Jerusalem just prior to the Third Crusade (1189–1192)
1187	Conrad of Montferrat, ruler of Tyre, grants Pisa extraterritorial jurisdiction over Pisan citizens
1250	Mamluks, a Turkish mercenary dynasty, overthrow Saladin's Ayyubid government in Cairo
1267	Genoese help to re-install Byzantine rule in Crusader-held Constantinople
1272	Marco Polo observes advanced rudders on ships in Hormuz
1273	Pera across the Golden Horne in Constantinople is given to the Genoese
1278	Nasrids of Granada grant the Genoese the right to trade inland, a fondaco, a church, and tax privileges
1289	Genoese notary Pietro Battifolio writes an account of Tunis noting the Italian presence
1304	Florentine chronicler Giovanni Villani observes Mediterranean shipwrights emulating Basque ships
1346	Genoese Simone Vignoso captures Chios and the two ports of Phokaia from the Byzantines
1355	Genoese diplomats Filippo Demerode and Bonifacio da Sori work as agents of the Ottoman sultan
1453	Ottoman capture of Constantinople
1532	Charles V signs a peace agreement with Protestant princes against the backdrop of Ottoman invasions
1541	Decree of the Venetian senate allowing Portuguese and Levantine Jews to settle in the city

1555	Pisaro's charter offers commercial privileges to five groups: Turks, Armenians, Greeks, "Moors," Jews
1586	Medici Oriental Press creates Arabic type for printing presses
1593	Ferdinando de Medici declares Livorno, close to Florence, a "free" port to attract foreign merchants
1597	Polish king Sigismund III finalizes capitulation agreement with the Ottomans detailing trade relations
1601	Ferdinando allows Greeks to establish a Greek church, La Santissima Annunziata on Via della Madonna
1608	Ferdinando de Medici battles an Ottoman fleet despite positive trade relations
1649	Livorno's first Hebrew-language printing press is established, called *La Stamperia del Kaf Nachat*
1795	French establish the Batavian republic in place of the Dutch republic
1814	Congress of Vienna: assembly in 1814–1815 of the four Great Powers (Austria, Great Britain, Russia, Prussia) negotiate European boundaries
1830	France annexes Algiers
1848	Grand Duke Leopold II agrees to a constitution with shared governance
1861	Italian kingdom is established
1881	France annexes Tunis
1923	establishment of the Republic of Turkey out of the Ottoman Empire
1946	establishment of the Republic of Italy out of the Kingdom of Italy
1952	establishment of the Republic of Egypt out of the Kingdom of Egypt

GLOSSARY

Aachen: one of the capitals of Charlemagne's Frankish empire on the borders of present-day France and Germany, also known in French today as Aix-la-Chappelle

abbot: an ecclesiastical title for the heads of monasteries, which were sites of socioreligious leadership throughout the Italian peninsula and France that helped recenter Rome and the bishop of Rome (the pope) in regional politics after the fall of Rome (*c.* 476)

Adriatic Sea: the northernmost portion of the Mediterranean Sea separating the Italian peninsula from the Balkans and Greek isles

Adrianopolis: one-time capital of the Ottoman sultanate (Turkish: Edirne) in the Thracian region separating present-day Greece and Turkey, named originally after Roman Emperor Hadrian

Almohads: a confederation of Berber tribes that captured various Islamic polities in Iberia and North Africa and that eventually lost territory to the Castilian kingdom

Anatolia: the peninsula that makes up present-day Turkey and that was once the heartland of the eastern half of the Roman Empire (Byzantine Empire)

Ancona: port city on the eastern coast of the Italian peninsula under the authority of the Rome-based Papal State and site of exchange with merchants from the Ottoman Empire

antipope: the title of a series of senior clerical figures in the Roman Catholic Church who claimed the title of pope in opposition to a concurrently serving pope during the heyday of political tension associated with the German kingdom's power over the Papal State

Antwerp: center of Dutch commerce and exchange connected with trade routes along the Baltic, North, and Mediterranean seas

Aragon: the kingdom and later Spanish province that was the site of extensive commercial exchange with the Italian maritime republics

archbishop: the ecclesiastical title associated with a higher-ranking bishop

Arsenale: the Venetian word for the site where the Republic mass-produced merchant galleys and war galleys

Babylonians: inhabitants of the ancient state of Babylonia based in the city of Babylon in Iraq and one-time home of influential kings Hammurabi and Nebuchadnezzar

Balearics: the islands off the eastern coast of Spain, including Mallorca, that were the site of several Muslim and Catholic frontier kingdoms

Benadetti (Tommaso): Italian nationalist and follower of Mussolini born in Alexandria (Khedivate of Egypt) at a time when clashing pro- and anti-Fascist factions lived in the Italian diaspora

Beyoglu:	district of Istanbul adjacent to historical Pera
bishopric:	the rank or office of a bishop in the Roman Catholic Church as well as the district under the bishop's ecclesiastical jurisdiction
Bjørgvin:	present-day Bergen (Norway) and one of a series of cities along the North and Baltic seas
Bohemond I of Antioch:	son of Norman adventurer Robert Guiscard of Apulia and Calabria (brother of Count of Sicily Roger) and his first wife, Alberada of Buonalbergo
Brescia:	city in present-day Lombardy that, despite being outside Veneto, was captured by the Republic of Venice and became intertwined with the pilgrimage routes through Venice
Bristol:	city in England connected with trade to Livorno in fish, cloth, and other British commodities
Byzantine:	modern English-language term used to identify the surviving eastern half of the Roman Empire that, after the fall of Rome in 476, was identified in various languages as the land of the "Romans" and "Greeks"
caesar:	Roman imperial title with origins in the persona and name of Julius Caesar with parallels in the way that the Frankish title Carolus draws on the legacy of Charlamagne (Latin: Carolus Magnus)
Carolingian:	Frankish dynasty named after Charlemagne (Carolus Magnus), grandson of Charles Martel (Carolus Martellus)
Castile:	present-day Spanish province named after the medieval and early modern kingdom that variously captured, annexed, and united with neighboring kingdoms (for example, Emirate of Granada, Crown of Aragon) in the formation of the Age of Exploration-era Crowns of Castile and Aragon across all of present-day Spain

cathedral:	the primary church associated with an ecclesiastical diocese of the Roman Catholic Church
Cervantes (Miguel de):	an early Castilian-language (Spanish-language) novelist and author of the influential *Don Quixote*
Ceuta:	one of two major Spanish-held ports on the coast of Africa adjacent to Morocco and close to British-held Gibraltar
Chalcedon:	ancient eastern Roman town south of Scutari (present-day Üsküdar) that was the site of the Council of Chalcedon and is currently located in Istanbul's Kadıköy district
Charlemagne:	Frankish ruler known in Latin as Carolus Magnus who governed during the height of the Frankish empire
Cleopatra:	ruler of Egypt (50–30 BCE) and paternal descendant of General Ptolemy, Macedonian general of Alexander the Great
Cluny:	a city in France northwest of Lyon that was the center of monastic reform since 909, when Abbot Berno sought to adhere more strictly to Benedictine rule and follow more closely the leadership of the pope to the exclusion of local kings and nobles
Constantinople:	second capital of the Roman Empire after Rome and, following the capture of Rome, sole Roman capital until its capture by the Ottomans in 1453
consul:	ancient title for the heads of the Roman Republic elected by the Senate centuries before the term was used for ambassadors of the Italian republics
Copenhagen:	city in Denmark and major center of Baltic Sea exchange during the heyday of the Hanseatic League
Cosimo de' Medici:	Florentine banker and namesake of the Medici dynasty that ruled Florence and the Duchy of

	Tuscany from the late 1300s until the era of Napoleon in the late 1700s
corsairs:	privateers or independent maritime adventurers who worked under the patronage of various Mediterranean powers from the 1500s to the 1700s, and lived a pirate-like existence in the world of maritime commerce and conflict
Crimea:	peninsula in the northern Black Sea just off the coast of present-day mainland Ukraine (north) and Russia (northeast), once the heartland of the Crimean khanate
Cristobal Colón:	Spanish-language name of Genoese mariner Christopher Columbus and namesake of the Portuguese and Spanish nobility associated with his son and one-time governor of Hispaniola island (present-day Haiti and Dominican Republic) Diego Colón
Ctesiphon:	principal capital of the Sassanian empire adjacent to ancient Hellenistic Seleukia (Aramaic: Saliq) located on the outskirts of present-day Baghdad
Darius:	Achaemenid emperor during the empire's height and namesake of later successor Darius III, who lost much of the empire's western territories in Anatolia just across the Greek isles to Alexander the Great
Deccan:	plateau across the central geography of the Indian subcontinent that was the center of several sultanates (the Deccan sultanates) later subsumed into the Mughal Empire
denarius:	a standard Roman silver coin and namesake of a related coin known in Arabic as the *dinar*
dhow:	ancient Arab trading vessel that transferred commodities such as porcelain between China and Iraq across the Indian Ocean and South China Sea

Diego Colón: son of Christopher Columbus and one-time governor of Hispaniola (present-day Haiti and the Dominican Republic)

doges: title used throughout the Italian peninsula for the elected ruler of several republics (for example, the Republic of Venice, Republic of Genoa) with origins in the military title *dux* (English: duke) in the ancient Roman Republic

dragoman: diplomat and translator (Arabic: *tarjuman*, Italian: *turcimanno*) typically in European service able to represent their home governments in the Middle East and North Africa using their skills in language and cultural literacy

Dubrovnik: capital of the Republic of Ragusa in present-day Croatia, formerly a crossroads of Slavic languages and the Romanian-like Dalmatian language along the Ancona–Dubrovnik–Istanbul trade routes

duchy: a dynastic monarchy led by an unelected duke (Italian: doge) that could be seen in the example of the Medici-led Duchy of Tuscany

duomo: an Italian term for "cathedral" that is used most famously in the English language for the cathedral of Florence

earthenware: a broad term for ancient varieties of glazed or unglazed pottery, including terracotta, that are made impervious to water through glazes and that have lower mechanical strength than stoneware, porcelain, and bone china

Elagabalus: name of an ancient Arabian deity (Arabic: *ilah al-jabal*, "deity of the mountains") and the name of a Roman emperor of the Severan dynasty descended from Septimius Severus of Lepta (Libya) and Julia Domna of Edessa (Syria)

exarchate: a territorial province of the surviving eastern Roman Empire that the emperor in Constantinople created to replace the various civil diocese of the former western Roman territories upon Constantinople's capture of those lands from the Visigoths, Ostrogoths, and Vandals

excommunication: an action, most famously used by the Roman Catholic Church, that officially excludes someone from participating in the services and sacraments of the Church

extraterritorial: a description usually for laws or rights that citizens of one territory are able to secure in another territory based on the second territory's extraterritorial agreements with the first territory

Fatimid: the descriptive title of a North African Muslim dynasty that founded Cairo on the outskirts of the early Muslim garrison town known as Fustat, which in turn was established close to ancient Memphis

Flanders: coastal region central to Hanseatic League exchange on the borders of present-day Belgium and the Netherlands across the North Sea from the British Isles

fondaco: the Venetian variety of a hotel or inn for visiting merchants from places like the Ottoman Empire

Gabès: Tunisian coastal city that was at the crossroads of Norman, Almohad, and later Ottoman politics

Futurism: a literary, artistic, and intellectual movement oriented around not only imagining the innovations and technologies of the future

Gagliano: the name of two brothers of Italian descent with an ability to move between Venetian and Ottoman subjecthood

Gattilusio:	a powerful Genoese family on a par with the Giustiniani family that, like the Giustinianis, controlled parts of the northern Aegean including the island of Lesbos through an alliance with the eastern Romans (Byzantines) in Constantinople
geniza:	a general term for a storage area of older Hebrew-language books and papers that, in the case of the famous Cairo geniza, preserved medieval Arabic-language documents in Hebrew script illustrative of the life of Arabic-speaking Jews
Genoa:	city on the Italian peninsula's Ligurian coast that was the center of the Genoese republic, one of several Italian republics that emerged from the shadow of Frankish German rule and eastern Roman (Byzantine) rule in the Italian peninsula
Ghassanids:	an Arab Christian tribe that lived in and governed part of the Levant region that was originally aligned with the eastern Roman (Byzantine) empire before changing alliance towards the rising Arab Muslims
Giustiniani:	a prominent Genoese family on a par with the Gattilusio family that controlled parts of the northern Aegean through an alliance with the eastern Romans (Byzantines) in Constantinople
Granada:	capital of the Emirate of Granada and, alongside cities like Barcelona, a center of Genoese commercial activity in the lead-up to the Age of Exploration
Habsburg:	German dynasty that came to prominence in the 1200s within the German Holy Roman Empire and that, by the lifetime of Charles V, was closely intertwined with Spanish and Portuguese royalty
Haracguzar:	a typically Christian or Jewish subject of the Ottoman sultan, including Roman Catholics of Venetian and Genoese heritage who, in the case of

	individuals like the Gagliano brothers, were sometimes able to move between Venetian and Ottoman subjecthood
Hafsid:	one of several dynasties in northwest Africa that traded with the Italian republics and that was subsumed into Almohad and later Ottoman territory
Hawran:	the North African city known in Spanish as Oran
Heraclius:	eastern Roman emperor in the early 600s during the rise of Islam and a supporter of the cultural Hellenization of the eastern Roman administration especially by changing the administrative language from Latin to Greek
Ilkhanids:	the Mongol dynasty that ruled the southwesternmost portion of the Mongol Empire around Iran in the 1200s and 1300s
Ifriqiya:	the Arabic word for the portion of North Africa overlapping with much of coastal Tunisia, eastern Algeria, and the ancient Roman province of Africa Proconsularis
Inquisition:	a set of offices established throughout the Roman Catholic Church that, particularly in Iberia and the Americas, attempted to investigate and prosecute Catholics suspected of observing "Judaizing" (*judaizante*) practices, Muslim customs, or any rituals or doctrines deemed a heresy (*herejía*)
Latakia:	Syrian city under various eastern Roman (Byzantine), Arab, and Ottoman histories
Leghorn:	the English-language word for Livorno
Liguria:	the coastal region connecting present-day Monaco in the south of France with the northwestern coast of Italy including Genoa, where the Ligurian language (Genoese: Zeneize) is spoken

Lombardy:	an administrative region in the Italian peninsula with a name that stems from the Germanic kingdom of the Lombards (*Regnum Longobardorum*) that reigned throughout the Italian peninsula in the aftermath of the Germanic conquests
Mamluk:	dynasty known as the Mamluk sultanate that governed Egypt and the Syrian Levant in the late medieval and early modern eras (1250–1517 CE)
Marrakesh:	city in Morocco that was a historical center of Atlantic and Mediterranean commercial exchange
Maronite:	description of the predominant Christian denomination of Lebanon
Mussolini (Benito):	former prime minister of Italy and head of the National Fascist Party (PNF)
Nabateans:	an Arabic-speaking nomadic north Arabian tribe and kingdom that fell under Roman rule
Napoleon:	French ruler who rose to prominence during the French Revolution
Nasrid:	Arab dynasty of the Iberian peninsula known in Arabic as Banu Nasr and, for much of its history (r. 1230–1492), a vassal of the Castilian kingdom
Normans:	French-speaking adventurers and conquerors of originally Norse-speaking Viking heritage that established dynasties in England (Normandy), the southern region of the Italian peninsula, and Crusader-era Syria
Odoacer:	Germanic conqueror of imperial Rome and one-time officer in the Roman army
Palaiologus:	eastern Roman ruler who was restored to rule by the Genoese
Palmyra:	a city in present-day Syria that, like Petra in Jordan, was one of several commercial cities

along north–south trade routes connecting the Levant with the Hejaz region in present-day Saudi Arabia

Podestà: a Genoese term for Genoese ambassadors or consuls in centers such as Pera (district of present-day Istanbul), which the Genoese secured as an independently governed port in the aftermath of the restoration of eastern Roman (Byzantine) power in the formerly Crusader-held Constantinople (*c*. 1200s)

Protestants: denomination of Christianity that grew out of the teachings of Roman Catholic clergy who protested certain political and theological trends associated with the early modern Roman Catholic Church

Ragusa (Republic of): independent Roman Catholic republic that was situated across the Adriatic from the Italian republics (around present-day Croatia)

Ravenna: city in the northern Italian peninsula that was once the center of the eastern Roman-held Exarchate of Ravenna

Risorgimento: the nineteenth-century cultural and political movement oriented around Italian unification and culminating in the establishment of the Kingdom of Italy in 1861

Safavid: a Persian dynasty of Turkish origins that governed much of present-day Iran from the 1500s to the 1700s (*c*. 1501–1736)

Samarqand: center of Persian-speaking culture and commerce along the historical silk routes connecting commerce around the Black Sea with commerce in China

Saraybosna: the official name of Sarajevo in Turkish during the city's four centuries of Ottoman rule

Sassanian: ancient Iranian dynasty that ruled Iran (*c.* 224–651) until its capture by the rising Islamic empires on the eve of the global Umayyad caliphate's establishment in Damascus (*c.* 661–750)

Tabriz: northern Iranian city in the historically Turkish-speaking regions bordering present-day Azerbaijan

Thalassocracy: a seaborne empire or maritime empire with primarily maritime domains similar to the Republic of Genoa and Republic of Venice

Theodoric: ruler of the combined Gothic realms following the capture of imperial Rome

Umayyad: Arab Muslim dynasty established in Damascus in 661

Vaballathus: the Latin name minted on local coins of the son of Zenobia, the Palmyrene queen who rebelled against the eastern Romans and established an independent empire

Valerian: Roman emperor (*c.* 253–260) who was famously captured by Persian emperor Shapur and represented on a Persian rock relief alongside future Roman emperor Philip of Arabia Patraea, known by later Roman writers for having potentially been the first Christian Roman emperor prior to Constantine

Zengid: Turkic Muslim dynasty with origins in present-day southern Russia that crossed eastern Anatolia into the Levant and Iraq and governed parts of the region in alliance with the Seljuk dynasty during the Crusader era until the eve of the Ottoman era

Zirid: Muslim dynasty of Berber origin in North Africa, especially present-day Tunisia, that established close diplomatic and commercial connections with both the Fatimid caliphate and the Norman kingdom

Zenobia: Palmyrene queen who rebelled against the eastern Romans and established an independent empire

SOURCES:
TEXTS, OBJECTS, ARTS

How do historians know so much about Italy's connections with the Middle East and North Africa from the days of Caesar to Mussolini? Why is it a challenge for writers to organize this material in a way that elucidates key patterns and trends that have impacted the modern world? The simplest answer is evidence, and specifically evidence from a variety of sources: texts, objects, architecture, inscriptions, memory, and the like. The task for archivists, archaeologists, and historians is to sort through this large volume of evidence, discern fact from fiction, and interpret these facts according to questions about biography, how society is organized, cultural practices and beliefs, and political power. The result is a book of history, like this one, rooted in fields like sociology, anthropology, and political science with evidence from the Florentine archives, Ottoman archives, and more than a dozen international archival collections and museums.

But what happens when sources about the same event disagree? For historians, this problem is captured by the term historiography—that is, the study of how people in the past observed, recorded, and interpreted events. In the case of the current study, for example, writing a history of Italy's encounters with the Middle East and North Africa requires an analysis of how and why travelers—writing variously in Italian, French, Arabic, and Turkish—recorded and interpreted the same events differently. The outcome, this book, illuminates not only the historiography of Italy, but also that of its maritime neighbors around the Mediterranean. And in the comparative story that this book recounts, Italy has as much to do with Western history as it does the worlds of the "East." Today, Italians are coming to terms with this duality as they debate Italy's place in Europe, and what the current study shows is that this debate has been in motion for 2,000 years.

The earliest sources used in this book are vestiges of the Roman Empire recorded in Latin. Among the most interesting are the many inscriptions, coins, and works of art that supplement what we can learn from Roman chronicles. In the case of Roman emperor Philip of Arabia, for example, the surviving Roman amphitheater in Philippopolis (Arabic: Shahba)—situated in the district of Aurantis (Arabic: Hawran)—illustrates the extent that southern Syria and Jordan were an important part of Roman politics on the eve of the establishment of Constantinople. The region remains dotted with Christian monasteries dating back to early Christianity, which contextualizes debates among Roman chroniclers about Philip's possible Christian identity. Prior to Constantinople's conversion, Christianity in Syria was a source of political contention for Rome that prompted the empire's construction of temples to suppress Christianity. The Temple of Apollo in Baalbek (Lebanon) remains the most spectacular example. Other political tensions in the region were connected with local power players, such as the family of Palmyrene ruler Zenobia (fl. *c.* 240s–270s CE), whose loyalty to Rome wavered.

Zenobia, the daughter of a Palmyrene ruler in alliance with the Romans, rebelled against the capital and established her own empire. Surviving coins of the Palmyrene ruler Zenobia, minted in her name and that of her son rather than the Roman emperor, tell us how contested Syria was as a region that was simultaneously semi-Romanized in its political culture and semi-independent. Coins in her own name are inscribed with the title *S. Zenobia Aug* (*Septimia Zenobia Augusta*), while those in the name of her son Vaballathus read *Im. C. Vaballathus Aug.* (*Imperator Caesar Vaballathus Augustus*). The use of the Latin terms *Augusta* and *Augustus* represent explicit claims to be rulers on a par with the reigning Roman ruler Aurelian in Rome, whose name and title (*Imperator Aurelianus Augustus*) appear on older Palmyrene coins during her rule.

Following the emergence of Constantinople as the empire's eastern capital, the activities of the Arab Christian Ghassanid tribe in the region (*c.* 400s–600s) echoed the extent that frontier rulers oscillated between alliance with the Romans and rebellion against them. Following the expansion of Islam in the 600s, the Arab Muslim Umayyad tribe similarly made Syria a new center of political rule in friction with the earlier Islamic capital of Medina and the contemporary eastern Roman capital of Constantionple. Surviving art and architecture in Umayyad Syria, from mosaics to surviving palaces and mosques, similarly tells the story of an early Islamic-era Syrian geography that was still very intertwined with its Roman and Palmyrene political past.

The expansion of Islamic political dominion across the once Roman-held lands of the Middle East and North Africa occurred simultaneously with the growth of Frankish rule in Europe. For the eastern Romans based in Constantinople, the expansion of the Frankish kingdom in the 500s and 600s was complex. Surviving legal codes tells us how far Emperor Justinian was willing to go in order to recenter the Mediterranean world's politics around Constantinople rather than Italy. Justinian's *Pragmatic Sanction* of 554 saw the old civil diocese network replaced with two new exarchates: the Exarchate of Ravenna (*Exarchatus Ravennatis*), based in the Italian peninsula's north; and the Exarchate of Africa (*Exarchatus Africae*), based in Carthage along the Tunisian coast. The ecclesiastical diocese network, however, remained in place, with bishoprics like Ravenna slowly pushing Rome's bishopric, that is, the papacy, into the region's periphery.

The abilities of the bishop of Ravenna to look eastward to Constantinople rather than to the bishop of Rome for ecclesiastical leadership demonstrated Constantinople's political reach throughout the Italian peninsula. In the end, Justinian's ambitions exceeded the abilities of his military and diplomatic corps. While the goal was to pull Italy into Constantinople's sphere of influence, the bishop of Rome, that is, the papacy, managed to consolidate connections with the Franks in a process that culminated in the establishment of a distinct Frankish-aligned Papal State and the coronation of Frankish king Charlemagne with the new church-approved title of Emperor of the Romans. The coins of Charlemagne read, in full, *Karolus Imperator Augustus* (*Karolus Imp Aug*) and omitted *Romanorum* ("of the Romans"), potentially out of caution against challenging the surviving eastern Roman emperor's own imperial claims to being "emperor of the Romans." The term *Romanorum* did appear in his documents, but in either case, the term Romanorum was simply absent from ancient imperial titles. Vespanian (r. 69–79 CE), for example, ruled in Rome as *Imperator Caesar Vespasianus Augustus*, with the titles *Caesar* and *Augustus* as well as other monikers—*princeps* (first) and *dominus*—being the typical corollary titles adjacent to *imperator* across the centuries between Caesar's rule and Odoacer's conquest.

In the end, however, neither the Franks nor the eastern Romans in Constantinople nor the rising Islamic kingdoms—stretching from Cairo into Sicily in the 800s—would be able to secure a long-term hold over Italy. In the many centuries since the fall of Rome (*c.* 476), ancient Roman cities had developed more elaborate systems of self-governance modeled after the ancient Roman Republic. Venice had a senate, which was part of a larger phenomenon of communes developing self-governing systems across the centuries of political change and turmoil after 476. By the 800s and 900s CE, many of these communes had declared independence from the Frankish kings and the local Frankish margravines (German: *markgraf*), and by the 1000s, the era of the Italian maritime republics was in fruition: the Republic of Pisa, the Republic of Genoa, the Republic of Venice, and the Republic of Florence among others.

At the level of text and archival documents, the way that these republics diverged in language is one of the most interesting stories of how the worlds of the former Roman heartlands simultaneously converged and diverged. On the one hand, Latin remained a key language of administration and culture that could be seen in Pisan texts from the Crusader era. *Carmen in Victoriam Pisanorum* (*Song on the Occasion of the Victory of the Pisans*), a mix of poem and chronicle, comes from this period and survives in the Albert I Royal Library in Brussels. Written in the aftermath of the Mahdia campaign, *Carmen in Victoriam Pisanorum* celebrates the heroism of Pisa's soldiers and their commitment to the faith. Its poet-chronicler author, likely a clergyman, describes the Genoese as having joined "the Pisans with great love; they do not care about earthly life (*de vita mundi*), or about their sons; [for] they give themselves to the dangers for love of the Redeemer (*pro amore Redemtoris*)." On the other hand, many of these types of administrative texts and chronicles began to diverge from Latin in places like Venice and Florence.

The Venetian archives, including collections of ambassadorial notes like the *Dispacci degli Ambasciatori e Residenti Costantinopoli*, are largely written in Venetian language. Venetian was a prestige language of speech and writing that left its mark in Italy's history of theater. Some of the most important plays in Italian history were written in Venetian. In the end, however, the language of Florence in the era of the Medicis became the peninsula's premier prestige dialect in a cultural context where Rome, center of the Roman Catholic Church, was a center of cultural and diplomatic exchange among ruling circles with estates in the city. With cultural centers in Florence and Livorno, the Medicis were among the most influential ruling families of the peninsula, but by the 1800s, Napoleon's state-of-the-art armies had captured much of the Italian peninsula, Europe, and even North Africa's Ottoman-aligned kingdoms including Tunisia.

Perched just across the Sicilian Strait, Tunisia was once the center of the ancient Roman Empire's North African territories, and, in the 1800s, was still a center of Maltese and Italian commerce and culture. With the establishment of the French protectorates in Algeria (1830) and Tunisia (1881), French texts began to document the eclipse of Italian cultural currency across North Africa and Egypt amidst a rapid acceleration of Francophone cultures throughout the Mediterranean. From Tunis to Alexandria, archives including those of the Alliance Israélite Universelle documented the transformation of the former Duchy of Tuscany's Livorno-based Jewish communities from Italian- and Arabic-speaking cultures into French-speaking cultures. Still, Italian culture remained a prominent part of the region's high and popular cultures in part because of the activities of new arrivals from the Italian kingdom in cities like newly industrializing Alexandria, Cairo, and Istanbul.

The Dante Alighieri Society's archives tell us how all the Italian citizens who traveled to these cities worked in industries including architectural design, construction, and music. The Cairo Opera House was an outcome of this exchange, as were many of the architectural projects of late Ottoman Istanbul. The Dante Alighieri Society also documented two world wars and the rise and fall of a new Italian empire, when much of the Italian diaspora navigated rapid changes in laws around citizenship and residency privileges across Italy, France, Egypt, and Turkey. Today, decades after the mass emigration of Italians to countries like France and the United States, what survives of Italian heritage in the Middle East and North Africa extends beyond texts, objects, and artistic architecture and includes something more global: memories preserved in music and film.

PREFACE

Italy and the Islamic World: From Caesar to Mussolini offers the first long-duration reconstruction of the Italian peninsula's forgotten millennia as a bridge connecting Europe with the Middle East and North Africa. Beginning with the rise and fall of the Roman Empire and the emergence of the Papal State, and with extensive analysis of the lives of the Pisans, Genoese, Venetians, Florentines, Livornans, the so-called Levantines (*gli levantini*), and the *Risorgimento*-era Italian citizens, *Italy and the Islamic World* traces the story of families from the Italian peninsula as they navigated culture and conflict in the shared pursuit of commercial exchange.

These centuries saw the Italian maritime republics emerge from the shadow of the Frankish kingdom (Francia, fl. 481–843), royal successors of the mighty Goths and Vandals who first captured the western Roman lands. By the Age of Exploration, the Republic of Venice and the Republic of Genoa could be seen building business connections from Seville to Istanbul in competition with the Medicis of Florence, legendary governors of the Duchy of Tuscany. By the nineteenth century, in the aftermath of Napoleon's conquests and the start of the Italian Unification (*Risorgimento*), Tuscany's port of Livorno became the cultural center of a global Italian-speaking diaspora that included Roman Catholics, Greek Orthodox, and Sephardic Jews. In the final decades of the Ottoman Empire, these Livornese networks connected western Italy with cities like Algiers, Tunis, Alexandria, and Istanbul.

But against the backdrop of competing nationalist pulls in cities like Paris and Alexandria, when the rising Italian kingdom lost much of its cultural influence around the Mediterranean, large segments of the Italian-speaking diaspora parted ways permanently with the peninsula as they began new lives as citizens of countries like Egypt, Turkey, France, and the United States. Many others returned to Italy in the aftermath of the Second World War to find a country that was still coming to terms with its ancient and medieval past.

1

ITALIANS IN THE EAST (*LEVANTE*) AND THE MAKING OF MODERN EUROPE

Figure 1.1 Istanbul's Galata Tower is an old Genoese tower in the city's Beyoğlu district. Beyoğlu is also known as Pera (Greek: Πέρα). In 1273, Byzantine Emperor Michael VIII Palaiologos granted the Republic of Genoa control over Pera in recognition of Genoa's support for the Byzantines against the Crusaders. Back in 1204, a Crusader army captured Constantinople and made it the capital of a short-lived Crusader kingdom (Latin Empire of Constantinople) that lasted until 1261.

Confluence and Conflict across the High Seas

In 1384, Florentines Leonardo Frescobaldi, Simone Sigoli, and Giorgio Gucci traveled to Egypt as part of an extended trip to visit the ports and sacred sites of the Middle East and North Africa. Their surviving accounts offer some of the most vivid European representations of North African and Middle Eastern cultures.[1] Frescobaldi was a diplomat in Tuscany. His trip to Egypt via Venice

I

took him, together with a large group of diplomats and pilgrims, to some of the most influential centers of culture and commerce across the eastern Mediterranean: Alexandria, Cairo, Gaza, Bethlehem, Jerusalem, Damascus, and Beirut. The maps they brought were dotted with historical churches and archaeological sites dating back to early Christianity and the ancient Roman era. Among the group's most interesting encounters was one with a dragoman (Florentine Italian: *dragomanno*) who worked in royal service in Cairo. At the time, dragomans were local diplomatic interpreters versed in European and Middle Eastern languages such as Arabic, Turkish, and Persian. When consuls and pilgrims from Europe traveled to Egypt, local authorities employed professional dragomans as diplomatic go-betweens and chaperones to help them navigate the city.

In this particular case, Frescobaldi's dragoman had a unique profile. The dragoman was a Venetian who learned Arabic and settled permanently in Cairo, where he lived and worked as a Muslim. The dragoman's wife, a Florentine, was also Muslim. Frescobaldi's dragoman worked specifically as the grand dragoman for one of the Mamluk-era (r. 1250–1517) sultans, which meant that the visit of Frescobaldi, Sigoli, and Gucci was a high-level affair. From a modern perspective, the sight of a Venetian–Florentine couple who were Muslim and spoke Arabic ought to have been striking to Frescobaldi, Sigoli, and Gucci. Surprisingly, Frescobaldi spoke of their encounter matter-of-factly. To him, their Venetian Muslim dragoman was simply "a renegade Venetian" married "to one of our Florentines," suggesting that the phenomenon of Europeans living and working as Muslims in the Middle East and North Africa was not rare.[2]

Indeed, fifty years before Gucci and Frescobaldi's encounter with the Venetian polyglot, the Irish Franciscan friar Symon Semeonis similarly wrote in the 1320s that his two local interpreters in the Levant were "outwardly renegades."[3] One was a member of the Knights Templar organization who became Muslim and married locally. Another was a Roman friar who likewise became Muslim while in the Levant. Semeonis imagined that these interpreters were only "outwardly" Muslim in an apparent hope that they might still be Roman Catholic.

One factor that explains why cultural boundaries were so porous between people in the Italian peninsula, the Middle East, and North Africa was that these regions were all part of a single empire—namely, the Roman Empire—from the time of Julius Caesar (*c.* 50s BCE) until the fall of the Roman heartlands to conquerors like the Vandals, Visigoths, Ostrogoths, and Franks (c. 500s CE). Both before and after the career of Julius Caesar, cities such as Carthage (Tunisia), Alexandria (Egypt), and Palmyra (Syria) were in commercial contact with European cities like Rome and Athens. This explains why ancient rulers of the Middle East and North Africa loomed large in ancient Greek- and Latin-language literature: Queen Dido (c. 700s BCE) of Tyre (Lebanon) and her Phoenician kingdom in Carthage (Tunisia), Queen Cleopatra (c. 50s BCE) of Alexandria (Egypt) and her Greco-Egyptian kingdom connected with Alexander the Great's conquests (c. 300s BCE), and Queen Zenobia (200s BCE) of the Palmyrene kingdom situated along the Roman-controlled northern sections of the Syrian–Arabian trade routes adjacent the legendary Via Traiana Nova route in Roman *Arabia Petraea*.

After the fall of Rome and expansion of the Paris- and Aachen-centered Frankish empire (Paris, c. 508–768; Aachen/Aix-la-Chappelle, c. 795–843), rulers like Charlemagne (c. 800s CE) and local governors like Matilda of Tuscany (c. 1000s CE) were keen to navigate continuing connections with the Middle East and North Africa for various reasons. Most important among them were commerce with merchants throughout Mediterranean ports, conquest for maritime control in the high seas, competition with Constantinople over Christian loyalties, territorial competition with the caliphates governing formerly Roman-held territories—the Umayyads of Damascus and Cordoba, the Fatimids of Cairo, the Abbasids of Baghdad—and the like.

The outcome was a degree of political fragmentation and flux that facilitated the rise of independent states in the Italian peninsula beyond the Frankish empire's direct rule: the massive Papal State stretching from Rome to Ancona on the Adriatic, the Venetian republic in the northeast, the Genoese republic in the northwest, the Amalfitan republic in the south, and others. Most of the maritime republics grew out of towns like Genoa that had become self-governing communes after the fall of Rome in 476, and they were never entirely under the direct control of the conquerors who eventually took over the Roman Empire's western lands – namely, the Visigoths, the Ostrogoths, the surviving eastern Romans of Constantinople, the Lombards, and eventually the Franks of the Frankish empire (Francia). It was out of those new republics, which modeled themselves after the ancient Roman Republic, that a new generation of diplomats and merchants emerged in search of new post-Roman trade agreements in familiar cities like Constantinople and Alexandria.

As was the case in the Italian peninsula itself, the administrative and popular cultures had shifted in those regional cities in the centuries since the fall of Rome. The result was the rise of polyglot merchants able to communicate in multiple varieties of vernacular Latin—French, Genoese, Tuscan, Venetian—as well as languages such as Greek, Turkish, Arabic, and Persian.

For merchants of the Italian peninsula, the importance of expertise in foreign languages grew out of the new administrative cultures that rose to prominence after the fall of Rome, from the increasingly Greek-speaking eastern Roman (Byzantine) administration of Constantinople to the Arabic-speaking Islamic caliphate administrations of Damascus, Cairo, and Cordoba. Venetian and Genoese diplomats began to conduct business not only in vernacular Latin and Greek, but also in Arabic and eventually in Turkish and Persian.

Against this backdrop, the activity of a Venetian–Florentine couple who were Muslim, spoke Arabic, and worked as translators in the service of the sultan was notable and maybe even remarkable to Florentine travelers like Frescobaldi, Sigoli, and Gucci. But it was not unheard of in the late 1300s on the eve of the Renaissance. At the time, Turkish had already become an important language of administration relevant to the business interests of Genoese merchants in Pera. In the decades before Constantinople was subsumed into Ottoman rule, Genoese merchants in the independently governed port city of Pera—site of the surviving Genoese tower in present-day Istanbul—were already conducting business in the former Ottoman capital of Bursa. They did so without paying import–export tariffs, as though they were naturalized Ottoman subjects of the Ottoman domains. And they eventually were naturalized when large segments of the Genoese population remained in and around Constantinople after it became the new Ottoman capital in 1453.

It was at this point when Turkish became a permanent part of the dragomans' linguistic repertoire. The Ottomans were one of the Turkish principalities in western Anatolia that began to use Turkish, not just Persian and Arabic, as administrative languages. This linguistic choice was evocative of the earlier Timurid khanate (*c*. 1360–1507) of Central Asia, which used its own Uzbek-like Turkish dialect as a literary language (Chaghatai). The fact that the Medicis in Florence were operating a printing press in Arabic just a century later, namely, the Typographia Medicea Orientale (Medici Oriental Press), fits perfectly into these linguistic trends.

It was across these connected worlds of confluence and conflict that monarchs like the polyglot Frederick II (r. 1220–1250), Norman–Hohenstaufen king of Palermo and one-time head of the German "Holy Roman Empire," could be seen speaking and writing Arabic fluently in his communications with Cairo-based Ayyubid sultan al-Kamil (r. 1218–1238) in Jerusalem. At the height of the Crusader era, Frederick II was one of the key patrons of Europe's Arabic–Latin translation movement on the eve of the Medicis' Renaissance-era activity in Florence (*c.* 1400s–1500s). His patronage of translators was part of a larger history of cultural transfer that saw Castilian Toledo and Norman Palermo become centers for the study of Greco-Arabic medicine and cartography in the lead-up to both the Renaissance (*c.* 1400s) and Age of Exploration (*c.* 1500s–1600s).

It was in this context that merchants and diplomats sometimes made a lifetime move towards what they thought of as the East (*Oriente*). At the peak of Ottoman–Habsburg rivalries in the reign of Spanish Habsburg King Philip II (r. 1556–1598), namesake of the Philippines, Spanish priest and one-time captive Antonio de Sosa (fl. 1538–1587) wrote about North African Muslims from Roman Catholic families in ways that evoked Frescobaldi's observations centuries earlier. The friar encountered these Catholic-heritage European Muslims in the late 1500s in Ottoman Algiers, where he described them as "Turks by profession" (*turcos de profesion*). By this term, which foreshadowed the writings of Cervantes (*c.* early 1600s), De Sosa meant "all the renegades who, [despite being] of Christian blood and parentage, have of their own free will become Turks (*de su libre voluntad se hicieron Turcos*)." He even claimed that these "Turks by profession" were greater in number than the "Moors, Turks, and Jews of Algiers."[4] In other words, with the rise of Ottoman dominion throughout the Middle East and North Africa, Roman Catholics from Europe were moving to Ottoman-held lands and becoming Muslim in numbers that seemed – to the friar's perhaps exaggerated observations – greater than the number of native Turkish-speaking Muslims ("Turks") and Arabic-speaking Muslims ("Moors").

By De Sosa's lifetime, however, what may have been more common than the Italian peninsula's Roman Catholics converting to Islam was a parallel phenomenon: families of the Italian maritime republics naturalizing as Catholic subjects of a Muslim sultan alongside larger Greek Orthodox communities who had naturalized previously. This phenomenon was seen above in the example

Figure 1.2 The military naval ensign used by the Italian navy on its flag points to Italy's continued memory of the global maritime republics. Clockwise from upper left to right is the Republic of Venice, Republic of Genoa, Republic of Pisa, and Republic of Amalfi. Amalfi, an early player in Cairo, lost its lead across the Middle East and North Africa to the Venetian and Genoese republics. Pisa was subsumed into the Republic of Florence, which in turn became part of the legendary Grand Duchy of Tuscany under the Medicis. The conquests of Napoleon brought a sudden end to many of the republics a century before the rise of a single Italian kingdom.

Source: https://en.m.wikipedia.org/wiki/File:Naval_ensign_of_Italy.svg, Public domain.

of the Genoese of Pera who became subjects of the Ottoman sultan after 1453. Many of these Genoese families were already linguistically Hellenized, living throughout the Aegean among largely Greek-speaking Orthodox populations. Their counterparts were Genoese who had naturalized as subjects of the Spanish and Portuguese royals, including Christopher Columbus' son Diego. One-time governor of the Indies based on the Caribbean island of Hispaniola, Diego's career was a testament to how Genoese mariners and merchants looked west and east for opportunities during the Iberian-led Age of Exploration and rising Habsburg–Ottoman rivalry in Europe, with the Italian maritime republics attempting to navigate this increasingly global world of transoceanic shipping.

The Italian Maritime Republics: Venice, Genoa, and Florence from the Age of Exploration to Napoleon

Confluence and Conflict between the Genoese and Venetian Republics

The Iberian-led Age of Exploration saw a major shift in European shipping patterns that dramatically challenged the dominance of Italian shipping in West–East exchange. Portugal and Spain were the centers of monarchy-supported shipping expeditions that successfully bypassed the Italian peninsula, the Middle East, and North Africa in pursuit of direct access to the Spice Islands (Maluku Islands, Indonesia). These islands were situated where the Indian Ocean meets the South China Sea and Pacific Ocean. The two kingdoms—Portugal and Spain—eventually developed two rival trade routes that began in the Atlantic. Spain developed the trans-Atlantic and trans-Pacific Seville–Acapulco–Manila route. Portugal secured the Lisbon–Goa–Macau route that went around the southern tip of Africa and across the Indian Ocean. Within fifty years, both kingdoms were conducting direct business with Beijing and Nagasaki and trading in commodities such as silks, precious metals, spices, and porcelain.

From the Italian maritime republics perspective, the development was tremendous. The Age of Exploration developed in the aftermath of the Almohad caliphate's territorial and naval losses in Iberia in the 1200s, when the Kingdom of Portugal expanded southward into Lisbon (Arabic: al-Ushbuna) and the rising Kingdom of Castile absorbed its Muslim client state, namely, the Emirate of Granada. The Italian maritime republics had a long history of business with the Almohads and the Nasrids in cities like Marrakesh and Granada, just as they did with the Roman Catholic kingdoms in cities like Barcelona. In fact, the loss of the silk industry in Granada was partly offset by the new northern silk industry in Barcelona built with Genoese help. It was this same Genoese presence that, in the 1400s, saw the rise of a Spanish and Portuguese military nobility descended from Christopher Columbus' son Diego stretching from Iberia to the Caribbean. The Venetians, in contrast to the Genoese, were less present in Spanish and Portuguese circles due to the Venetian republic's activities in the eastern Mediterranean: securing diplomatic connections with the rising Ottomans of Istanbul, building trade alliances with the Safavids of Isfahan, conquering the Italian peninsula and Greek isles like the ancient Romans before them, and building a high-speed commercial traffic system.

This contrast in Genoese and Venetian activity could even be seen in shipping technology, which was a core driver of the Age of Exploration. Venice's mass-production of high-speed low-walled galley ships at the renowned Arsenale complex diverged from Genoa's growing preference for high-walled transoceanic cog ships at this time. It was this latter variety of shipping technology that allowed Spanish- and Portuguese-funded mariners to chart a shipping route across the Atlantic to the Caribbean and, during the expedition of Magellan, routes across the Pacific to from Acapulco to Manila. The contrast in shipping technologies pointed to the many ways that merchants and mariners from the Italian maritime republics built momentum in both international business and technology after the Renaissance in a way that was only truly interrupted by the shock of Napoleon's state-of-the-art military in the late 1700s.

What gave the Venetians an advantage in the Mediterranean was the special relationship they developed with the region's two most important regional players. The first were the Ottoman sultans, one-time competitors and ultimately conquerors of the surviving eastern Roman Empire of Constantinople. The second were the Safavid shahs, Muslim self-styled successors of the ancient Achaemenids and Sassanians and recent inheritors of the Iranian lands previously held by the Timurid khanate. Venetian activity in Ottoman Istanbul illustrates how much the Genoese had come to abandon their earlier attempts to build a sprawling territorial empire in the Mediterranean. It was a feat that the Venetians continued to pursue as they captured more and more territory on the Italian peninsula itself.

But the Venetians were not willing to abandon entirely the possibilities of the Age of Exploration to the new global empires of Spain and Portugal. With the rise of the Dutch Republic (est. 1581) and the United Kingdom (est. 1603), when the government-supported Dutch East India Company (est. 1602) and the British East India Company (est. 1600) began pushing the Spaniards and Portuguese out of Asian waters, the Venetians found new ways to capitalize on global trade networks. In a decision implemented by the Venetian state, the Venetians provided a variety of globetrotting merchant groups with access to the city center: Muslims from the Ottoman Empire,

Armenians from Safavid Iran, Aegean Greeks, Germans active in the cities of the Hanseatic League, and, most notably, Sephardic Jews and Jewish-heritage *conversos* (Jewish-heritage New Christians) fleeing the Spanish and Portuguese empires. The outcome was the Venice–Spalato–Istanbul trade route that crossed the Adriatic port of Spalato (Croatian: Split) north of Dubrovnik (Republic of Ragusa), and that saw the exchange of commodities like red pigment (cochineal) from the Spanish New World (Mexico) and Iranian silks used to create Venetian red velvet.

What limited the possibilities of Venice's Venice–Spalato–Istanbul trade route was how easily its traffic was replicated by the other Italian republics and states. The Adriatic coastal city of Ancona, part of the Papal States, followed Venice's lead by allowing—in competition with Venice—foreign merchants from Iberia and Ottoman Istanbul commercial and residency privileges. The result was the Ancona–Dubrovnik–Istanbul trade route that passed through the Republic of Ragusa (*c*. 1358–1808) and that was further south than the Venice–Spalato–Istanbul route. Interestingly, the popes involved in relaxing Ancona's residency restrictions were citizens of the Florentine republic and, specifically, members of its most powerful ruling household: the Medicis. The Medici household supplied four political administrators to the Roman Catholic Church who all rose through the ranks to become bishop of Rome, that is, the pope. Perhaps unsurprisingly, it was this same ruling Medici family of Florence that managed, by the 1600s, to outdo both Venice and Ancona in the very same game of building a two-way trade circuit with Istanbul by rebuilding the storied Florentine-held port of Livorno in Tuscany.

The Medicis, the Republic of Florence, and the Duchy of Tuscany

The Florentines under Medici governance (*c*. 1434–1737) had been following closely behind the Genoese and Venetians in pursuit of commercial exchange with both the Ottomans of Istanbul and the Mamluks of Cairo (r. 1250–1517). The Medicis were Tuscans like their Pisan compatriots half a millennium earlier during the First Crusade (1096–1099). During the Ottoman era of Istanbul (*c*.1453), they were poised to dominate exchange between Europe, the Middle East, and North Africa first via Florentine merchant networks and eventually via the port of Livorno. In the lead-up to transforming Livorno into Florence's own international port for merchants from all empires, the Medicis managed to cultivate Florentine relations with a variety of powers—Rome's Papal State, Cairo's Mamluk sultanate, Istanbul's Ottoman sultanate—in order to rebuild Tuscany's central position in global trade half a millennium after Pisa rose to prominence.

Having managed to serve as pope for an almost continuous and historically pivotal twenty-year period (1513–1534), the Medici family built an enterprising Florentine trade circuit during the early Ottoman period that connected Florence with the papal-held Adriatic port of Ancona. Florence's connections with Ancona allowed the city access to the Ancona–Dubrovnik–Istanbul trade route. It was the Medici popes who played a key role in relaxing restrictions on residency for Ottoman subjects in Ancona, and by the end of the 1500s plans were underway to apply the same logic in the Medicis' own ports. In a move that challenged both the Ancona–Dubrovnik–Istanbul and earlier Venice–Spalato–Istanbul route, the Medicis built a global trade center in Tuscany that would be on a par with Venice: Livorno.

Livorno: Tuscany's First "Free Port"

By 1580, half a century after the Florentine republic became the more prestigious Grand Duchy of Tuscany with papal blessing, the Grand Duke of Tuscany Ferdinando I de' Medici came up with a new plan that was even more profitable than pushing Florence towards the Ancona–Dubrovnik–Istanbul trade route: pulling the region's trade diasporas to Tuscany itself, and specifically to the port of Livorno. Livorno had the disadvantage of being on the Italian peninsula's western coast, as opposed to Venice and Ancona's Adriatic location. At the same time, it shared an advantage with its northern neighbor Genoa: it looked out to northern and western Europe, which in the 1600s saw the rise of powerful Dutch and British trading operations.

Evoking nearby Pisa's global heritage, and going further than Venice's ability to attract foreign merchants, Ferdinando I declared Livorno a "free port" in 1580. That is, he allowed a variety of merchants—Greeks, Armenians, Jews, Muslims from the Ottoman sultanate ("Turks" in the charter), Muslims from Iberia and North Africa ("Moors" in the charter), and Protestants from the north—to conduct business in Tuscany without the burden of high taxation duties. Ferdinando de' Medici additionally offered residency privileges, which in the 1600s and 1700s turned Livorno into an international city on a par with Istanbul and Venice.

To make Livorno more of an economic and cultural hub of the Mediterranean rather than a transitory site of exchange, groups like Sephardic Jews escaping the Spanish Inquisition as well as formerly Byzantine-era Greek Orthodox operating across the Venetian and Ottoman Aegean were welcome to remain permanently in Livorno, where they built churches and synagogues. Under Medici governance, the Grand Duchy of Tuscany became a veritable trade competitor of the sprawling Venetian republic, and Livornese Jewish networks in particular played a major role in bridging Tuscany with major trade emporia like Fez, Algiers, Tunis, and Alexandria.

In its heyday, however, Livorno ran into the same tumultuous outcome that impacted neighboring Venice and Genoa: the rise of Napoleon at the end of the French Revolution (1789–1799), and the Napoleonic armies' invasion of southern Europe. The spread of the Napoleonic armies throughout the early 1800s left a profound impact on the political and social networks of both the Italian peninsula and the worlds of North Africa across from it. From Middle Eastern and North African perspectives, the rise of Francophone North Africa was the most obvious outcome of France's rise to prominence in the early 1800s.

From the Italian peninsula's perspective, Napoleon's impact was both seismic and elusive. In the short term, the Genoese and Venetian republics came to a sudden and inglorious end in 1797. Paintings of the Venetian doge's resignation, dressed in a scarlet robe and descending the palace stairs for the last time, would evoke black and white photographs of the last Ottoman sultan saluting his guards as he left Topkapi palace in 1923. In the long run, the Napoleonic invasions of the northern Italian peninsula left the same type of enduring and elusive impact that drove the Ottoman Empire's nationalist movements. Specifically, it propelled far beyond Paris the French Revolution's language of anti-monarchism, parliamentary democracy, and liberal citizenship. Politically powerful Italian centers, including Genoa, Venice, Florence, and Livorno, became centers of local political and intellectual reforms that culminated in the rise of a unified Italian kingdom in 1863. This outcome shaped and was shaped by the Greek and Balkan nationalist movements across the Adriatic, which in turn shaped varieties of Ottoman, Turkish, and Arab nationalisms. One of the lesser known dimensions of this process in the Italian case was what happened in the Italian diaspora among the so-called Levantine Italians. While some went through a process of "becoming Italian," others lost their ties with the Italian peninsula.

Figure 1.3 Alexandria was one of the many places where Italians with recent and more distant connections to the Italian peninsula debated the rise of Mussolini-era fascism. Filippo Tommaso Marinetti (left), whose parents came to Egypt as legal advisors during Egypt's modernization era, left Egypt to become a formative player in the Italian literary and artistic movement known as futurism. Marinetti became a supporter of Mussolini's Fascist Party at a time when other Italian Alexandrians, including Fausta Cialente (right), were vociferous critics.

Sources: https://en.wikipedia.org/wiki/Filippo_Tommaso_Marinetti#/media/File:FilippoTommasoMarinetti.jpg, public domain; http://www.voxmilitiae.it/2016/12/fausta-cialente-il-destino-di-una-scrittrice-straniera-dappertutto, public domain after fifty years.

Becoming Italian and the Debate in Rome about the Levantines

From Pisa and Genoa to Venice and Florence, and in the decades leading up to the Italian kingdom's establishment (est. 1861), families connecting the Italian peninsula with the ports of North Africa underwent a process of "becoming Italian" during the *Risorgimento* (Italian Unification). Tuscan-speaking Livornese Jews in early nineteenth-century Tunis, for example, founded schools where Italian was taught at a time of growing French–Italian rivalry for political influence in the region. At the same time, there one outcome of these post-Napoleonic reforms of the 1800s was even more elusive: as much as the *Risorgimento* movement appeared to unveil a shared Italian-ness hidden behind the peninsula's many political cultures and diverse social customs, it also magnified—both in the peninsula and abroad—a certain ambiguity over whether certain groups were more Italian than others.

This debate about who was truly Italian was a question fraught with complexities, and it played out long after the rise of a unified Italian kingdom. Among its most enduring outcomes was that many so-called Levantine Italians (*gli Italiani Levantini*) in the 1900s never returned to the homelands of their parents and grandparents, who immigrated across the Mediterranean in large numbers in search of work during the *Risorgimento* era. The "Levantine" diaspora included everyone from older generations of Tuscan-speaking Livornese Jews active in 1800s Tunis to Roman Catholic Lombards in 1900s Istanbul and Cairo. In Algeria and Tunisia, which became French protectorates in 1830 and 1881, respectively, Livornese Jews found themselves subsumed *en masse* into the linguistic and legal gallicization policies of the new governors who encouraged Francophone learning among Tuscan Jews. Jews from a wide variety of backgrounds, including Arabic-speaking Jews and Italian-speaking Livornans, became simultaneously French speakers and French citizens by virtue of new laws around education and citizenship.

A segment of Tuscans in the North African diaspora, in other words, increasingly became French in a growing and culturally multivalent French empire of the twentieth century that stretched as far as Hanoi in Vietnam. At the same time, in the decades leading up to Tunisia's transformation into a French protectorate (1881) just a few years later, the Duchy of Florence was pushing Livornese Jews to naturalize in North Africa as subjects of the Tunisian bey after residency of only one to two years. In other words, throughout the Italian peninsula, a process of political and cultural border delineation was underway in the decades between Napoleon's French Revolution-era occupation of the peninsula's northern regions (*c.* early 1800s) and the declaration of a united Italian kingdom (1861). Livornese Jews, native speakers of the rising Italian national dialect and a group with deep transnational connections with Jews in North Africa, were among the first groups to navigate the outcomes of new post-French Revolution discussions of liberal citizenship—that is, citizenship defined not in terms of a communitarian identity (Livornese Jews, Livornese Greeks, Livornese Catholics) nor in terms of being the subject of a king or duke, but rather in terms of ideas about "equality" and democratic governance.

The French Revolution's "liberty, equality, brotherhood" would permeate antimonarchist movements throughout the eastern Mediterranean in the 1800s and early 1900s. That some Livornese Jews became French in the nineteenth-century diaspora, while one member of the community became the Kingdom of Italy's prime minister, points to how the outcomes of these nineteenth-century debates about being Italian were still in formation. Still, the case of diasporic Livornese Jews becoming French foreshadowed something that would happen in Ottoman Istanbul and Khedival Cairo and Alexandria: many would remain in the Middle East and North Africa and never return.

The phenomenon of families from the Italian peninsula living in the Middle East and North Africa lasted longest where the British Empire had its greatest influence: the cosmopolitan port cities of late Ottoman Istanbul and Khedival Alexandria (Egypt). In both cases, *Risorgimento*-era Italians resident in the cities in the late 1800s and early 1900s became subsumed into the expanding exterritorial laws governing British and French foreigners. The result was complex: for many of the so-called Levantine Italians (*gli Italiani Levantini*) who arrived after Italian Unification, the diverse circumstances of their local residence, career pursuits, and marital choices meant that they—like their Genoese, Venetian, Florentine, and Livornan forebears in earlier centuries—acculturated to local milieus in ways that British officers and diplomats did not. Legally, however, Italian citizenship meant that they remained as technically foreign throughout the Middle East and North Africa as the British. Unlike the British, however, Italian acculturation to the cosmopolitan local milieu meant that not every Italian was willing to forgo the kind of business and residency privileges that foreigners were increasingly restricted from keeping. That is, moving into the tumultuous decades between the First and Second World Wars, Levantine Italians in early twentieth-century Istanbul and Alexandria were frequently in the complex position of being both culturally local and legally foreign, and the choice to leave or stay was mediated by this tension.

On the Ottoman side, the Levantines (*gli Levantini*) were deeply involved as artists, artisans, and business owners in the industrialization and development of the Ottoman capital for some fifty years after the establishment of Italy (*Regno d'Italia*). In the late 1800s, the legendary residence of the Venetian ambassador (*bailo*) became the site of the Italian embassy, which oversaw the affairs of Italians living in the city. For much of the community, however, their activities came to an abrupt end with the outbreak of the Italian–Ottoman war of 1911. By then, Italy was living out pretensions to become one of Europe's

Great Powers, jumping into an attempted conquest of Ottoman Libya (1911). The invasion led the Ottoman administration to fulfill its threat of responding with the expulsion of Italians resident in Istanbul and the Levant. However, for many of these Italians, like the Greeks of late Ottoman Izmir, there was another option outside the empire: Alexandria.

Egypt, especially Alexandria, saw the last large community of Levantine Italians moving into the 1952 revolution. Governed by the khedives and their administration, Egypt was nominally Ottoman and increasingly British-influenced in the late 1800s. The port city of Alexandria was legally and culturally pluralistic, with law and popular culture articulated in Italian, French, English, and Arabic. By the late 1930s, however, new reforms under the khedivate—now a constitutional monarchy—began to restrict extraterritorial privileges for foreigners, and the antimonarchist nationalist movement that carried out the 1952 revolution was already taking root. Alexandrian Italians, like their Greek neighbors, were faced with an interesting question: should they naturalize as Egyptians within Alexandria's cosmopolitan, international, and multiconfessional Muslim and Christian landscape? Alternatively, should they head to Italy, the economically struggling and politically turbulent home of their parents and grandparents? Might there be a middle position of remaining in the city and navigating the change in laws governing foreigners, particularly as the Italians and Greeks were not nearly as culturally foreign as the British and French?

To the surprise of the Italian consulate, many Italians in the late 1930s naturalized as Egyptians. The political and social landscape of both Italy and Egypt at the time makes this decision look less surprising in retrospect. For the many Italians who did not naturalize as Egyptians, however, the first of two major blows to the community occurred in the early 1940s: military conflict between Mussolini-led Italy and Britain in western Egypt.

At the time, Mussolini decided to invade western Egypt in continuity with Italy's short-lived experiment with being an imperialist power. In the eyes of the British side of Egypt's administration, Italians in Egypt were a suspect community. Many Alexandrian Italians were arrested and interned, including the father of singer Iolanda Gigliotti—better known as Dalida. Born in Cairo to Calabrian parents, Dalida was an actress in Arabic-language cinema until 1954, when she moved to France and cultivated a singing career in French, Italian, and Arabic well into the 1980s. Her father Pietro, a late arrival to Egypt from Calabria in the 1920s, was among the many Italians interned despite having careers outside politics. Pietro was a violinist for Cairo's Khedival opera house. Dalida's mother Giuseppina, a seamstress, came to Cairo together with Pietro from their economically hard-hit town in southern Italy.

The episode of Britain's internment of Italians in Egypt in the 1940s, aimed officially at Alexandrian Italians who supported Italy's Fascist Party, was the first of two major blows to the last major community of Levantine Italians. The other came soon after the declaration of the Arab Republic of Egypt in 1952, which was a year before Dalida—Miss Egypt in the Miss Universe competition of 1954—moved permanently to France. The key policy change in the 1950s was rising president Gamal Abdel Nasser's nationalization of foreign-owned large and small businesses, which followed the tumultuous nationalization of the British-held Suez Canal. Underlying the policy shift was a synthesis of Egyptian nationalism, which had a long history in Egypt, with two new elements that had an economic and cultural effect across industries: the first was socialist-inspired economic reform, which was widespread in British and French colonial territories around the world. The second was pan-Arab nationalism. Since the late 1800s and early 1900s, Egyptian nationalists associated pan-Arab nationalism with the late Ottoman-era Syrian Levant and with the many Syrian Christian and Muslim émigrés living in Egypt since the late 1800s. By the 1950s, Egyptian nationalist Gamal Abdel Nasser argued that pan-Arab nationalism should be a key component of Egyptian nationalism. Egypt's 1952 revolution, which occurred shortly after the Syrian Arab Republic emerged from French Mandate Syria and Lebanon (1920–1946), identified the new Egyptian republic as the "Arab Republic of Egypt." Its socialist policies were shared by newly independent Syria to the north.

By the end of the decade, Nasser began nationalizing large and small foreign-owned businesses as part of an attempt to lift help Egypt's largely Muslim and Coptic Christian countryside achieve upward social mobility. The reforms saw the disappearance of the country's British and French presence. Alexandria's Aegean Greeks expected to be excluded from nationalization policies given their century and a half role in building Egypt's industries under the khedives, and also given their participation in the Egyptian armed forces during the British invasion of Egypt following the Suez Canal dispute. The Italians had a similarly multigenerational role building Egyptian industries and were widely seen as the most acculturated European minority to Alexandria and Cairo's Arabic-speaking milieus. In the end, neither the Greeks nor Italians were excluded.

From an Alexandrian perspective, the most striking outcome of the new Egyptian republic's policies was the trickling away of Alexandria's and Cairo's Greek and Italian communities throughout the 1950s and 1960s. The departure of the Italians and Greeks from the ancient port city of Alexandria, where Italian and Greek were heard alongside French and English throughout the 1800s and early 1900s, transformed a decidedly cosmopolitan city of the 1940s into a ghost of its former self by the 1970s. By then, France had just given up control of its North African and Levantine holdings, the British likewise withdrew from the region, and Europe saw the rise of a variety of new post-Second World War industrial centers: Bedford (England), Lyon (France), Milan, Munich, and others that grew in parallel with American centers like Detroit and Buenos Aires. With the pull of Mediterranean labor and talent to the north and west, including Italian talent from centers like Alexandria and Cairo, the millennium-long history of families from the Italian peninsula residing in the Middle East became a living memory.

Writing Western History in its Global Context

The Industrial Revolution and its Global Origins

For decades, the study of Italy's connections with the Middle East and North Africa has attracted the attention of writers interested in economic globalization and the nature of Europe's past, present, and future. One question related to the Industrial Revolution has been of particular interest: how did European centers like ancient Rome and medieval Paris, one-time capitals of the Roman Empire and Frankish empire (Francia), emerge in the twentieth century as global centers of industry and design. One answer traces a genealogy of progress that is entirely European: Italian and French industrialization in the twentieth century developed in dialogue with innovation in London. In the heyday of the global British Empire, London became a center of the Industrial Revolution built on well-funded advances in steam engine technology and mechanized mass production in factories.[5] These advances, which were in continuity with the Renaissance and Scientific Revolution, facilitated England's industrial-era export of mass-produced commodities like ceramics, tea, and textiles to new import markets across Asia. Paris and Rome, centers of the European Renaissance and Scientific Revolution, were the beneficiaries of these later advancements in London as European administrators consciously attempted to emulate the British in cities like Paris, Lyon, Rome, and Milan.[6] By the late twentieth century, these French and Italian cities were centers of state-of-the-art innovations in technology and design, from multinational automobile manufacturers like Fiat (Turin) and Renault (Paris) to nanotechnology-driven textile innovators like Benetton (Ponzano Veneto near Venice).

But there was a certain complexity to this story of the British Industrial Revolution, one that points to origins that are as global as the British Empire itself. The type of ceramics, textiles, and teas that the British produced and exported to China and Japan were actually Western emulations of higher-cost commodities imported directly from China and Japan since the Age of Exploration, namely, Fujianese black tea, Japanese porcelain, Southeast Asian silks, and the like. In the case of tea, for example, the British East India Company successfully pushed the Dutch East India Company out of the tea import business by monopolizing access to Chinese tea exporters, but there were fundamental problems in satisfying European demand. The Qing-era Chinese government placed limits on tea exports in part because the British East India Company had nothing of value to sell back to Chinese tea exporters beyond contraband items like opium, which was illegal in China. The Chinese government kept a close watch over illegal opium imports in the decades leading up to the Opium Wars, when the Chinese government's destruction of an opium cargo sparked the start of British–Chinese military hostilities and British influence over Chinese economic policy in the late 1800s.[7] Even before the Opium Wars, however, what allowed the British to get around China's supply limitations was certain technological innovations in the realm of botany and horticulture: the British East India Company managed to transfer the secrets of tea cultivation from Fujian to British India and build tea plantations within and across the British Empire using hybrid seeds, including the renowned Sino-Indian Darjeeling seed.[8] They then, drawing on industrial steam technology, used machines to depart from the older handcrafted Chinese methods of cultivating, harvesting, and shaping small batches of tea. These technological innovations in horticulture and mechanized production allowed a move towards manufacturing machine-harvested and machine-processed black tea at scale all across the plantations of British India. The same story of European innovation with global origins could be seen in how porcelain-like Staffordshire ceramics drew on the ceramics of Delft, which were in turn based on close studies of highly prized imported Chinese and Japanese porcelain with their sophisticated under-the-glaze design.

Western industrial innovations, in other words, developed in close dialogue with innovations to the east, and the same could be said for the mechanized technology associated with the steam engine. The steam engine was one of various engineering advancements in mechanical technology that impressed global observers and included mechanical firearms, which allowed the British invasion of China. Ironically, it was China where gunpowder and cannons were invented. And when Europeans invaded China, they noted in encounters with foot soldiers that the once mighty Chinese military had grown oddly outdated in both technology and strategy. The Japanese, meanwhile, were observing the firepower of European weapons technology with alarm despite being closely connected with Dutch medicine and military innovations.

This technological gap between the West and the so-called East points to an earlier era when European science, once behind its counterparts in cities further east, began to advance ahead with engineering feats that facilitated the Industrial Revolution. For global historians, those centuries are the era of the Latin-language Renaissance and Scientific Revolution, when Newton's physics made an unprecedented set of advances that were central to modern steam-driven and electrical technology. It is across these centuries where Europe's forgotten dialogue with its neighbors in the East is most obvious. Global historians have documented in detail how the massive momentum of Latin language during the Scientific Revolution epitomized by Newton drew directly on the Arabic–Latin translation movement of Toledo and Palermo, which in turn drew on the Greek–Arabic translation movement of Damascus and Baghdad.[9] Global historians have realized, in other words, that advancements during the British Industrial Revolution were borne out of its global exchange with neighbors near and far, and that an understanding of the present and future of this innovation requires the same global approach.

In the case of Rome and Paris, one-time centers of the bygone Roman and Frankish empires, historians with a more global perspective have discovered that these cities' modern transformations were as much a product of innovations in the British Industrial Revolution as they were the countless innovations central to the French and Italian Renaissance: glassblowing and textile manufacturing in Aleppo under the Umayyad caliphate, surgery and pharmacology in Alexandria under the Fatimid caliphate, shipbuilding and weapons manufacturing in Baghdad under the Abbasid caliphate, cartography and navigation technology in Mamluk Cairo, the chemical extraction methods of aromatic and medicinal oils in Ottoman Arabia and East Africa, the spice-processing techniques of Southeast Asia's sultanates, the gunpowder and silk manufacturing of China; and the ceramics and tea cultivation of Japan. It is this global picture of the world of Europe and its neighbors that this book seeks to explore, and in doing so, it takes a specifically maritime approach to understanding global geographies and trade routes that passed through Italy.

Towards a Maritime Understanding of Italy's Past and Present

French historian Fernand Braudel was among the first modern researchers to investigate an understanding of Europe's past and present through a global maritime lens, and he did so in continuity with past writers who connected geography with politics and culture.[10] From Anatolian writer Herodotus in Greek to Andalusian writers Ibn Khaldun and Ibn al-Khatib in Arabic, chroniclers and political philosophers have observed for centuries how the sea links disparate regions together in a way that shapes politics and human behavior: the Baltic Sea linking Scandinavia with present-day Russia, the North Sea around the British Isles and coastal Iberia, the Atlantic Ocean linking the Iberian and West African coasts, the Black Sea connecting the Greek isles with the Crimean Peninsula across the Sea of Marmara, and the most storied of all in European history, the Mediterranean Sea with its links to the Adriatic Sea, Aegean Sea, and Sicilian Strait.

According to Braudel's approach, an understanding of Europe's past and present meant understanding the innovations of merchant networks who operated across these seas. There was, for example, the Hanseatic League with their high-sided carrack ships in the North Sea and Baltic Sea ports. Their activities linked cities like London and Amsterdam with Bergen, Copenhagen, and Stockholm, regions once dominated by the Vikings and Normans. For Braudel, these networks gave northern Europe a story that was clearly distinct from developments further south along the Mediterranean and Adriatic seas, where low-sided, high-speed Venetian galleys raced up and down the Italian and Balkan coastlines in pursuit of commerce and conquest across very different linguistic worlds: vernacular Latin, Slavic languages, Greek, Turkish, and Arabic. At the same time, Braudel recognized that these histories were not entirely disconnected, and that understanding European history required investigating innovations where these trade routes met.

In the case of transnational innovations in laws around trade and residency, Venetian archives and architectural history tells us that the innovation of the *fondaco*, that is, the warehouse-inn, played a key role in allowing global travelers short-term access to Italian cities. Short-term residency privileges via the Venetian *fondaco* offered merchants from the Middle East and North Africa access to southern European markets while providing the city with profits from taxable imports and exports. The Venetian *fondaco* drew on the Middle Eastern and North African *funduq*, which served a similar function in allowing Venetian merchants access to Asian markets. German traders from the north were similarly welcomed in Venice at the German warehouse-inn (*fondaco dei tedeschi*), where they were able to do business with Turkish-speaking merchants staying at the Turkish warehouse-inn (*fondaco dei turchi*).[11] The intersection of these same trade routes further west along the Iberian Atlantic is what facilitated innovation among the Genoese, who moved away from the low-sided galleys popular in Venice in favor of the high-sided carracks used by the Genoese. It was this type of ship was used by Genoese mariners Christopher Columbus and his son Diego—one-time Admiral of the Indies in Santo Domingo (1506–1526)—to traverse the treacherous Atlantic Ocean. Tracing the origins of these shipping innovations, historians have rediscovered an encounter between medieval European mariners with those of the Middle East and Southeast Asia. Sailing back and forth across the Indian Ocean, merchants from the Arabian Peninsula trading in Chinese commodities moved away from the ancient steering oar in favor of the rope-operated rudder, which in turn paved the way for modern mechanical rudders on boats and airplanes. Italian shipping mastered techniques from both West and East, building on innovations seen in the Hanseatic League's cog ships, Roman galleys, and Arabian dhows in the construction of their own state-of-the-art vessels. Western innovation, in other words, is an outcome of centuries of global encounters, and the past and present trajectory of those encounters is best understood through a global understanding of history.

Since Braudel, a variety of historians have applied this maritime approach to understanding the past and present. Janet Abu-Lughod's analysis has shown how the world's West-centered political and economic ascendancy is in fact a very modern phenomenon, making the resurgence of centers in Asia unsurprising.[12] Andre Gunder Frank and Peter Borschberg have shown how the biographies and innovations that make up modern Europe and Asia were in fact borne out of encounters centered especially in Southeast Asia in cities like Singapore.[13]

Taken together, all these works illustrate that just as modern Europe can be understood only in the context of its past trade connections throughout the world, so likewise the story of Italy's present and future appears most clearly when examining the peninsula's historical links with the Middle East and North Africa. These connections are ancient and go back to the early centuries of the Roman Empire, when Roman Carthage and the province of Roman Arabia linked global trade between West and East. It is in this world where this book's story begins in a saga about Italians in the East (*Oriente*) and the making of modern Europe.

2

AFTER CAESAR: THE ROMAN EMPIRE AND ITS ARABIAN FRONTIER

Figure 2.1 Christian Bedouin in Jordan (right) have been written about for centuries because of their cultural connections with multiple histories that link the ancient Roman Empire with its Arabian frontiers around Petra: the childhood of Roman emperor Philip in Awrantis (Arabic: Hawran) in Arabia Petraea, the culture of early Aramaic- and Arabic-speaking Christianity where Philip came of age, the childhood of Roman imperial matriarchs Julia Domna and Julia Maesa of Emessa (Arabic: Homs), the Christian Arab Ghassanid tribe once in alliance with the eastern Romans in the sixth century, the seventh-century Muslim Arab tribes that secured the Ghassanids' counter-alliance, the north–south trade routes from Palmyra and Petra to northwest Arabia (Hijaz) during the revolution of imperial ally-turned-rebel Queen Zenobia of Palmyra, and in the days of Julius Caesar and Cleopatra (c. 100s BCE), the ancient Nabatean kingdom associated with Petra's most famous archaeological site (left). The culture and history of Christian Bedouin serve as a reminder of how northern Arabia's deserts and oases, like the fertile south, were the crossroads of global exchange long before the Age of Exploration and even before the Islamic caliphates. In the early decades of Roman rule in Petra, the mausoleum of Nabatean king Aretas IV (Nabatean Arabic: Haritha) was built in a Hellenistic style that drew on the region's even older connections with Alexander the Great's conquests (c. 300s BCE), and it has stood in present-day Jordan across all of these centuries as a testament to the Levant and northern Arabia's continuous ties with centers to the west—Rome, Athens, Alexandria, and Carthage.

Sources: https://tinyurl.com/42htwtbm & Library of Congress, public domain; https://www.loc.gov/item/2003653622, public domain; http://www.mariamhotel.com/family.html, public domain after fifty years.

Imperial Rome's Expansion into the Ancient Middle East

In 476, a high-ranking soldier in the Roman imperial army carried out a military campaign that Julius Caesar (d. 44 BCE) could never have predicted: the conquest of Rome itself. The soldier's unique name, Flavius Odoacer, pointed to his origins in the Roman Empire's Germanic frontiers beyond the Danube.[1] In a series of moves that shocked the Mediterranean world, Odoacer deposed Roman emperor Romulus Augustus, declared himself king of Italy (*Rex Italiae*), and pledged nominal allegiance to the eastern co-emperor Zeno (r. 474–491) in Constantinople. Odoacer's successor Theodoric, born in present-day Austria, would reign as king of Italy, king of the Ostrogoths, and king of the Visigoths (r. *c.* 475–526).

The fall of Rome represented a sharp contrast to the city's fortunes two centuries earlier, when Roman emperor Marcus Aurelius Claudius "Gothicus" (r. 268–270) earned his unique moniker for a successful military campaign against the Goths. Rome's fall was in even sharper contrast to the city's initial expansion from city-state to global empire almost a millennium before Odoacer's career. The Roman Republic's ancient military transformation from a city-state to regional power player occurred across the same centuries in which Alexander the Great's generals (*c.* 320s BCE) captured Anatolia, Egypt, the Middle East, and Central Asia from the mighty Achaemenids based in Iraq and Iran. The city of Babylon on the Euphrates River, legendary capital of the ancient Babylonian kingdom (*c.* 1800s–500s BCE) became the Achaemenids' capital when they moved westward from Fars in Iran to Iraq in the 500s BCE. Under founder Cyrus the Great (r. 559–530 BCE), the Achaemenid empire extended westward far beyond Iran and Iraq and even beyond Syria and Anatolia, reaching Anatolia's Aegean frontier with the Greek isles. The ancient Persians loomed large in ancient Greek literary and oral culture, and their proximity to Athens set the stage for history's most legendary Greco-Persian encounter: the clash of a young Alexander the Great with Achaemenid emperor Darius III just two centuries before Julius Caesar extended Rome's political authority into the local kingdoms that Alexander and Darius had captured.[2]

It was from the Aegean kingdom of Macedon where Alexander, one-time student of the Athenian philosopher-scientist Aristotle, set out to conquer almost all of the Achaemenids' territory as far south as Egypt and as far east as the Achaemenid capital (Babylon), reaching even present-day Afghanistan and Pakistan. Alexander died in Iraq, where General Seleucus (d. 281 BCE) established Seleucia on the outskirts of the future Parthian capital of Ctesiphon (est. 120s BCE). The twin cities of Seleucia–Ctesiphon would become, in turn, the capital of both the Sassanian empire (*c*. 224–651 CE) and a major church in early Christianity: Iraq's Nestorian Church of the East. The Abbasid caliphate's capital of Baghdad (est. 762 CE), in turn, would be built on the outskirts of Seleucia–Ctesiphon (Arabic: *mada'in*) and became the adoptive new home of the Church of the East. For the Church's Aramaic speakers, Seleucia–Ctesiphon was known simply as *Saliq*. Among Arabic speakers further south, where Syria and Iraq met present-day Jordan and Arabia, the twin cities were known as *Mada'in* (The Cities) and marked an ideal site along the Tigris River for a new city in the 700s: Baghdad, capital of the Abbasid caliphate. Among the Abbasid caliphate's first diplomatic contacts were the Franks of the Frankish kingdom (Francia), who governed much of the Italian peninsula by the 700s CE in alliance with the bishop of Rome based in the Papal State.

This connection between the Franks and the Abbasids in the 700s was new in Islamic history, but it was not the first time the Italian peninsula had been linked with Iraq and its frontiers in Syria and Arabia. A millennium earlier, Julius Caesar's conquests were in many ways the start of Italy's continuous geopolitical and cultural encounters with the Middle East that continued well into the era of Mussolini. Caesar's conquests were part of a larger Roman strategy in the East directed towards Iraq, where the Seleucid dynasty's Parthian vassals usurped Seleucid rule (247 BCE–228 CE). In the lead-up to Julius Caesar's conquests in the East, after the Romans captured the heartlands of North Africa from the ancient Phoenicians of Carthage (209 BCE), both the Romans and Parthians eyed the remaining Middle Eastern and North African territories once held by Alexander. Julius Caesar's capture of Cleopatra's Egypt was a sign that the Romans were doing well. Like the Seleucids, the Ptolemies of Egypt (305–330 BCE) were a long-lasting descendant of Alexander's conquests. Seleucus and Ptolemy were two of Alexander's most successful generals, and the ultimate collapse of the Ptolemaic dynasty during the reign of its last ruler—Queen Cleopatra

IV—was a direct outcome of Julius Caesar's push eastward. Roman conquests during Caesar's generation finalized a half-millennium process that saw the once humble city-state of Rome take control of Mediterranean Europe, North Africa, and much of the Middle East.[3] Julius Caesar himself formalized the Roman Republic's pretensions to rule with the kind of grandiose militaristic authority seen among the great Hellenistic, Phoenician, Babylonian, and Persian empires of the Middle East and North Africa. In what officially transformed the sprawling Roman Republic into the Roman Empire, Caesar—given emergency powers as "dictator in perpetuity" (*dictator in perpetuo*) by the Senate—curtailed the power of the ancient Senate and sidelined the rule of governing consuls in Rome.[4] With the Senate and consuls out of the way, the republic-turned-empire was governed as a semi-dynastic imperial autocracy from the 100s BCE to the 300s CE. Beginning with Caesar's adopted son Octavian "Augustus," his successors began using titles like "first" (*princeps*), "lord" (*dominatus*), and the old military-turned-imperial title of "emperor" (*imperator*).[5]

Against this backdrop, Rome's fall in the late 400s CE to the Visigoths and Ostrogoths was, on the one hand, a major break in the Italian peninsula's connections with the Middle East and North Africa. On the other hand, it was a sign that Roman imperial borders had become expansive and unwieldy. They were large enough for one Roman emperor, namely, Constantine, to decide to establish a second capital further east a century before Rome's fall and several centuries after the life of Julius Caesar. The second capital, aptly named Constantinople, was built on the ancient port of Byzantion and was situated across the Aegean from Alexander's old homeland in Macedon. Its location as a second capital further east offered something Rome to the west could not: a way of monitoring both the Germanic frontiers of the Danube, where the rising Visigoths and Ostrogoths would eventually advance southward, and the Syrian frontiers with both Sassanian Iraq and Arabia. It was throughout these Syrian frontiers with Arabia, specifically in the Roman provinces of *Syria-Palestina*, *Syria-Phoenicia*, and *Arabia Petraea*, where a variety of local figures rose through the Roman administrative ranks in an illustration of how closely Rome became intertwined with the Middle East in the centuries after Julius Caesar's conquests in the region. In the centuries between Julius Caesar's capture of Egypt and Constantine's establishment of a second capital, a certain Julia Domna and her

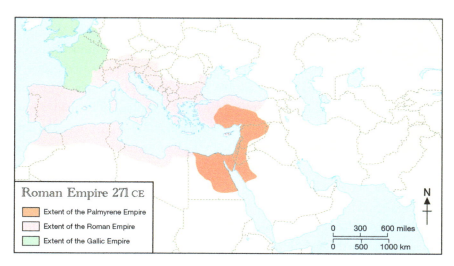

Figure 2.2 In the aftermath of Gothic incursions from the German Danube and Zenobia's rebellion in Palmyra along the Syrian–Arabian frontier, the promises of a new eastern capital in the ancient port of Byzantion (c. 300s) included closer administration of the increasingly sprawling empire's periphery. By the 400s, contemporary with Odoacer's capture of Rome, the empire was already administratively divided into western and eastern provinces with co-emperors in each of Rome and Constantinople.

relative Julia Maesa of Emessa (Arabic: Homs) became empress and imperial matriarch, respectively, during the rule of Roman emperor Septimius Severus of Leptis Magna (Libya). A few decades later, Philip of Awrantis (Arabic: Hawran) became Roman emperor. The ability of local patricians in the Middle East and North Africa to wield power in the Roman Empire was a phenomenon that Rome knew well and even cultivated in an attempt to lead through local aristocracies. But in the lead-up to the establishment of Constantinople, it was a strategy that was risky. In the same regions of Roman Syria and Jordan where Roman emperor Philip rose to prominence for his military feats in Iraq, Roman citizen and Palmyrene ruler Zenobia undertook a shocking rebellion against Rome with major territorial conquests that stretched from the Egyptian coast in the south to the heartlands of inner Anatolia in the north. A closer look at this history points to how later encounters of the Italian peninsula with the Islamic world, which began in the era of the Francia and Abbasid caliphate, were ultimately rooted in the deep political and cultural connections that Rome established in the Middle East after Caesar.

After Caesar: Zenobia of Palmyra

Along the Syrian–Arabian trade routes, local players remained influential even after Julius Caesar's arrival two centuries later. What illustrated this pattern most clearly was a contrast between two figures from present-day Syria and Jordan: one was a Palmyrene aristocrat named Zenobia of Roman *Syria-Phoenice*. In contrast to Cleopatra in the age of Julius Caesar, Zenobia two centuries later reneged on her partnership with the Romans and rebelled, minting coins that named herself *Augusta* as if she were herself Roman emperor and, at the height of her power, conquering much of the eastern Mediterranean. The other figure was her contemporary Philip of Roman *Arabia Petraea*, which was situated just south of Palmyra closer to Petra. Philip was older than Zenobia and, in his youth, rose through the ranks of military leadership after successful campaigns against the Sassanians. In a story that is frequently forgotten in history, Philip was actually named Roman emperor, earning the moniker "Philip the Arab" among later Roman chroniclers interested in his roots in *Arabia Petraea*. The stories of Zenobia and Philip, coupled with a slightly earlier story of two imperial matriarchs who hailed from Emessa (Homs, Syria), sheds light on how Rome found creative ways to pull the eastern provinces under its control before eventually establishing an eastern capital (Constantinople) as an answer to its problems in frontier governance.

Zenobia of Palmyra

Palmyra, like nearby Petra and Emessa, was a wealthy city on the northern tip of the Syrian–Arabian trade routes. It was also a key frontier city in the Romans' competition with the Sassanians of Iraq. In the 200s CE, Rome was keen to secure the loyalties of the Palmyrene leadership in the same way that the loyalties of Christian Arab tribes became an imperial strategy from the 300s CE onward. But in what foretold the growing independence of Christian Arabs such as the Ghassanids and their alliance with Muslim Arabs like the Umayyads (*c*. 600s CE), the leadership of Palmyra moved towards independence and territorial expansion under the rule of a certain Palmyrene governor named Zenobia (fl. 240–274). At a time when Emperor Aurelian was bogged down by conflict with the Goths in the Balkans, Zenobia declared the independence of Palmyra and its surrounding regions in 272 CE and even appointed her own governors as far away as Egypt. The multilayered cultural dimensions of Palmyra were most obvious in the Roman-style coins she had minted and, in particular, their various Latin, Greek, Palmyrene Aramaic, and Arabic linguistic dimensions.

More specifically, at the height of her rule, Zenobia minted Roman imperial coins in her own name—*S. Zenobia Aug* (*Septimia Zenobia Augusta*)—and in the name of her son Vaballathus—*Im. C. Vaballathus Aug.* (*Imperator Caesar Vaballathus Augustus*). The Latin terms *Augusta* and *Augustus* represented an explicit claim to be rulers on a par with the reigning Roman ruler Aurelian in Rome, whose name and title (*Imperator Aurelianus Augustus*) appeared on older Palmyrene coins during her rule. The Greek dimension could be seen in the use of her Greek name Zenobia rather than her Palmyrene Aramaic name Bat-Zabbai. The name *Zenobia* is the feminine form of *Zenobios*, which means "one whose life derives from Zeus." The name was not a translation but a kind of spinoff of her Palmyrene name Bat-Zabbai, which had the very different meaning of "daughter of Zabbai." The name Zabbai, in turn, was like other Palmyrene names including Zabeida and Zabda, which meant "divine gift." That meaning echoed the meaning of her son's name Vaballathus, which was a Latinized version of the Palmyrene Aramaic and Arabic phrase meaning of "Gift of Allat." In Arabic, the Latin Vaballathus reads as *Wahb al-lat*, and the Palmyrene Aramaic cognate sounds nearly identical. *Allat* was one of the various Arabian deities whose veneration extended across the Syrian–Arabian trade routes and who, in Palmyra, was represented visually in the "Temple of Allat" as the Greek deity Athena. In fact, surviving inscriptions indicate that the Temple of Allat in Palmyra was identified among locals as both the Temple of Allat and Temple of Athena, which paralleled the way the Latinized name *Vaballathus* had a Greek counterpart in the eastern Mediterranean: *Athenodoro* (Gift of Athena).

In other words, in the linguistically Greek, Palmyrene Aramaic, and Arabic worlds of Zenobia's Syria and the Syrian–Arabian trade routes, Zenobia wanted all her subjects to know that Palmyra—not Rome and certainly not Seleucia–Ctesiphon in neighboring Iraq—was the ultimate center of political power in the eastern Mediterranean world. And for any families who were Roman citizens within the rising Palmyrene empire, whether at home in Syria or further away in Egypt or southern Anatolia, their new imperial rulers were

Figure 2.3 Roman emperor Philip of Aurantis (Arabic: Hawran), like imperial empress Julia Domna Augusta of the Severan family (above), came from the same part of the Roman Empire as Zenobia. All these figures came from the Syrian–Arabian trade routes linking Petra and Palmyra with northwest Arabia in the decades before Constantine established a second capital in the eastern provinces, namely Constantinople.

Source: https://en.wikipedia.org/wiki/Julia_Domna#/media/File:Julia_Domna_(Julia_Pia),_inv._2210,_Roman_-_Braccio_Nuovo,_Museo_Chiaramonti_-_Vatican_Museums_-_DSC00897.jpg, public domain.

the two rulers represented on the new Roman-style Palmyrene coins: *Septimia Zenobia Augusta* (Zenobia) and *Imperator Caesar Vaballathus Augustus* (Vaballathus).[6] Roman emperor Marcus Aurelius Claudius "Gothicus" (r. 214–270), whose moniker recalled Rome's contemporary problems with the rising Goths of the Danube, no longer had authority in the region. The Palmyrene empire, stretching from Anatolia to Syria and Egypt, was the new player with which the Romans and Sassanians had to contend, and Rome would have to figure out another way of asserting its cultural and administrative dominance throughout the faraway eastern provinces.

Before Constantinople: Philip of Arabia and the Severan Matriarchs

The fact that there were powerful families in Roman Syria who were attuned to the politics of Rome is obvious from the story of Zenobia's earlier contemporary: Roman emperor Philip of Aurantis (r. 244–240 CE) in

Roman Arabia–Petraea. Both Philip and Zenobia came from the same region of the empire as three even earlier Roman imperial matriarchs: Julia Soaemias (Arabic: Suhayma), Julia Domna (Arabic: possibly Dumayna or Dumna), and Julia Maesa of the imperial Severan dynasty. The Severan matriarchs were originally from Emessa in Roman Syria–Phoenice, which bordered Aurantis in Roman Arabia–Petraea. The three centers—Emessa, Palmyra, and Aurantis—formed an upside down triangle pointing southward towards Petra along the Syrian–Arabian trade routes to northwest Arabia. Philip came specifically from the town of Shahba on the present-day borders of Syria and Jordan, and like Zenobia in Palmyra, Philip sought to elevate his hometown into a world-class city and gave it the name Philippopolis. Unlike Zenobia, he did so in his capacity as Roman emperor while Zenobia was still a child and not yet an imperial revolutionary.

Philip rose to prominence as a general who helped to secure Rome's Syrian border with Sassanian Iraq and Iran in the early 200s. This border was the very frontier that was breeched decades later close to Palmyra, where Zenobia's father similarly helped to secure the Roman frontier with the Sassanians and was rewarded with Roman imperial status. Philip's earlier work was famously depicted by the rival Sassanians on a rock relief in Persepolis, where he is represented standing next to Roman emperor Valerian during a loss against Emperor Shapur. During Zenobia's childhood, Philip was already emperor in Rome in a reign that was characterized by exceptional and curious tolerance of Christianity almost a century before Constantine became the first Christian emperor. That tolerance was pronounced enough for Roman writers to wonder if Philip was, in fact, Rome's first Christian emperor. Christianity was widespread along the Syrian–Arabian trade routes. At a time when the Romans had only recently installed colossal temples for the deities Jupiter and Bacchus in Baalbek (Lebanon), where early Christianity and a variety of Arabian priestly religions were already deeply rooted, it comes as no surprise that Christian chroniclers contemporary with Constantine debated whether Philip the Arab may have been Rome's first Christian emperor. What suggested the possibility was what one chronicler—Eusebius, bishop of Caesarea in Roman *Syria–Palestina*—described of Philip's tolerance of Christians and visit to a church.[7] The description would fit the context of his origins as well as Zenobia's later reputation for the tolerance of Christians.

If Philip's tolerance of or close familiarity with Christians was an outcome of his origins in Arabia Petraea, it would not be the first time that an administrator from the region brought something of their heritage with them to Rome. A generation before him, Roman emperor Marcus Aurelius Antoninus, born Varius Avitus Bassianus, could be seen undertaking the curious task of having a temple built in Rome for the Arabian deity known in Latin as Elagabalus (Arabic: *Ilah al-jabal*, "deity of the mountain"). Notably, his origins lay in Emessa (Homs, Syria), close to his younger contemporary Philip's own origins in Aurantis and later Zenobia's Palmyra. Antoninus was among a series of Roman emperors immediately preceding Philip who were, variously, the grandchildren and nephews of a certain Julia Maesa.

Maesa was the Emessa-born (Homs, Syria) daughter of an Arabian priestly family serving as custodians of the solar deity Elagabalus (Arabic: *ilah al-jabal*, "deity of the mountain"). Maesa was the elder sister of Julia Domna, who became Roman empress through her marriage with the Latin- and neo-Phoenician-speaking (Punic) general-turned-emperor Septimius Severus of Leptis (coastal Libya). Maesa's own marriage to Emessa-born nobleman in Roman military service, coupled with her connection to her imperial sister Domna, allowed her a major political role during the reigns of multiple emperors who were either of her own or her sister's descent in the early 200s. Maesa's image appears on a 2-denarius antoninianus coin, which reads *Iulia Maesa Aug* (*Julia Maesa Augusta*) in reference to her position in the imperial family. Her sister Julia Domna, wife of Septimius Severus, was honored upon her husband's death with titles like *Mater Senatus*, *Mater Patriae*, and *Pia Felix* (dutiful, auspicious) *Augusta*.[8]

Taken together with the stories of rebel queen Zenobia of Palmyra and Roman emperor Philip of Arabia Petraea, the story of the Severan matriarchs of Emessa adds context to why Emperor Constantine established the eastern capital of Constantinople in ancient Byzantion a few decades after the reign of Aurelius "Gothicus," against whom Zenobia and the Goths fought separately. Political stability across the eastern frontiers with the Sassanians was as important to Roman imperial longevity as was the frontier with the Goths north of the Balkans. In fact, Septimius Severus was himself ahead of Constantine in already eyeing Constantinople's original site (Byzantion) as an eastern capital, which would additionally facilitate Roman governance of the Syrian–Arabian frontiers with the Arabian world and its links to the lucrative East African and Indian Ocean trade.

The establishment of Constantinople was, in other words, as much a show of force as it was a realignment in defense of the borders dating back to Julius Caesar's era. Constantine's establishment of two capitals in the 300s CE simultaneously fortified the empire and facilitated its division into two manageable parts. The establishment of co-emperors, one in each capital, laid the framework for a long-term division in administration and eventually political culture. After the eclipse of the Palmyrenes, new vassal groups such as the Christian Arab Ghassanids (*c.* 300s–600s) would govern under the authority of Constantinople, not Rome, and the use of Latin in coins and documents would begin receding into the past in favor of the more exclusive use of Greek.[9]

For the Romans themselves, even if the move to the east in the 300s was a belated one, it would prove useful upon Odoacer's capture of Rome. Odoacer's successor Theodoric's rule as "King of Italy," "King of the Ostrogoths," and "King of the Visigoths" signaled the long-term absorption of the Italian peninsula into the rising world of German politics around the Danube. Constantinople would be left to begin simultaneously rolling back German conquests in the 500s CE under its Latin-speaking emperor Justinian, while simultaneously doubling down on its precarious hold over the Syrian–Iraqi frontier with the Sassanians. Not only would Constantinople see an emperor, namely, Heraclius, formally change the language of administration from Latin to Greek in the days of the early caliphates, but also one emperor would rise to prominence, namely, Leo III, who was a bilingual Greek and Arabic speaker in parallel with the Umayyad caliphate's early Greek- and Arabic-speaking bilingual administration. In the end, however, these efforts proved unsuccessful as Rome was ultimately captured in 476 and, within a few years, subsumed into the rule of Goths and later Franks.

Odoacer's conquest of Rome in 476 was transformational in how it brought to an end the western half of the ancient empire and left Roman involvement in the Middle East and North Africa to the eastern Romans, that is, the so-called "Byzantines" in modern historical writing. But that would not be the end of Rome's direct connections with the Middle East and North Africa.

From the 500s to the 700s, the Roman bishopric – that is, the papacy – worked with painstaking precision to carve out a new and autonomous political center in Rome that would be independent of both the German states to the north and Constantinople in the east. It was from that position of independence that Rome would pursue a new and independent political and commercial policy with the rising caliphates, one that saw both the Crusades in collaboration with rising Italian maritime republics and, during the Renaissance, attempts to attract Muslim and Jewish merchants from the Ottoman Empire through short-term residency agreements in the eastern papal port of Ancona. What facilitated all of this activity was the ability of the papacy to negotiate with the Goths' Frankish successors for independent governance of a large strip of land, which stretched across the Italian peninsula from Rome to Ancona. The success of those negotiations were rooted in the papacy's preservation of the Roman Church and, specifically, success in simultaneously pushing Chalcedonian Christianity on Arian Christian rulers and recentering regional Christian loyalties on Rome after Odoacer's conquest of the capital and the rise of Ravenna, which became the preferred capital of the Goths.

The fall of Rome in 476, in other words, was transformational not only in how it facilitated a political division between the Italian peninsula and the eastern Mediterranean, but also in how it marked the start of a new and enduring era when the Italian peninsula would become the new crossroads of three geopolitical worlds. The first was the world of the increasingly Romanized Germanic kingdoms based in the north, where the Lombards and Franks would begin overtaking the Ostrogoths, Visigoths, and Vandals in the 500s and 600s. The second was the world of Constantinople to the east, which competed with the Germanic kingdoms for influence in the Italian peninsula until the very last days of the eastern Romans (Byzantines) in 1453. The third was based within the Italian peninsula and, specifically, in Rome itself: the ancient Roman Church.

In Rome, the once powerful bishopric governed by the bishop of Rome, that is, the pope, slowly lost control over each ecclesiastical diocese in the 500s as the bishop of Ravenna and other bishoprics became more closely aligned with regional political circles like the Ostrogoths, Franks, local patricians in communes like Genoa, and even Constantinople across the Adriatic. As early as the 500s, Constantinople's ecclesiastical identity as the second center of Chalcedonian Christianity was beginning to challenge the leadership of Rome's bishopric, with an official schism erupting in 1066 that left two distinct churches: the Latin-language Roman Catholic Church and the Greek-language Eastern Orthodox Church. Part of what secured the longevity of the Roman Catholic Church long before the schism was the political strategy of the bishop of Rome immediately following Odoacer's conquest. While the conquest sidelined Rome as a political and ecclesiastic center, the office of the bishop of Rome managed to reemerge as one of the peninsula's most powerful political figures by the 700s and 800s. This recentering was the outcome of a painstaking process that saw the pope or Rome recenter Rome's religious authority among the many churches, monasteries, and abbeys that stretched from post-Roman capitals of Francia in the north to the Frankish-held Italian peninsula in the south, and even formerly Vandal-held post-Roman Carthage across the Sicilian Strait.

What made the bishop of Rome's efforts to recenter Rome particularly complex was the rise of a fourth geopolitical world: that of the Islamic caliphates, which managed in the 600s to capture Constantinople-held provinces from the Syrian Levant in the east to North Africa and even Iberia in the west. These two worlds became known in Arabic as the geographical west (*Maghrib*) and east (*Mashriq*). The outcome of the caliphates' expansion in the 600s into formerly western Rome was, centuries later, the unique phenomenon of Roman Catholic clergy in southern Iberia and North Africa operating in a bilingually Arabic- and Latin-speaking administrative milieu. Letters to Rome were written in Latin, while letters to local authorities were written in Arabic. The long duration story of Rome, in other words, was its fall in 476 and subsequent resurgence in a new form in the following centuries, with the bishop of Rome at the head of a sprawling Papal State rather than part of an imperial Roman administration governing a Mediterranean empire." The story of how the pope built the kind of regional alliances necessary to secure an independent Papal State and, with it, the loyalties of regional political and ecclesiastical leaders, illustrates one of the most important political phenomena that shaped Italian connections with the Middle East and North Africa between the fall of Rome and the rise of modern Italy: despite the centralized rule of post-Roman rulers like the Goths in Ravenna and Franks in Paris, local power in the Italian peninsula was deeply fragmented after Odoacer's conquests to an extent that facilitated the rise and independence of the Italian communes-turned-republics, that in turn further empowered the post-Roman Papal State and became partners in a new millennium of exchange—both in conflict and confluence—with the newly Islamic political world of the Middle East and North Africa.

3

THE FORMATION OF THE PAPAL STATE DURING THE EARLY CALIPHATES

Figure 3.1 During the reign of Justinian and Theodora in the 500s, Constantinople recaptured much of the European and North African territory once held by Rome that fell under the rule of the Goths and Vandals in the late 400s. Following the campaigns, Constantinople created two new administrative regions in the Italian peninsula and North Africa known as the Exarchate of Ravenna (r. 584–751) and Exarchate of Africa (r. 591–698). While the latter was based in Carthage and was eventually subsumed into the Islamic caliphates, the former was based in an unexpected location: Ravenna. The choice of Ravenna on the peninsula's Adriatic coast pushed Rome to the peninsula's political and cultural periphery and magnified Constantinople's influence in the region's ecclesiastical leadership.

Sources: https://commons.wikimedia.org/wiki/File:Emperor_Justinian_and_Members_of_His_Court_MET_LC_25_100_1a-e_s01.jpg, public domain; https://www.worldhistory.org/image/1421/theodora-i, public domain.

The Provincialized Papacy

The fall of Rome in 476 was a shock felt across the Mediterranean world, and the choice of Ravenna as the conquerors' new capital pushed Rome to the region's periphery. In many ways, however, the Roman Empire was still alive and well: the eastern emperor, Constantinople's emperor Zeno, still reigned and became the sole political inheritor of Rome's imperial past. Zeno commanded enough respect across western Roman administrative and popular circles that the Goths and Vandals, the new rulers in Ravenna and Carthage, respectively, trod carefully around him. But there was another figure with a claim on the Roman past: the bishop of Rome, that is, the pope. The survival of the papacy together with its ecclesiastical network of Roman bishops meant there was a path for Rome's revival as a political and cultural center in the region. Over the next few centuries leading up to the Crusades, the story of Rome's resurgence as part of powerful Papal State was complex, and it began with a key strategy: building a political alliance with the so-called "barbarian" conquerors and turning the religious loyalties of regional bishops and abbots away from the ruling circles of Gothic Ravenna, Vandal-held Carthage, and Constantinople, and back towards Rome.

In the long run, Constantinople became the biggest obstacle to Rome's resurgence. In the immediate aftermath of Odoacer's arrival in Rome (476), Constantinople found early success in its attempts to pull the western Roman lands' political and religious loyalties eastward. Justinian (r. 527–565), one of the last native Latin-speaking emperors in the increasingly Greek-speaking administrative world of Constantinople, led a series of campaigns that captured both the Italian peninsula as well as the Tunisian coast from the various Germanic kingdoms that controlled the Italian peninsula and North Africa. What occurred next demonstrated how small a role that Constantinople envisioned for Rome or its bishop in a fully restored Roman empire, and why the bishop of Rome looked for an ally in a third group of conquerors: the Franks.

The Papacy under Constantinople's Exarchate of Ravenna 568–751 and the Rise of a Papal–Frankish Alliance

Justinian's capture of the western Roman lands from the Goths and Vandals had a transformative effect on the region in how it set the stage for a Papal–Frankish alliance. In a major break from Rome's past, Justinian dismantled the ancient Roman network of administrative civil diocese on both sides of the Strait of Sicily. That is, Justinian administratively restructured the fallen western half of the ancient Roman Empire in order to centralize both halves in Constantinople. Specifically, Justinian's *Pragmatic Sanction* of 554 saw the old civil diocese network replaced with two new exarchates: the Exarchate of Ravenna (*Exarchatus Ravennatis*) based in the Italian peninsula's north, and the Exarchate of Africa (*Exarchatus Africae*) based in Carthage along the Tunisian coast.[1] Constantinople even installed its own duke (Latin: *dux*, Greek: *doux*) at a local level in various cities, including Rome itself (*c.* 536–756). Before the Papal State, in other words, there was the long-forgotten "Duchy of Rome" under Constantinople's authority. During those two centuries, the pope was politically subordinate even to the local duke. The duke, in turn, answered to the exarch in Ravenna, who answered to Constantinople.

"Duke" was an ancient Roman imperial title that endured after the fall of Rome with the combined meanings of governor and general. During Constantinople's governance of the Italian peninsula and North Africa beginning in the late 500s, Constantinople-appointed dukes in the Italian peninsula were under the authority of the two exarchs based in Ravenna (*c.* 584–751) and Carthage (*c.* 585–698), who, in turn, were under the authority of Constantinople.[2] Ravenna was where Odoacer's successor Ostrogothic king Theodoric (r. 476–493) had earlier governed the peninsula, making the city a natural choice as the capital of Constantinople's exarchate. Its position on the Adriatic just north of Venice also made it a strategic dual window looking out to both the Italian peninsula and the Germanic world in the north. Justinian's choice of Ravenna, however, was also an affront against Rome's previous place as the historical capital and later co-capital of the splintered empire's political and religious authority. Justinian, in other words, sought to push Rome to the periphery of the ancient Roman heartlands, which in turn displaced the ancient papacy. Rome was now relegated to being the capital of a peripheral duchy rather than an imperial center on a par with Constantinople, and the bishop of Rome's role was diminished.

In sum, the bishop of Rome, once the most important figure in the Roman Empire's church and head of the ancient network of ecclesiastical dioceses, was under Justinian's successors increasingly just a local patriarch among patriarchs, that is, a kind of chief regional cleric on a par with or lower in rank than

Constantinople-appointed clergy based in Antioch, Jerusalem, Alexandria (Egypt), and Carthage. From 537 to 752, Constantinople appointed each new pope in the same way that clergy were sent from the eastern capital to sideline the Coptic Christian clergy in Alexandria and the Syrian Christian clergy in Antioch. Even the visual and material culture of Rome, like its changing political culture, became intertwined with what was by the 600s an increasingly Hellenistic and specifically Greek-speaking administrative and ecclesiastical world in Constantinople.[3] In cities that were closest to Rome in the 500s and 600s, Rome's ecclesiastical network of bishops was increasingly outside the papacy's control.

By the mid-600s, tensions between the bishop of Rome and the ecclesiastical leadership of Constantinople erupted. In a development that foreshadowed the Catholic–Orthodox schism of 1054, Pope Vitalian (657–672) excommunicated Archbishop Maurus of Ravenna shortly after the archbishop's refusal to travel to Rome in submission to the papacy's theological and ecclesiastical authority. The dispute had its origins in Rome's theological dispute with Constantinople over a new iteration of Christological debates since the Council Chalcedon. Emperor Constans II (r. 641–668) encouraged Ravenna's ecclesiastical independence from Rome during this dispute. The emperor even secured the archbishopric's independence (Greek: *autokephalía*) in accordance with the emperor's position on the Christological controversy and his interest in having Ravenna's archbishopric fall under the authority of the city's resident exarch. The debate was known as the controversy over monothelitism, and it would reappear in the ensuing centuries before erupting again during the official schism of 1066.

Throughout the era of the exarchates, it was not only other bishoprics in the peninsula that challenged the papacy's authority. Various other players took over the authority of making appointments, including a revolving door of appointed and self-styled kings, dukes, and landowning patricians from the Venetian coast and Ravenna to Tuscany and the German frontier. With the rise of monastic orders and abbots, these power players would likewise have more authority over abbots than would the papacy. Under Constantinople's governance in the 500s and 600s, the papacy in Rome was in its weakest political position since Odoacer's capture of the city.

The extent that the papacy's aspiration of recultivating Rome's political and religious authority was an uphill battle could be seen in cities like Venice in the 700s. There, as in older cities in the peninsula, there were signs that Constantinople had totally transformed the Italian peninsula's political culture away from its western Roman past. In the example of ruling titles, for example, the first of Venice's 117 independent governors—namely, Orso Ipato (r. 742-755)—reigned simultaneously with the titles of *dux* and the Greek title *hypatos* (consul). The Greek title *hypatos*, in contrast to the older Roman title *dux*, came from the Hellenistic administrative world of contemporary Constantinople. Under later Venetian governors, as Venice cultivated more formal independence from Constantinople, Greek titles fell into disuse in the city, leaving the simpler title *dux* (Venetian: *doge*).[4] Behind the power of the *dux* were the city's patricians, who throughout the 800s and beyond had more control over the appointment of the city's bishops and surrounding abbots than the papacy in Rome. In other words, the authority of the papacy had become detached from the ancient ecclesiastical diocese network in the era of the exarchates, as it was pushed into the margins of the more centered political authority of Constantinople's Exarch of Ravenna (*c*. 584-751) and the increasingly powerful patronage of local patricians across the Italian peninsula.

But despite Constantinople's power, the papacy managed to capitalize on a fundamental weakness in Constantinople's political and religious leadership: the unmanageable size of Constantinople's empire in the 600s and 700s, which had created problems for the original Roman Empire in the 200s and 300s. It was this size that allowed Constantionple's rivals—the Frankish kingdom and rising Arab caliphates—to exploit its territorial and administrative weakness in the 600s and 700s. By 698, Exarchate of Africa in Carthage was subsumed into the Umayyad caliphate, and by the 750s, the Exarchate of Ravenna was under Frankish control. Frankish territories even bordered Umayyad territories on the western edge of France, because by the 720s the old Visigothic kingdom of Iberia had become a frontier province of Damascus known as al-Andalus. And just as the Roman Empire and later eastern Roman Empire of Constantinople were too unwieldy in size to govern, Umayyad Iberia became effectively independent in 751 with a rebellion in the Middle East.

That rebellion saw the rise of the Abbasid caliphate with centers in Baghdad and Cairo. The Franks, keen to exploit chaos in the eastern Mediterranean, entered into talks with the Abbasids in order to manage the enduring threat in the western Mediterranean. In the end, the Umayyads of Spain were unable to secure a foothold in Frankish domains. Frankish King Charles Martel's victory

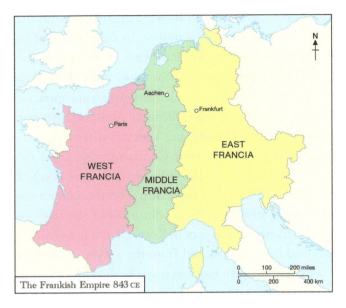

Figure 3.2 The Frankish Kingdom, based in present-day France and Germany, had its origins in the 400s close to Tournai (present-day Belgium). It moved its capital to Paris (508–768) and eventually to Aachen (Aix-la-Chappelle, 795–843). By the late 800s, it was also known as the Carolingian Empire in reference to its most famous ruler Charlemagne (French: Charles le Magne; English: Charles the Great; Latin: Carolus Magnus), grandson of Charles Martel. At its height in the 800s, the Empire was divided into three regions (above) in a fragmentation that facilitated the independence of Italian communes like Genoa further south. The Frankish Kingdom played a central role in the collapse of the Exarchate of Ravenna (584–751) and, in the same decade (750s), the simultaneous rise of an independent Papal State based in Rome (756–1870). By then, the Exarchate of Africa in Carthage (591–698) had been captured by the Muslim Arab Umayyad caliphate based in Damascus, with Carthage becoming a district of larger Tunis.

at the Battle of Tours (732) was decisive, but perhaps more consequential was a revolt among Berber tribes who came to dominate North African politics well into the Crusader era. The papacy in Rome became the key beneficiary of chaos on all sides.

The Papal–Frankish Alliance

Where the opportunity for the papacy's ecclesiastical independence emerged was in the advance southward of the Lombards and Franks, Germanic groups who by the 600s were far more intertwined with the sociocultural world of Latin-speaking Roman Chalcedonian Christianity (Roman Catholicism after 1066) than with the Arian Christian Ostrogoths, Visigoths, and Vandals were in the 400s. Ravenna, capital of the Exarchate of Ravenna, fell in 750 to the Lombards, who in turn lost it to the Frankish kingdom. Conveniently for the papacy, this turn of events meant that the office of the Constantinople-appointed *dux* of Rome (*c.* 536–756) fell into disuse. The pope, in fact, had already taken on the exarch's responsibility of appointing Rome's *dux* in the final years of the exarchate. What occurred in the aftermath of the fall of the exarchate was almost paradoxical: an alignment of the papacy towards the same Germanic sociopolitical world from which Rome's ancient conquerors—the Visigoths, Ostrogoths, Vandals—originated. That is, the papacy in the 700s opted for a Papal–Frankish alliance against Constantinople that in the 300s would have been inconceivable. What made the turn less paradoxical was the fact that the Franks, as mentioned, were unlike the Goths and Vandals in that they were the Christian followers of the liturgically Latin-speaking variety of Chalcedonian Christianity preached in Rome.

Rome's formal geopolitical realignment away from Constantinople and turn towards the northern Germanic states occurred in the three decades leading up to the Exarchate of Ravenna's official collapse (751) and the establishment of an independent Papal State in Rome (est. 756) just five years later. It began specifically during the reigns of Pope Gregory II (r. 715–731) and his successor Pope Gregory III (r. 731–741). One of the key episodes facilitating this Papal–Frankish nexus was the rise of Lombard king Liutprand (r. 712–744), the first Chalcedonian Christian king of the Lombards. In accordance with multiple centuries of Roman–Germanic cultural convergence in the region, Liutprand oversaw institutional reforms in favor of Roman law. In a key victory for the papacy, Liutprand transferred the city of Sutri and surrounding hill towns, that is, towns along Rome's northern road to Tuscany, to the papacy as a "gift to the blessed Apostles Peter and Paul."[5] Along similar lines, Pope Zacharias (r. 741–752) endeavored to put Rome more on a par with Constantinople in the realm of iconography and saints, the representations of which he miraculously discovered in the papal archbasilica (Archbasilica of St. John Lateran) during his reign. In what foreshadowed the way Venice would similarly appropriate the sanctity of St. Mark of Alexandria (Egypt) and bring the saint into the post-exarchate (post-Byzantine) world of Rome's pre-Renaissance visual and material culture, Pope Zacharias had the newly and miraculously discovered head of St. George—a central saint in Constantinople—placed in the Lateran Church of Rome.

By 754, in sum, in the aftermath of the Lombards' and Franks' capture of the Exarchate of Ravenna's core territories, and as the Exarchate of Africa—including Carthage—became fully subsumed into the Umayyad caliphate of Damascus, Pope Stephen II (r. 752–757) managed to transform the small Constantinople-run Duchy of Rome (est. 533) into the core of the Papal State. Stephen II did so through continued diplomacy with the Lombards and in political collaboration with the Franks, who captured most of the previously Lombard-held territories.[6] By the end of the century, with the rise of a larger Frankish kingdom extending across all of present-day France and Germany, Pope Leo III (r. 795–816) took it upon himself to invest the Frankish leader Charlemagne (r. 768–828) with a new title: "Emperor of the Romans" (*Imperator Romanorum*).

The papal coronation of Charlemagne as "Emperor of the Romans" was in many ways the final act in the papacy's long road to recentering Rome in the Italian peninsula, but it was also the start of a new road expanding Rome's authority far and wide across the peninsula, across the German frontiers, and even as far as the still active Roman Christian diocese of Carthage on the outskirts of the administratively Arabophone city of Tunis. The coronation of Charlemagne (800) was the cornerstone of the papacy's newly achieved church–state alliance, which would reach the climax of its rivalry with Constantinople's own church–state nexus in the decades that saw both the Latin–Greek schism (1054) and the start of the Crusader invasions of eastern Roman and Muslim-held territories (1096).

Charlemagne's Papal Coronation

On December 25, 800 (Christmas Day), the Frankish king Charlemagne (Latin: *Karolus*, French: *Charles le Magne*) could be seen kneeling before Pope Leo III in Old St. Peter's Basilica (est. *c.* 300s CE) and receiving the title *Imperator Romanorum*. The newly crowned emperor would mint coins with the words *Imperator Augustus* (*Imp Aug*) as if the fall of the western Roman Empire had never happened in 476, and as if the two Roman cultural centers were Rome and Frankish Aachen (Aix-la-Chappelle) as opposed to Rome and Constantinople. The event constituted a major change of fortunes in Rome's political clout, but the precise outcome of that shift was complex.

In theory, the image of the bishop of Rome investing Frankish king Charlemagne with the title *Imperator Romanorum* represented the political revival of the ancient Roman Empire's western provinces, with the papacy gaining an unprecedented degree of authority in a new church–state nexus. In practice, there were clear indications that the event was far removed from the ancient Roman Empire, from the Frankish dimension of the church–state nexus to the novelty of the title *Imperator Romanorum*. The title was evocative of ancient titles only, and was actually a neologism. More specifically, the coins of Charlemagne read, in full, *Karolus Imperator Augustus* (*Karolus Imp Aug*) and omitted *Romanorum* ("of the Romans"), potentially out of caution against challenging the surviving eastern Roman emperor's own imperial claims to being "emperor of the Romans." The term *Romanorum* did appear in his documents, but in either case, the term *Romanorum* was simply absent from ancient imperial titles. Vespasian (r. 69–79 CE), for example, ruled in Rome as *Imperator Caesar Vespasianus Augustus*, with the titles *Caesar* and *Augustus*, as well as others such as *princeps* (first) and *dominus*, being the typical corollary titles adjacent to *imperator* across the centuries between Caesar's rule and Odoacer's conquest.[7] The pope's investiture of Charlemagne as *Imperator Romanorum*, in other words, was new, and it was more specifically four new things: it was an affront against Constantinople's own claim to the Roman past, a declaration of a new Frankish–papal partnership against Constantinople's rival empire–church nexus, a striking culmination of papal evangelism in the once Arian Christian and enduringly pagan Germanic states, and a sign that Rome—in its new papacy-led German-aligned form—was again a major political player in the Mediterranean world some 700 years after Latin-speaking emperor Constantine—who relied on Greek translators—moved away from Rome to his new capital in Hellenistic Constantinople.

Figure 3.3 In the immediate lead-up to the Crusades, following the fragmentation of the Frankish Kingdom, the papacy based in Rome managed to cultivate a broad degree of religious and even political authority across rising communes in centers like Pisa, Genoa, Florence, and Venice. Bishops and monastic abbots, frequently appointed by local patricians, were among the most influential figures who looked to the papacy as a center of virtue and sociopolitical reform. Ruling circles in communal governments, interested in cultivating naval and political independence over their communes in the hope of establishing Roman Republic-like local republics, increasingly saw Rome as a political counterbalancing force to the enduring authority of the German states to the north and Constantinople to the east. The pull of Rome coincided with local alliances with the papacy during the Crusades. By 1115, with the passing of Tuscan March governor (*markgraf*) Matilda of Canossa and with the first Crusader kingdoms already established, Tuscan communes like Pisa and Florence could be seen charting their own independent political and commercial roads throughout the Mediterranean.

The Communes' Turn to Rome on the Eve of the Crusades

While the pope's investiture of Charlemagne was a mutually beneficial arrangement, Rome and the papacy were in many ways the more immediate beneficiaries. Specifically, the Franks' partnership with the papacy bolstered the sacred dimensions of the Franks' kingship, and, in return, Rome was assured a measure of security, geopolitical importance, and, most importantly, political autonomy under papal leadership. What tipped the balance of long-term benefits in Rome's favor was the fact that the Frankish empire began to break up internally in 843. Once that occurred, the papacy took the opportunity to accelerate Rome's political hold over the Italian peninsula by exercising as much religious authority as possible across the ancient and sprawling network of bishop-led ecclesiastical dioceses. Although the parts of the network newly under Muslim rule—Iberia (al-Andalus), Carthage (Tunis), Sicily—were furthest outside the realm of papal control, and although the German states exercised considerable authority over the appointment of bishops in their own domains, the many bishop-led dioceses and surrounding monastic orders of the northern Italian peninsula were still susceptible to the political and cultural pull of the papacy in the 800s and 900s in the context of the pope's role as virtuous reformer in the time of vice and decay. This appeal intersected with the appeal among local communal governments of a papal alliance as local Italian cities like Pisa and Florence sought to establish their own independent states.

More specifically, two phenomena explain the papacy's successful pull on the northern Italian cities in the two centuries leading up to the papacy: first, as mentioned, the peninsula was still a crowded geopolitical world, which meant that northern Italian governing circles in the 800s and 900s were willing to leverage their connections with the papacy in Rome to offset the political hold of the German states and Constantinople. The Venetians, committed as early as the 700s to independence from all regional powers, managed these connections with the greatest sophistication in what facilitated the early rise of both the Venetian republic and a bishopric under the republic's control.[8] The Pisans, likewise, were the beneficiaries of Tuscan March governor (*markgraf*) Matilda's commitment to Tuscany's close connections with the papacy, culminating in the rising Pisan Republic's ecclesiastical diocese being transformed into an archdiocese and, in turn, its new archbishop Daimbert (Dagobert) becoming a leading figure (Latin patriarch) in Crusader-era

Jerusalem (est. 1099). In the long run, the Pisan–papal alignment of the 1000s facilitated the expansion of Pisan political authority in the Crusader-era Syrian Levant, and by the 1200s, Pisa was at the center of a sprawling network of Pisan settlements stretching from Seville to Crusader Syria. In other words, papal-held Rome in the 800s and 900s offered the rising Italian communes of the north an appealing counterforce to the German states and Constantinople in an era when both still had official administrative control over parts of the peninsula. That the Republic of Florence was able to officially declare independence from the formerly Frankish "Tuscan March" upon March governor (*markgraf*) Matilda's death in 1115 was a reflection of how governing circles in the 1000s and 1100s were still, in the Crusader era, navigating their place between the peninsula's three main frontiers—the German states, Constantinople, and Rome—as they began building their respective communes-turned-republics' commercial empires in the region's fourth frontier: the Arabic Mediterranean.

Apart from Rome's place as a counterbalance to the German states and Constantinople, the second key factor that explained the papacy's ability to pull northern Italian cities into its own political sphere in the 900s was the expansion of church-related sociocultural institutions. The most prominent were the monastic orders, which were based in monasteries led by abbots. While bishops were part of the imperial Christian world back in the 300s and 400s, abbots were not. The earliest monastic communities in the old Roman imperial domains could be seen in fourth-century Egypt and fifth-century Syria, while the rise of organized monasticism in Europe, that is, autonomous congregations with abbots based in stand-alone monasteries, appeared later in the sixth century.[9]

Only at the end of the eighth century did monastic orders really begin to proliferate in Europe, with Charlemagne and his son Louis the Pious having played a foundational role in supporting their existence and their administrative autonomy.[10] Far from isolated mountain or desert communities, the orders in their European context were geographically close to cities and played a key role in the growth and urbanization of the Frankish kingdom. They were self-sufficient centers of agriculture and craft production, with monks and nuns frequently in town to sell everything from surplus agricultural produce, clothing, and household or agricultural equipment. Centuries later, English boroughs (small towns) owed their entire origin to monasteries, which frequently had a public hospital attached and were often one of the primary sources of employment for craftsmen and various domestic and agricultural workers.[11] From the start, they were also centers of learning. Abbots were in frequent contact with ruling circles, with court–cloister relations being a key dimension of Frankish politics during the reign of Charlemagne's successors.

Paradoxically, despite the central role played by Charlemagne and Louis the Pious in the proliferation of monasteries in the central Frankish lands (present-day France and Germany), the papacy managed to begin pulling monasteries and monastic orders into Rome's networks of patronage and loyalty in the 800s and 900s. The epitome of the papacy's centralizing pull could be seen in the reformist movement of the ancient Benedictine order at Cluny Abbey (eastern France), where Abbot Saint Odo (c. 878–942) and the so-called Cluniac reformers pushed for the disentanglement of monasteries from local landlords and political patrons in favor of closer monastic–papal connections.[12] In other words, in the same way that patricians of the rising Italian cities looked to Rome as a counterforce to the German states and Constantinople, abbots in local monasteries looked to Rome in order to offset the authority of any number of local players, especially landlords.

In the immediate lead-up to the early Crusades (c. late 1000s), the final outcome of the papacy's centripetal pull was that a wide variety of influential figures in the northern Italian cities looked to Rome for both political alliances and cultural connections. The key example was Matilda of Tuscany (r. 1052–1115), the Tuscan March governor (*markgraf*). In theory, the very office of a March governor in a March (*mark*) was a vestige of Frankish administrative logic, and should have been the apex of a framework of leadership and loyalty that was centered around German ruling circles in the north. In practice, the case of Matilda illustrated how the nexus of local rulers, bishops, and abbots could move in the opposite direction in favor of either local independence or, as was common in the lead-up to the Crusades, local independence in alliance with Rome. Despite being Tuscan March governor under German authority, Matilda was a prominent ally of the papacy at a time of German–papal tensions, and she used her position to manifest that alliance at a local sociocultural level in the realm of monastic orders and bishoprics.

More specifically, Matilda was patron of a variety of surviving monasteries throughout present-day northern Italy that became closely intertwined with the papacy, and she even pulled the bishop-led Pisan diocese away from the hold of German ruling circles in favor of the papacy. As mentioned, it was under Matilda's patronage that Daimbert (Dagobert) of Pisa, originally intertwined with the patronage of German ruling circles, became bishop and an associate of the pope. It was this Daimbert at the start of the 1100s who became the first uncontested patriarch of the Crusader-era Latin Patriarchate of Jerusalem, when the rising Republic of Pisa – partly through Daimbert's commitment to the city's interests – cultivated an unprecedented degree of political authority in the Crusader Levant.[13] What's more, Matilda was the founder, or at least foundational patron, of a military order—the Hospitallers of St. James of Altopascio (est. *c.* 1070s)—at a time when rising military orders such as the Knights Hospitaller and Knights Templar were learning to navigate the same worlds of loyalty and leadership that brought bishops and abbots closer to the papacy.[14] The orders were evocative of the monastic orders but provided a different variety of services. Matilda's order, like others, combined protection for pilgrims in the Levant and northern Iberia (Santiago) with medical and military services. All of these developments came prior to the prolific activities of the most global religious orders active during the Age of Exploration (Jesuits, Benedictines), which points to how the new millennium saw the papacy successfully turn Rome into the center of an increasingly global Roman Catholic world.

In sum, in the aftermath of Odacer's sacking of Rome in 476, the pope's ability to secure an independent Rome-based Papal State from the Franks in the 700s became the most impactful episode of the millennium that ensured Rome's return to political prominence and facilitated the Italian communes-turned-republics' own independence from the old German and eastern Roman frontiers. By the 1000s, in its new papal-led form, Rome was at the forefront of a striking and culturally impactful geopolitical move that evoked the days of Julius Caesar: the Crusader-era invasion of the once Rome-held territories of the Middle East and North Africa. With an early campaign on the Tunisian coast close to Carthage (1087) and a subsequent campaign in Jerusalem (1095), papal Rome's campaigns evoked ancient imperial Rome's successful attempts to capture North Africa and the Syrian Levant in the century before Jesus rose to prominence in the Roman Levant. The players, however, had mostly changed. Long gone were the Phoenician (Punic) empire of

North Africa, the Hellenistic Ptolemaic kingdom of Egypt, and the vassal-turned-rebel Palmyrene kingdom of Queen Zenobia (*c.* 260–272) along the Syrian–Arabian frontier. Rome, likewise, was no longer a center of Greco-Roman deities, commissioning temples for Apollo and Bacchus in the Syrian Levant in what might sideline early Christianity and local Phoenician and Arabian spiritual traditions.

Rather, the Crusades saw the Roman Catholic papacy, newly in schism with fellow Chalcedonian Christians of Constantinople, invade the caliphates and emirates that were the new governors of the ancient centers of Christianity. With that shift came a new pretext for the capture of the Middle East and North Africa: sacred glory in the name not of Caesar or Greco-Roman deities, but in the name of God, whom local bishops and abbots talked about in their teachings throughout the Italian peninsula. For local bishops like Daimbert in Pisa, glory in the name of God was determined not simply through territorial gains or losses, but through more abstract conceptions of heroism and martyrdom. For the rising communes-turned-republics, whose navies in the 1000s were just a century away from dominating Mediterranean commerce, a short-term intercommunal alliance with the papacy became a worthy experiment on the road to building their own empires across the Middle East and North Africa.

4

A NEW TURN TO CARTHAGE (TUNISIA) AND THE START OF THE CRUSADES

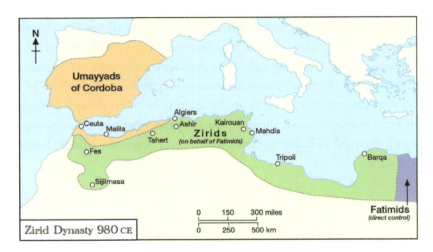

Figure 4.1 At its height (c. 980s), centuries after Berber- and Phoenician-speaking families could be seen becoming Romanized in cities like Phoenician-turned-Roman Carthage adjacent to Arabic Tunis, a semi-Arabized Berber family known as the Zirids cultivated wide political authority between the Andalusian Umayyad caliphate's capital in Cordoba and the Fatimid caliphate's capital in Cairo. The newcomer Normans of Palermo, just across the Sicilian Strait from Zirid Mahdia, established close commercial relations with the Zirids just as the papacy in Rome led a Pisan- and Genoese-led invasion of the Tunisian coast. According to the Normans' one-time courtier al-Idrisi and several of his predecessors, vernacular Latin (North African Romance) from the Roman era was still spoken in various coastal and inland parts of Roman-turned-Arabic *Ifriqiya* (coastal Algeria, Tunisia, Libya). Al-Idrisi, echoing older encounters of Arabic-speaking writers with Berber Christians in the 600s, described the local Christians as "Berberized" (*tabarbara*) Christians. The ancient Roman ecclesiastical diocese in Carthage, at that point on the outskirts of Tunis, was still active and in contact with both Rome and other regional ecclesiastical dioceses. The campaign in Mahdia, in the end, failed to establish the equivalent of a series of Crusader kingdoms that were created a decade later in the Syrian Levant.

An Early Crusade in Mahdia

In some ways, the papacy's invasion of Mahdia in 1087 was both a trial run for the First Crusade in Jerusalem (1095) and a reflection of the papal capital's enduring connections with ancient North African cities. There were bishops in nearby Carthage, by then the outskirts of Tunis, before and after the start of the Crusades. That continuity of Roman Christianity in North Africa contextualizes why Pisan writers likened papal Rome's campaign against Mahdia to ancient Rome's capture of Carthage. In a sense, the papacy in Rome never lost interest in maintaining political and religious connections with old imperial centers in North Africa despite the many groups that captured the region between the 500s and the 1000s, from the Vandals and eastern Romans to the caliphates and Normans conquerors.

The campaign to capture Mahdia was carried out by Pisan and Genoese naval forces that, notably, flew the Papal State's flag of St. Peter (*vexillum sancti Petri*). In the end, the invasion was unsuccessful in its inability to hold onto the city, and the event faded into historical memory next to the more famous conquest of Jerusalem ten years later.[1] But although it was short-lived, the campaign nonetheless illustrated two trends underway in the Italian peninsula that were in tension. On the one hand, some 300 years since the establishment of the Papal State based in Rome, the coalition to capture Mahdia demonstrated the very real and far-reaching pull of the papacy's political and religious authority across the rising northern Italian communes: Pisa, Genoa, Venice, Florence, and their neighbors. On the other hand, with the newcomer French-speaking Normans boldly eschewing the campaign altogether and even cultivating commercial connections with Mahdia's Muslim rulers, the campaign also demonstrated the limits of papal authority within Roman Catholic ruling circles. The Normans' independent policy in Tunisia also foreshadowed how the northern communes-turned-republics could—and very soon did—defy the papacy's political orders and trade embargoes in order to pursue their own futures across the Crusader-era Middle East and North Africa.

At the time of the invasion, Mahdia had been under the administration of an administratively Arabized Amazigh (Berber) dynasty, namely, the Zirids, for a century. For much of their history, the Zirids governed the Tunisian coast in a vassal–patron relationship with the powerful Fatimid caliphs of Cairo. The Fatimid caliphate, which built Cairo (est. 961) just outside the old Arab garrison town of Fustat and in the vicinity of ancient Memphis (est. before 3100s BCE), originally built Mahdia as their first capital in 921. With the global expansion of the Arab caliphates (Umayyads, Abbasids) in the 600s and 700s CE, the Tunisian coast became a major center of commerce linking cities in the Arabic east (*Mashriq*)—Aleppo, Damascus, Baghdad—with cities in the Arabic west (*Maghrib*)—Fez, Seville, Bougie, and beyond. Against this backdrop, Pisa and Genoa's ownership of Mahdia would mean controlling a port city along the overland and maritime trade routes connecting the Atlantic coast with the Persian Gulf and Indian Ocean.

For the papacy, Rome's authority in North Africa would offer an outcome that had not been seen for 600 years: Rome's political and religious authority in what was once the Roman province of Africa (Latin: *Provincia Africa proconsularis*). In the 1000s, despite the reigns of several ruling circles on the coast since Odoacer's conquest (Vandals, Constantinople's exarchs, the Arab caliphates), the ancient Roman past was still very present. Not only did Arabic speakers still call the coastal region by its Roman name "Africa" (Latin: *Africa proconsularis*, Arabic: *Ifriqiya*), the ancient Phoenician-turned-Roman city of Carthage—on the outskirts of Tunis since the 700s—remained the center of an active Chalcedonian Christian bishopric connected with Rome's papacy. Even vernacular Latin (North African Romance) was still spoken on the Tunisian coast as late as the 1000s in a phenomenon that was described in detail by Arabic-speaking writers like al-Idrisi, one time courtier in the Norman court of Palermo.

More specifically, in the lead-up to the Mahdia campaign, the ancient bishoprics in Carthage and elsewhere on the Tunisian and Algerian coast were still functional and in contact with Rome. In 1053, specifically, just three decades before the Mahdia campaign, Pope Leo IX (r. 1049–1051) sent a surviving letter to a certain Bishop Thomas, likely of Carthage, confirming his authority over bishops elsewhere along the Tunisian and Algerian coast: cities like Gummi near present-day Sousse (Arabic: *Susa*) and others.[2] The pope also sent a surviving letter to those other bishops, including Bishop Petrus and Bishop Ioannes, confirming the former bishopric's authority. As for the continued use of vernacular Latin (North African Roman) in the region, Norman King Roger II's one-time courtier Muhammad al-Idrisi described—only decades later—the existence of "Berberized" (*tabarbara*) Christians who spoke Latin in the inland oasis town of Qafsa (Latin: *Capsa*).[3] Drawing on observers before him, he also noted several other inland and coastal towns throughout present-day Tunisia and Algeria where vernacular Latin was spoken by "Berberized" Christians: Gabès, Beja, Biskra, and Monastir.

In other words, the papacy's control of greater Arabic Ifriqiya—corresponding with both ancient Roman Africa (*Africa Proconsularis*) and the more recent Constantinople-held Exarchate of Africa (*Exarchatus Africae*)—would revive Rome's place as a political center on both sides of the Sicilian Strait. It would restore the late ancient Roman Christian cultures of Carthage and Hippo (c. 300s CE), which had been in the process of being eclipsed since the 600s by the newer Arabic-speaking cities of Tunis and Annaba (Algeria). Bishop Augustine of Hippo (d. 430) was a product of that still recent era, and his legacy loomed large in Rome during the Umayyad and Abbasid caliphates.

Of likely Romanized Amazigh (Berber) heritage on his mother's side, Augustine in the early 400s wrote and spoke vernacular Latin (North African Romance) and had a career that stretched from Hippo and Carthage to Rome and Milan.[4] He lived less than 200 years after the reign of Roman emperor Septimius Severus. Emperor Severus was the Phoenician- and Latin-speaking Roman citizen from the Libyan coast who married Julia Domna. Domna was seen earlier as the Emessa-born (Homs, Syria) daughter of an Arab priestly family associated with the temple of Elagabalus (Arabic: *ilah al-jabal*) along the Syrian–Arabian frontier. The papacy's Islamic-era letters to Carthage suggest he hoped to recultivate that Roman past after many centuries (c. 400s–900s) of rule by the Vandals, Constantinople-appointed exarchs, and Arab caliphs. But that task would be an uphill battle given how deeply Arabized the culture and commerce of North Africa had become.

In the centuries leading up to the Crusades, the Tunisian coast's cultural and political center of gravity had turned sharply away from Rome and much more in the direction of coastal and inland cities along the trade routes between the *Maghrib* and *Mashriq*: Granada, Seville, Fez, Kairouan, Tunis, Mahdia, Cairo, Baghdad, and beyond. The history of the Amazigh (Berber) Zirid family in Mahdia was closely intertwined with the culture and commerce of these cities. One side of the family governed part of Iberia after the fall of the Andalusian Umayyad caliphate in the 1000s CE, which occurred just one century after another part of the family governed Tunisia as vassals of the Fatimid caliphate in Cairo. At the height of their power in the 980s, the political reach of this Arabized Amazigh (Berber) family network stretched across the same geography governed by the ancient Phoenician (Punic) empire of Carthage just before Rome's conquest of the city (146 BCE). A successful crusade in the 1000s would bring not only Carthage, but also the still functional diocese in the city, the remaining pockets of polyglot vernacular Latin-speaking (North African Romance) Christians, and the many commercial worlds of North Africa into the authority of the papacy in Rome and the governors of the various Rome-allied Italian maritime republics. In other words, the ancient Roman bishopric would again command direct religious authority in North Africa, and individual popes would continue their predecessors' work in evangelizing new communities and centralizing the Papal State's political and religious authority.

Even though the capture of Mahdia turned out unsuccessfully, the project of bringing North Africa and especially the Tunisian coast back into Rome's political sphere was not entirely far-fetched. Not only did the Normans of Sicily manage to turn Zirid kingdoms into vassal states more than a century later, but also Rome itself accomplished a similar project only ten years after the Mahdia campaign. More specifically, Rome's aspirations of political and cultural hegemony in Tunisia resembled what occurred ten years later in the Latin Kingdom of Jerusalem (Latin: *Regnum Hierosolymitanum*, c. 1099–1291), that is, the Crusader kingdom that was established following the Crusader conquest of Jerusalem (1095). The residential Latin patriarch of Jerusalem (c. 1099–1347, 1847–present) was in many ways a political arm of Rome in the Middle East both during the Crusades and the immediate centuries that followed. What culturally offset that project was the cultural currency of the *Mashriq*. Crusader-era European ruling circles and merchants, whom Arabic speakers called the "Franks" (*afrang*) with a broad brush, found the intellectual, material, and visual culture of the new Arabic-language cities of the *Mashriq* something to marvel and even assimilate into their own Crusader kingdoms and, upon their frequent return home, the Italian peninsula and southern France. This paradigm of Arabic cultural currency in the 1100s, seen among the Arabized Roman Catholic Christians of Umayyad Iberia, contrasted to ancient Roman cultural currency that saw the rise of Romanized Arabs in the examples of Julia Domna (c. 200s CE) of Emessa (Arabic: Homs).

In the end, however, while the papacy secured political and limited cultural gains in Jerusalem in the 1090s, the failed Pisan-led invasion of

Mahdia back in the 1080s meant that Rome was never able to cultivate a new Rome-affiliated Christian sociopolitical culture and ecclesiastical leadership across Roman-turned-Arab Ifriqiya. What doomed the project from the start, and what likewise beleaguered the later Crusader states in the long run, was the reality that the navies of central and southern Europe in the early 1100s were still a century away from being able to overpower their counterparts in the Middle East and North Africa. The massive industrial complex where the Venetians built their high-speed armed galleys, the Arsenale complex, only began its construction in 1104. The peak of their production and efficiency occurred much later in the sixteenth century during the height of Venetian competition with the Genoese.

The naval power of the Italian republics, in other words, were still on the rise in the late 1000s. By the late 1100s, Jewish writers in Arabic—active between southern Europe and the Middle East—would begin noting how ubiquitous Italian merchant ships had become in the region. Saladin (r. 1174–1193), the general who famously overthrew the Fatimids and later captured Crusader Jerusalem, even secured arms from these merchants and noted the sophistication of their craftsmanship. This picture was in sharp contrast to the way earlier writers in Arabic represented the first Crusaders in the late 1000s as disorganized. In that earlier era, before the Fatimid navy sharply declined, the Fatimids still commanded one of the most powerful naval fleets in the Mediterranean. Even though the Zirids were no longer in a vassal–patron relationship with the Fatimids in the 1000s, the waters around the Tunisian coast were still traversed by the Fatimids.[5] Disturbances in the region were relevant enough to politics in Cairo that only decades after the Pisans began barreling into Mahdia in the 1080s, Norman king Roger I—son of the Norman conqueror of the Sicilian emirate—was writing to the Fatimid caliph to explain his own territorial incursions into Gabès across the Sicilian Strait. It was precisely this mismatch in naval power, coupled with the possibilities of trade in the wealthy *Mashriq*, that made the Normans of Palermo operate very carefully around the Tunisian waters as they cultivated trade relations with the Zirids during the early Crusades. The fact that the Normans, French-speaking Roman Catholics, cultivated a fierce political and military independence of all other players in southern Europe facilitated this independence of the papacy.

In the end, given the Islamic principalities' naval power and the possibilities of trade in Muslim-held ports, and given how obvious these trade opportunities were to the earlier Amalfitans and contemporary Normans in Palermo in the late 1000s and early 1100s, why would the Pisans partner with Rome in an invasion at all? Why not take a page from the Normans' playbook in political and commercial diplomacy, which the Pisans did ultimately pursue in North Africa just fifty years later? The answer has something to do with Pisa's political culture in the late 1000s and how closely the papacy managed to shape northern Italian political cultures in the early decades of the Crusades. It was a degree of power and authority in Rome that was not seen even in the last decades of the Roman Empire.

Figure 4.2 Monasteries, like San Zeno Abbey in Pisa, were among the key socioreligious institutions in the 1000s that aligned local communes with Rome's papacy in accordance with the belief that the papacy was a center of virtue and reform. San Zeno Abbey included a hospital, which illustrates the formative role monastic orders played in local society. Monasteries even produced wares and produce in surplus for their own use and for sale in local markets. Monasteries were under the leadership of abbots, and were in many ways a counterpart to bishop-led cathedrals and markets in the way they served as go-betweens connecting local communities with both ruling circles and the papacy. Echoing examples of churches in Amalfi, and pointing to how interconnected Mediterranean commerce and material culture remained in the post-Roman era, the example of San Zeno Abbey pictured here originally featured inlaid ceramic basins that were imported from the Islamic world and fixed into the roundrels above the windows.
Source: https://pixabay.com/photos/italy-tuscany-abbazia-di-sant-antimo-3603925, public domain.

The Early Peak of Crusader Political Culture in Pisa

Rome-aligned bishops in Pisa during the early Crusades articulated specific beliefs about the glory of sacred heroism and Christian martyrdom at a time when local socioreligious institutions—monastic orders, bishoprics—were both politically influential and loyal to the papacy. Like the commune of Florence in the days before it officially declared independence as the Republic of Florence (1115 CE), the Pisan commune in 1087 was still decades away from being the Pisan republic of the mid-1100s. In this latter iteration, the Pisans built a sprawling presence around the Syrian Levant's Crusader kingdoms and reached the peak of their naval might and political independence. By then, the Pisans began paving a Norman-like independent path towards political and diplomatic relations across the Arabic Mediterranean. Back in the 1080s, however, the Pisans were still emerging from the Germanic Tuscan March (*mark*), and the reputation of Italian shipping was still in formation. The papacy, in the same decades, was reaching the zenith of its centuries-long effort to direct the loyalties of the peninsula's political and religious leadership—bishops, abbots, patricians, local governors—away from the Germanic states and towards Rome. Where this papal effort reached its peak was during the career of the last Tuscan March governor (*markgraf*) Matilda, who turned away from her superiors in the German states in favor of Rome. This turn occurred during the peak of German–papal tensions over control of Roman Catholic ecclesiastical institutions.

As much as Matilda became a catalyst for Pisa and neighboring Florence's independent trajectories outside the shadow of the Franks in Aachen and Paris, the medium of that rising independence—namely, a Pisan–papal alliance via its bishopric—positioned the commune as a key site of the papacy's early Crusader-era fervor for invasions. What made this fervor somewhat short-lived was the reality that the northern communes-turned-republics, in continuity with the rising Norman county-turned-kingdom of Palermo, were moving in the direction of total political independence and territorial expansion beyond the old shadows of the German states, Constantinople, and the papacy alike. The epitome of that later independence could be seen in how the northern communes-turned-republics began to violate the papacy's trade embargoes with Muslim powers, going as far as selling arms to Saladin—one-time conqueror of the Latin Kingdom of Jerusalem—in a way that would have scandalized the Pisans a century earlier. In other words, the historical fourth frontier of the peninsula, namely, the Arabic-language Islamic Mediterranean, was emerging in the 1100s as a place for profits and commerce rather than just plunder and conquest.

Markgraf Matilda and Pisa's Alliance with Crusader-era Rome

In the lead-up to the Mahdia and Jerusalem campaigns, Tuscany was still under the nominal authority of the German states, while local socioreligious institutions like monastic orders and bishoprics were increasingly loyal to the papacy's religious authority in Rome. Papal religious authority, in turn, bolstered the pope's rising political authority as the Papal State geared up for an invasion of the Tunisian coast. That is to say, in the late 1000s northern cities like Pisa and Florence— each with an ancient Roman ecclesiastical diocese— were at a political crossroads between the German states and the Papal State, but they were not yet in the position of Norman-held Palermo (r. 1061). The Normans' military might underpinned a remarkably independent political and commercial trajectory dating back to the start of their momentous conquest of the emirate of Sicily. The Pisans, in contrast, were like the other communes that were still building their military and naval power in the 1070s and 1080s. The outcome was that in the years immediately preceding the Crusades, what facilitated the Pisans' independence from the German states was an entrenchment, albeit a short-lived one, into the depths of Rome's expansionist Crusader-era political culture. The key figures who facilitated that turn were Tuscan March governor Matilda and, under her authority, bishop-turned-archbishop Daimbert (Dagobert) of Pisa.

Whether for reasons of faith or political strategy, and more likely both, Matilda cultivated connections with the papacy in Rome at a time when growing German–papal tensions erupted. The reigning German "Emperor of the Romans" (Latin: *Imperator Romanorum*), later known by the English as the Holy Roman Emperor, was in the centuries after Charlemagne just a king among regional German kings. In the public eye, what endowed the office with a degree of religious authority was, among other things, the role of the papacy in reenacting the ancient Roman church–empire relationship in the pope's investiture of the German emperor with the title *Imperator Romanorum*. Since the days of Charlemagne, despite the extent that this investiture genuinely signaled the papacy's expanding political and religious authority, Germanic circles continuously contested the ground-level control of bishoprics, monastic orders, the peninsula's communal governments, and even the process of appointing the papacy itself. The later picture of the Florentine Medicis' activities in Rome, where the Medicis managed to have multiple politically influential family members serve either as pope or as clerics close to the pope, points to the extent that powers based outside Rome were able to co-opt the core of the Church's administrative infrastructure. This phenomenon was especially obvious in the lead-up to the Crusades, when the centralized political and religious authority of the papacy made control of the office desirable to regional powers.

In a remarkable development that was neither the first nor last of its kind, Pope Gregory VII (r. 1073–1085)—reigning just prior to the Mahdia campaign—excommunicated German emperor Henry IV (Heinrich IV) three times in a dispute over control of the Church's ecclesiastical network.[6] Henry IV, in turn, appointed an alternative pope: namely, the so-called "Antipope" Pope Clement III (r. 1080–1100), former archbishop of Ravenna who contested the authority of both Pope Victor III during the Mahdia campaign and Pope Urban II during the Jerusalem campaign.[7] Tuscan March governor Matilda made the key decision of not only siding with the papacy, but also positioning Pisa's ecclesiastical diocese in alliance with the papacy rather than the German states. As part of this policy, she oversaw the appointment of Daimbert (Dagobert) of Pisa as the Pisan bishop (1088). Daimbert was a major player in the Crusades, both preaching zealously for the Crusades in Tuscany and rising to a position of political prominence on behalf of both Pisa and the papacy in the Crusader kingdom of Jerusalem.

More specifically, Matilda's appointment of a Rome-aligned bishop, one who was a key advocate of the Crusades, secured the Pisan communal government both long- and short-term rewards. In the long run, following the successful Crusader campaign in Jerusalem (1095), Daimbert established the politically powerful position of Latin patriarch in Jerusalem. Daimbert's position ultimately facilitated the Pisan commune-turned-republic's ability to build wide and independent legal jurisdiction in the Crusader Levant. In the short run, the close Pisan–papal alliance during the Mahdia (1087) campaign—and more specifically the role of the papacy-aligned clergy in defining

Pisa's political culture—facilitated the possibility of the Pisan communal government and navy to be seen locally as heroes in spite of continuous losses dating back to a failed crusade against the emirate of Sicily and earlier.

In specific terms, the Christian values Daimbert and wider clerical circles preached defined the Pisans' power and glory not simply in terms of wealth, but sacred heroism. Where the clergy's articulation of the Pisans' sacred glory found its most public form was in all the oral and visual cues embodied in war stories, sermons, sacred art, architecture, and city insignia. In the case of war stories and legends about Christian martyrs, local and regional clergy played a role in making public meaning of military losses by articulating them in the language of salvation.

Carmen in Victoriam Pisanorum (*Song on the Occasion of the Victory of the Pisans*), a mix of poem and chronicle, comes from this period and survives in the Albert I Royal Library in Brussels. Written in the aftermath of the Mahdia campaign, *Carmen in Victoriam Pisanorum* celebrates the heroism of Pisa's soldiers and their commitment to the faith. Its poet-chronicler author, likely a clergyman, describes the Genoese as having joined "the Pisans with great love; they do not care about earthly life (*de vita mundi*), or about their sons; [for] they give themselves to the dangers for love of the Redeemer (*pro amore Redemtoris*)."[8] The poem makes space for celebration in the aftermath of human loss by highlighting how those who lost their lives ultimately secured a place with God.

Similar celebratory poems written after Pisan battles include the *Liber Maiolichinus de Gestis Pisanorum Illustribus* (*Majorcan Book of the Deeds of the Illustrious Pisans*), which recounts the story of Pisa's conflict with the *taifa* of Mallorca and Ibiza (1113–1115). That campaign occurred just two decades before the Pisans quietly returned to the Tunisian coast to secure a trade agreement, including a hostel-inn (*funduq*) and residency agreements. Similar trade agreements with the Balearics occurred in the 1200s.

The fact that the author of the *Liber Maiolichinus* was likely a cleric is significant, as it points to how Pisan governing circles and the Roman Church worked synchronously in cultivating popular support for military campaigns. Among the more tangible outcomes of this heroism was, even in cases where lives were lost, captives of the same faith were freed and brought home in an era when Mediterranean conflict saw the rise of captives across the Mediterranean's Latin–Greek–Arabic administrative boundaries. In other words, from a Christian perspective, the stories of the soldiers' brave devotion to the faith and the ability to overcome fear—in spite of military losses and what it suggested about the rulers' lack of planning or ability—translated not only into promises of salvation, but also the possibility of tangible faithful outcomes like the return home of long-lost captives.

From this perspective, Christian visual cues embodied in art, architecture, and city insignia added even more tangible visual cues that even a failed military campaign was a success. The most obvious example in Pisa could be seen in the construction the central cathedral, which stands adjacent the more famous leaning tower. The cathedral was built over three decades from 1063 to 1092 and was the seat of one of Tuscany's most important ecclesiastical dioceses. Notably, its construction and expansion was paid for, in part, by the spoils of war coming from a failed campaign to capture emirate of Sicily (1063) and the failed campaign the Mahdia (1087).[9]

That is, more than just a set of visual cues for the faithful to ponder God's grace upon their city (Pisa), the foundation and increasing grandeur of the Pisan cathedral during the three decades of its construction offered a visual picture of the sacred rewards secured by Pisa's Christian martyrs who fought in the name of both Pisa and God. From the Church's perspective, where they failed Pisa's territorial ambitions, they were still victors in the eyes of God and the papacy.

The Pisan cathedral, in other words, was a kind of spatial go-between that served the intertwined interests of Pisan governing circles, on the one hand, and the papacy in Rome, on the other. Each bolstered public support for the other in the late 1000s as they continued to cultivate their respective independence from the powerful German states to the north. As much as the cathedral—and specifically its bishop—articulated sacred meanings of Pisan politics and social affairs, the cathedral was also the theater where Pisan governing circles paid public homage to the papacy. It was here at the cathedral, for example, where bishops preached the Crusades in the 1100s and 1200s.

The political motivations and public meanings associated with the Pisans' invasion of Mahdia in 1087, in sum, were intertwined with the papacy in Rome in ways that distinguished Pisa from the more militarily powerful and politically independent Norman kingdom in Palermo. From the late 1000s through the early 1100s, contemporary with the first Crusades, Norman kings Roger I and II were in a position to rule in independence of all of the major players the region: the German states that governed the north through their March governors, the eastern Romans (Byzantines) who governed Sicily and the Italian Adriatic coast before the Arab conquest of the island, the Arab emirs whom the Normans ousted from Sicily, and the papacy.

While the papacy-aligned clergy in Pisa's cathedral celebrated the sacred heroism of fallen naval officers in the 1080s and 1090s, the Norman cathedral in Palermo was in the process of representing visually a political culture that excluded the pope. In the cathedral's famous mosaic, count-turned-king Roger II could be seen being invested with the divine right of kingship by Jesus directly, that is, without the intermediary authority of the popes. In the 1100s, the papacy still invested the German *Imperator Romanorum* (Holy Roman Emperor) in a

Figure 4.3 Roger II was the patriarch in a line of polyglot Arabic-speaking Norman kings in Palermo who oversaw a similarly polyglot administrative bureau (Arabic: *diwan*) inherited from the earlier Sicilian emirate. The Normans were French-speaking newcomers in the Italian peninsula in the 1000s who established one of two major southern Mediterranean polities. The other was the Norman Crusader principality in the Syrian Levant governed by Roger's uncle Robert Guiscard's son. Despite being Roman Catholic, Roger II cultivated a political and ecclesiastical independence of Rome's ancient bishopric, and even went to war with the pope over disputed territories around Naples. In a visual illustration of that independence, a mosaic of Roger II in Palermo's central cathedral represents him being invested with the divine right of kingship by Jesus, that is, without the intermediary authority that the pope had successful claimed and expanded since the papacy's famous investiture of Frankish King Charlemagne with the archaic title Emperor of the Romans (*Imperator Romanorum*) in the 800s. The mosaic even records his name and title in Greek: *Rogerios Rex*.

Source: https://commons.wikimedia.org/wiki/File:Chiesa_della_Martorana_Christus_kr%C3%B6nt_Roger_II.jpg, public domain.

tradition dating back to Charlemagne's day. Roger II, in stark contrast, went to war with the Papal State over disputed territory around present-day Naples and even captured the pope.[10] Like the Normans' unique gold dinars, which were the only coins of their type outside of Muslim ports, the depiction of Roger's investiture from Jesus himself was part of a broader political and material culture in early Crusader-era Palermo that illustrated the city's unique position southern Europe: As early as the 1070s, almost a century before the communes-turned-republics demonstrated their total independence of the papacy and the old frontier powers (German states, Constantinople), the Normans in Palermo were already elbowing both Rome and Constantinople out of their own affairs and cultivating close commercial relations with the southern Mediterranean's emirates and caliphates. In the history of exchange between the Italian peninsula and the Middle East, what makes early Crusader-era Norman political culture significant is how it closely foreshadowed the depth and sophistication of the northern republics' later commercial diplomacy (*c.* after the late 1100s) once their governing circles were able to carve out their own independent political and commercial trajectories throughout the Mediterranean's many worlds.

The Normans of Sicily and the Caliphate

By the time the Rome-sponsored Pisan–Genoese campaign just across the Sicilian Strait was underway (1087), the Normans in Palermo had already cultivated deep connections with the Berber Zirid dynasty that had controlled Mahdia and much of North Africa since the late 900s. The Normans were also in close contact with Cairo's Fatimid caliphate, the Zirids' one-time political patrons. The Norman–Zirid connection went back to the earliest years of the Norman presence in Sicily. Just one year before Zirid ruler Tamim ascended to power in Mahdia in 1062, Norman adventure Robert Guiscard de Hauteville and his brother Roger I invaded Tamim's allies in the emirate of Sicily.[11] The Norman brothers captured the Sicilian emirate's capital of Palermo some ten years later in 1071, almost a decade after the Pisans withdrew from their own failed campaign in the island.

Over the next two centuries (*c.* 1100s–1200s), Tunisia and Sicily's shared Strait of Sicily became a Latin–Arabic administrative boundary that would be crossed by multiple Norman rulers in search of military and commercial gains. As early as the reign of Roger I himself (r. 1071–1101), the Normans of Palermo were distinguished from all other powers in the Italian peninsula by their uniquely polyglot Arabic-language administrative bureau (Arabic: *diwan*). Rather than disband Arabic-speaking courtiers after the conquest, Roger I maintained the entire administrative machinery of the emirate and used them in service of his own trade aspirations in North Africa. The move was illustrative of the cultural currency that the *Mashriq* had cultivated in the early centuries of the Arab caliphates (Umayyads, Abbasids).

In what similarly demonstrated the political versatility of Palermo's Arabic chancery, many of the most influential Arabic-speaking administrators in Roger II's service came from the earlier emirate's Christian communities, especially the Melkites. The Melkites were Arabic-speaking Byzantine-rite Christians from the Syrian Levant associated with the old Constantinople-era Chalcedonian-turned-Orthodox Church, which remained active under the caliphates.[12] In what likewise demonstrated the depth of the Norman court's connections with Arabic political and intellectual cultures, the career of Ceuta-born cartographer Muhammad al-Idrisi in Roger II's court actually began in North Africa. He traveled northward across Arabic–Latin boundaries to work for Roger II in Palermo.

It was under Roger II's patronage that al-Idrisi penned the most influential work of cartography in the medieval world: the Arabic-language *Book of Pleasant Journeys into Faraway Lands*, translated into Latin as the *Tabula Rogeriana*. Roger II, in other words, was neither the first nor the last Norman sovereign to patronize Muslim and Arabic-speaking administrators. He was the son of pioneering patriarch—Roger I—who cultivated a dynasty of polyglot Arabic-speaking Sicilian Norman kings that eventually produced Frederick II.

In the 1200s, Frederick rose to prominence across Arabic–Latin boundaries as the renowned patron of Greco-Arabic sciences who, by virtue of his mixed Hohenstaufen–Norman parentage and strategic relationship with both the papacy and the German states, managed to secure the German "Emperor of the Romans" (Holy Roman Emperor) title. He even met and spoke personally, almost certainly in Arabic, with one of Saladin's successors in Jerusalem—al-Kamil—during a late Crusader-era negotiation deemed treasonous back in Europe. That is to say, the Normans of Palermo cultivated an early, deep, and enduring political and cultural connection with the worlds of the Arabic Mediterranean, and it became a major thorn in the papacy's plans to capture North Africa ports during the Mahdia campaign.

Specifically, the early Norman–Zirid connection dating back to Roger I shaped the Normans' early refusal to join the Pisans in Mahdia. According to the Egyptian chronicler Ibn al-Athir (d. 1233), the connection began at the very start of the Norman administration (1072), some fifteen years before the campaign. When the Pisans initially appealed to the Normans for assistance in the conquest of Mahdia, Roger I responded coolly:

> Suppose they [the Pisans] conquer the land and become masters of it, then [commerce] in foodstuffs will pass from Sicilian hands to theirs. Meanwhile we shall have to send them provisions from Sicily and I shall lose to them the money I draw each year from the sale of my produce. And if instead the expedition is unsuccessful, they will return to Sicily and cause me trouble.[13]

Indeed, there was as much for the Pisans and Genoese to gain from the Mahdia campaign in 1088 as there was for Roger I to lose. When the Pisans and Genoese captured Mahdia, they secured only briefly what the Normans had cultivated for themselves in the long term: payment in gold as well as access to North Africa's coastal and trans-Saharan markets. During the Normans' administration of Sicily in the early Crusader era, Norman Sicily became *North Africa's Ifriqiya's* foremost supplier of grain. Administrators throughout North Africa purchased Sicilian grain with gold, giving the Normans exclusive access among European states to North Africa's precious metals.[14] Any shortage risked edging North Africa towards famine. The Normans showed off the fruits of their diplomatic and commercial labor by minting and circulating gold quarter-dinars, which only the Normans among European dynasties were able to mint. While the Italian communes-turned-republics were busy barreling into Mahdia and Jerusalem, Roger I and II were cultivating a sophisticated knowledge of the Arabic Mediterranean's complex political workings.

The Fatimid Caliph's Letter to Roger II and the Politics of Norman Syria

Surviving correspondence between the Fatimid caliphs and Roger II illustrate the extent of the Palerman administration's knowledge of the worlds across the Sicilian Strait. In a letter addressed to King Roger II in the name of Fatimid caliph al-Hafiz (r. 1132–1149) in 1137, a picture of the southern Italian peninsula's global twelfth-century world emerges. The letter makes reference to Roger's vizier George of Antioch, who was a Syrian-born Melkite (Eastern

Orthodox) Arabic speaker working at the head of Roger's multilingual administrative bureau. On the Fatimid side was Armenian vizier Bahram al-Armani in Cairo. The content of the Fatimid letter indicates that it was a response to a previous one, now lost, sent by Roger via his Arabic administrative bureau. The Normans' letter appears to have addressed two issues, one of which is striking for what it indicates of Roger's close familiarity with Fatimid politics. The first issue is related to Roger's capture of a Tunisian island, pointing to a Norman encroachment on the North African trading world of the Fatimids. The second, oddly, was related to Roger's defense of the Fatimids' Armenian vizier Bahram, whom the caliph had just dismissed. While the first illustrates Roger's interest in maintaining the favor of the Fatimid caliph, the second points to the extent that Roger sought to manage the interconnected relationships that linked the politics of Sicily and Egypt with the rising Crusader Levant.

In the case of Roger's capture of the Tunisian island of Gabès, it seems that Roger wanted to explain himself to the Fatimid caliph. The caliph did not directly control the Tunisian coastline, but his administration did operate trading vessels in the area and managed relationships with local governors like the Zirids in the region. The island of Gabès (Qabis) and surrounding gulf are perched along the lower third of Tunisia's long longitudinal coastline. While Tunis in northern Tunisia is directly south of the Italian island of Sardinia and almost due west Sicily's southern coast, Gabès looks northeast to Sicily and Malta. What motivated Roger's capture of Gabès by 1137 was local piracy targeting not only Sicilian–Tunisian trade across the Strait of Sicily, but also security along the northern Zirids' Tunisian domains themselves. The caliph wrote in approval of the way Roger handled Gabès, and in reference to the caliph's own trading vessels in the region, the letter shows the caliph thanking Roger for having provided security for the ship and restoring some apparently lost cargo.[15] The caliph approved Roger's handling of the piracy problem in the island's gulf, and even rewarded the Normans with duty-free trade in the Fatimid port of Alexandria and, further inland, the capital of Cairo itself.

The Normans, therefore, commanded a sophisticated diplomatic operation that far outshone the Pisans' abilities in North Africa. Where the Pisans were beginning to make inroads in the context of blending naval power with commerce and diplomacy was in the rising Crusader Levant (c. 1095–1291), where events in Crusader Syria in the 1100s appear to explain the other major topic of the Fatimid letter: Roger's interest in the caliph's vizier choices.

In the case of this second topic of Norman–Fatimid exchange, the Fatimid caliph oddly explains to Roger why he had to dismiss Armenian vizier Bahram around 1137. What explains Roger's interest in the vizier was the shared activities of the Normans and Fatimids in the Crusader Levant. Roger's uncle established a Norman Crusader state along the Anatolian–Syrian frontier in Antioch (*c.* 1098–1268), where the Norman principality of Antioch (Latin: *Principatus Antiochenus*, Norman French: *Princeté de Antioch*) remained one of the longest Norman polities in Norman history. Despite the apparent military resilience that its long duration suggests, it was a vassal state of a variety of Anatolian powers throughout its history: Constantinople to its north (*c.* 1138–1183), the later Armenian Kingdom of Cilicia (1254–1260) to the northwest, and eventually the Mongol ilkhanate (1260–1268)—one of four successor states of Genghis Khan's original empires—coming from the Anatolian northeast. It in its early days in the early 1100s, however, the Norman Crusader principality was powerful and independent enough to hold fellow Norman Roger II's political attention over in Palermo. It appears that Roger II aspired to build what the Pisans, Venetians, and Genoese only later began to create: a semi-centralized commercially profitable maritime empire linking a home city, Palermo, with various ports throughout North Africa and the Levant.

More specifically, it appears that despite Roger II's connections with the Zirids along the Tunisian coast during Pisa's invasion of Mahdia in the late 1000s, and despite his absence from the Jerusalem campaign moving into the start of the 1100s, Roger II's first cousin's governance of a Norman principality in Crusader Syria may have prompted an eastern pivot that would have been facilitated by Palermo's close diplomatic relations with the Fatimids in Cairo. Sicily was both the furthest south and furthest east land of the Italian peninsula, and it was technically a distinct island. That geography put Sicily reasonably close to the Aegean and, further east, to the Anatolian–Syrian Levant. The outcome was that after a Norman principality was established in Crusader Syria during the First Crusade, one that was governed by his uncle Robert Guiscard's son, the possibilities of devoting more attention became worthwhile. An opportunity emerged in 1130 when his cousin died. In Roger's favor, the succession crisis that followed was part of a world with which both his own vizier George of Antioch and the Fatimid vizier Bahram were intimately familiar.

George began his career in Antioch before moving to Norman Palermo. Fatimid vizier Bahram was from a town close to Aleppo. Both George and Bahram had originally moved westward years earlier after beginning their lives and careers around the Crusader-era Syrian–Anatolian frontier. Bahram was an Armenian noble and commander who was well known and respected across the Crusader states prior to his career in Cairo.[16] It appears Roger II may have hoped that the forbearance Bahram showed Palermo following Roger's capture of Gabès on the Tunisian coast would likewise reappear if Roger traced his uncle's steps eastward, where Roger might be able to inherit his cousin's Levantine territories. What points to that possibility is evidence from archbishop William of Tyre, whose surviving writings indicate that Roger had involved himself in Crusader Syria's crisis of succession.

According to William of Tyre, Roger attempted to intervene in Crusader Syria's crisis of succession by preventing the marriage of a certain Raymond of Poitiers to Constance, the daughter of Roger's now late cousin. Roger even detained one of Raymond's key supporters, namely, Antioch patriarch Raoul de Domfront, who was on his way to Rome. Upon his release and return trip from Rome to Antioch, Raoul was sent by Roger with a squadron of Sicilian ships that William of Tyre believed was intended to force Raoul to transfer Crusader Syria to Roger's dominion.[17]

In the end, Roger II was never able to insert himself into the succession crisis, which meant he was never able to absorb distant Norman Syria into Norman Sicilian domains. The Sicilian–Egyptian diplomatic exchanges, however, did secure duty exemptions for Norman Sicily-based merchants in Alexandria and Cairo. The privileges, offered by the Fatimid caliph to Roger in the same letter, were a reward for Roger's work protecting Fatimid trade vessels around Tunisia as well as the Normans' long-standing commercial diplomacy in the region.

In sum, in what shed contrasting light on how far the northern Italian communes-turned-republic had to go before they would match the diplomatic sophistication of Roger II, the Fatimid letter addressed Roger II with the diplomatic respect normally accorded to Muslim rulers, and it agreed on the importance of maintaining stability around Ifriqiya, that is, the coastal lands connecting present-day eastern Algeria with Tunisia and Libya.[18] The Sicilian Normans, in other words, established an early foothold in the region that facilitated a long history as key political and economic players in the *Mashriq*. Interestingly, however, it was precisely as the Normans reached the apex of their commercial diplomacy with Tunis and Cairo in the 1130s, shortly after Roger II's brief pivot to Norman Syria was cut short, that he began to experiment with what the Pisans tried fifty years earlier in Mahdia: outright conquest of several North African cities.

Having cultivated their naval power and commercial leverage around the Zirid domains in the late 1000 and early 1100s, Roger II and his immediate successors subsumed the governing circles of the Tunisian coast under their direct authority in Palermo in the late 1140s. The move seemed to illustrate the Normans' own Roman Republic-like imperial pretensions in competition with the papacy. Their authority on the coast collapsed just a decade later, however, amid the expansion eastward of the mighty Almohads (r. 1121–1269) from Marrakesh. In the shadow of all these developments since the papacy's activities in Mahdia and Jerusalem were the Pisans, who quietly returned to the Tunisian coast to make their own arrangements with the Almohads. This time, the Pisans were interested not in conquest, but in diplomatic relations in order to secure trade privileges. In a sense, the Pisans were ready to take a page of the Norman strategy in the region. By the late 1100s and 1200s, the Pisans were in close contact with figures like Saladin in Cairo and had begun to secure a sprawling network of trade hubs stretching from the Muslim-held Balearic Islands and the Algerian coast to the ports of Egypt and the Syrian Levant.

5

PISAN TRADE HUBS FROM SEVILLE TO CRUSADER SYRIA

Figure 5.1 The Cathedral of Pisa, adjacent to the leaning tower, was built partly with funds that came from the spoils of the failed Mahdia campaign (1087). By the 1100s, with Pisan Archbishop Daimbert (Dagobert) serving as the politically and socially influential patriarch of the newly established Crusader-era Latin Patriarchate of Jerusalem, the Pisan commune-turned-republic began to pursue an independent political and commercial trajectory around both the *Maghrib* and *Mashriq* that disregarded papal embargoes against Latin–Arabic commerce. By the 1500s, in the era of the Medici popes, even the papacy would cultivate trade with the Muslim sultanates (the Ottomans) in papal-held Ancona. The Ancona–Ragusa–Istanbul route developed in competition with the Venice–Spalato–Istanbul route.

Source: https://pixabay.com/photos/architecture-pisa-building-italy-3108306, public domain.

When Pisa and its port were sold to the neighboring Republic of Florence in 1402, images of the city's glory days were a distant memory. The central cathedral's bell tower, leaning since the earliest days of its construction in 1173, offered a kind of metaphor illustrative of the Pisan republic's varied victories in Mediterranean conquest, diplomacy, and commerce. At its peak in the 1200s, Pisa was the center of a sprawling network of Pisan merchant communities stretching across ports from the Iberian coast to Tunis, Cairo, and the Syrian Levant. Pisa was never quite the Roman Republic during Julius Caesar's political career (59–44 BCE), when Rome extended its earlier conquests of the Italian peninsula into the entirety of the European and North African Mediterranean. Still, Pisa in the 1100s and 1200s was a formidable power with a strong navy. Its legacy in the Italian peninsula was so strong that its city flag, that is, its coat of arms, remains one of the four coats of arms featured on Italy's naval flag today. The earliest history of Pisa's flag, however, tells a story of the city's more humble origins in the shadow of Rome.

Perched today atop its famous leaning tower, Pisa's flag first came into public use in the 1000s. Its design, featuring a cross on a vermilion banner, points to Pisa's connections with the Roman Catholic Church based in Rome. A Latin chronicle on a Pisan campaign in Mallorca makes reference to the flag's origins. That text is known as the *Liber Maiolichinus de Gestis Pisanorum Illustribus* (*Majorcan Book on the Deeds of the Illustrious Pisans*). The fact that it was written in ancient Rome's classical Latin language, rather than the local Tuscan variety of vernacular Latin (Tuscan Romance) used by later Renaissance-era authors, points to how early the text was in the region's history. Its author, writing in the 1100s, indicates that the Pisan flag's design dates back to the 1000s, when Rome bestowed upon Pisa a sacred object that came to represent the city: a cross.

Pope Benedictine VIII (r. 1012–1024), the text explains, gave a processional cross to the Pisan archbishop as well as banners to the Pisan military commanders during one of their naval campaigns abroad. More than just an illustration of Pisa's Christian identity, the flag's cross tells a more specific story about how Rome still commanded political authority in Pisa in the 1000s. The early decades of the new millennium (1000s CE) saw Pisa, like its neighbor Florence, emerge as a semi-elective independent republic in the shadow of both the German kingdoms to the north and the Rome-based Papal States to the south. With closer political alignment towards Rome serving as a convenient alternative to an alliance with the German states, the Pisans and their Genoese neighbors became close partners of the papacy in their failed attempt to capture Mahdia—close to ancient Carthage—and in their more successful campaign to capture Jerusalem. What followed next in the first half of the 1100s was something that would have surprised Matilda Canossa, the Tuscan March governor (*markgraf*) who helped to align Pisa more closely with the papacy. The Pisans, while participating in the capture of Jerusalem and the establishment of a political and commercial presence in the Levant, worked in collaboration with Muslim emirates and caliphates to construct a sprawling network of trade hubs from the *Maghrib* to the *Mashriq*.

A Sprawling Trade Network from Seville to Tunis and Cairo

Between Conquest and Diplomacy in the Maghrib

The Pisans quietly returned to the Tunisian city of Mahdia in 1157, just four years before the Almohads (r. 1121–1269) ousted the Sicilian Normans and their short-lived "Kingdom of Africa." The Pisans' agreement with the Almohads in Mahdia, half a century after they had tried to conquer the city, marked the culmination of a new strategy in armed commercial diplomacy that the Venetians would later master. In a sense, the Pisans and Normans had traded strategies. While in the 1080s the Normans had originally refused to join a papal-supported Pisan–Genoese Crusade to conquer Mahdia and risk damaging Sicilian–Tunisian trade relations, fifty years later it was the Pisans who were closing commercial deals in Tunisia while the Normans were faltering in their belated territorial conquests. By the end of the 1100s, the had Pisans managed to construct a sprawling set of trade settlements from Iberia to Byzantium and the Levant complete with warehouses, consuls, and direct access to local markets.

Throughout the twelfth-century, in a pattern that paralleled their activity in the *Mashriq*, the Pisans' presence along the western half of the southern Mediterranean port cities slowly transitioned from short-lived Crusader conquests to more enduring mercantilist diplomatic missions. The case of Pisa's two ventures into the Balearics, several decades apart, illustrates this shift. In the case of Pisa's initial expedition to the Balearics (1113–1115), it occurred in the form of a papal-sponsored Pisan-commissioned crusade against a Muslim ruler. That is, decades after their initial engagements in Mahdia (1088) and the Levant (1095–1099), the Pisans were still pursuing outright conquest of Muslim-held territories in the name of revenue and sacred glory. The Balearics campaign, far out to the west of their North African and Levantine ventures, began in 1115.

While a largely Pisan–Catalan joint force captured Ibiza and reached as far as Denia on the Alicante coast in 1115, the Pisans lost control of the territories in 1116 to Marrakesh's Almoravid dynasty, that is, the Almohads' predecessors in Iberia and western North Africa. The outcome echoed the lessons, and specifically the shortcomings, of the joint Pisan–Genoese Mahdia campaign in 1087. Interestingly, when the Pisans returned to the Almoravids in 1133, they arrived in the context of the very different circumstances of a diplomatic negotiation for trade privileges. Many of the sources for both campaigns were written by the Pisans themselves, and their use of Latin in contrast to the later Venetian and Florentine use of Venetian and Tuscan, respectively, points to how early the Pisans' expansionist project was in global history.

The Pisan *Liber Maiolichinus de Gestis Pisanorum Illustribus* (*Majorcan Book of the Deeds of the Illustrious Pisans*), a Latin epic chronicle completed in 1125, is one of the key sources of the campaign. It indicates that the Pisans' first expedition to the Balearics occurred in 1114 in the context of a joint expedition that included "Catalans," one of the first references in Latin to the group. In the geographical context of eastern Spain, references to "Valencians," "Aragonese," and the people of Barcelona were more frequent in the eleventh and twelfth centuries. According to the text, the Pisan-led campaign had support from Catalonia, Occitania, and several regions on the Italian peninsula. Catalan duke (*dux Catalanensis*) and leader of the Catalan armies (*rector Catalanicus hostes*) Raymond Berangar III, who reigned as the Count of Barcelona (r. 1086–1113) and neighboring cities, contributed a large force to the Pisan-commissioned venture.[1] While the Crusader fleet of several hundred ships captured Ibiza within two months of the initial raid in June, the siege of Majorca degenerated into a stalemate that ended the following year with the island's fall to Pisa.

In what illustrated the limitations of Pisa's synthesis of conquest and commerce, the Almoravids of Marrakesh—predecessors of the Almohads—conquered the islands and waited almost a generation before allowing Pisa access to its ports.[2] It was only in 1133, some twenty years later, that the Almoravids considered a trade deal with Pisa. The Almoravids sent ambassadors on two galleys to Pisa, where one of the first of a variety of Pisan–North African trade agreements would be established in the context of Pisan trade diplomacy, that is, outside the scope of Pisan Crusader conquest.[3]

Pisa and the Almohads

It was against this backdrop that the Pisans' relationship with the Almohads developed. In 1168, in negotiation with the Almoravids' Almohad succcessors in the *Maghrib*, the Pisans managed to secure a degree of access to western North African ports that was nearly unprecedented for an Italian maritime power. The surviving renewal of the treaty in 1186, negotiated between the Pisans and Abu Yaqub Yusuf's successor Mansur, offers a picture of the arrangement: access for Pisans to four key ports in the *Maghrib*, namely, Sibta (Ceuta), Wahran (Oran), Bijaya (Bougie), and Tunis.[4] An additional stipulation indicated that distressed ships flying Pisan flags were allowed to anchor at any port under Islamic rule, and that the crew and passengers would be allowed free access to the nearest port necessary for the continuation of their journey on the condition that crew members and passengers did not engage in the commercial activities restricted to the four commercial ports.

What made these developments nearly unprecedented was the fact that the Genoese, one-time partners in the attempted Crusader conquest of Mahdia in 1087, had likewise learned the art of commercial diplomacy and secured trade privileges from the Almohads in 1161.[5] This Genoese–Almohad agreement of 1061 was likely a renewal of a 1053 agreement, and it was indicative of the very early inroads the Genoese made throughout the western Mediterranean's Latin–Arabic frontiers centuries before they became key players in Habsburg Spain's Atlantic world commerce.

Still, despite how quickly the Genoese would outdo the Pisans by the 1200s and certainly the 1300s, Pisa remained a pioneering trading force for both the wide geography of its commercial portfolio and the degree of Pisan commerce into the Arabic Mediterranean's urban landscape. Indeed, in the years leading up to the Almohad capture of Tunis, when the city was under the post-Zirid rule of the Banu Khurasan and when the Sicilian Normans were struggling to maintain a hold over their short-lived African holdings, the Pisans concluded a treaty with Tunis' governors that provides evidence of Pisan residents living in either a specially designated quarter, compound, or inn-warehouse (*funduq*). The longer Arabic version of the treaty, concluded between the Khurasanid ruler and the "most respected Archbishop of Pisa" (*al-ark al-jalil al-akram Ark Bisha*) refers specifically to the "walls" (*sur*) of the Pisans' residence in the city.[6]

What points to the fact that this compound or quarter was a nascent center of bustling Pisan and Genoese activity in the city is surviving written evidence from a contemporary observer. Genoese notary Pietro Battifolio, writing a little more than a century later in 1289, writes about the Genoese community in the city as a large group of soldiers, merchants, priests, and "fallen women."[7] He even describes a tavern that they owned, and that the Almohads taxed.

Still, despite the Pisans' commercial advances, there were clear restrictions about which Almohad ports in particular were open to them, and what activities they could undertake. The 1186 Almohad–Pisan agreement itself points to two sides of these privileges. On the one hand, access to Ceuta, Oran, Bougie, and Tunis meant broad access across the entire western half of the *Maghrib* and its Iberian frontier, where the Pisans' had secured trade privileges from the Muslim ruling circles of the Balearics. Outside these ports, however, the restrictions on what distressed ship crews and passengers could do in cities where they anchored as an emergency were very strict: not only were Pisans forbidden from buying or selling anything, but they were also allowed to anchor only as long as they refrained from speaking with any of the local inhabitants (*dun an yukallimu ahad min ahlih*).[8]

The restrictions are unsurprising given continuing Almohad questions of security. A Pisan–Genoese force had attempted to capture the coastal Algerian port of Annaba (Bône) only decades earlier in 1136, which was just two years after the Genoese attempted to invade Bougie. These were approximately the same years when Norman king Roger II captured Gerba (1137) and wrote to the Fatimid caliph in Cairo to explain himself, unaware apparently that the real power broker would be the Almohads coming from the other direction in Marrakesh. The Almohads' expulsion of the Normans from Mahdia, the one-time capital of the Fatimids and a Norman protectorate (1148–1159) during the Almohad expansion eastward, meant that the Almohads were well aware of the danger and benefit of Latin relations. For the Almohads, the

Pisans, Genoese, even Sicilian Normans would be commercially tolerated, but they would remain politically suspicious.

In the end, in spite of these restrictions and suspicions, ports like Bougie and Tunis began to see during Almohad era (1100s–1200s) a phenomenon epitomized in fifteenth-century Nasrid Granada and Ottoman Istanbul: frontier cities connecting Europe with the Islamic worlds on either side of the Mediterranean were not only centers of commodity exchange but also sites of cultural transfer. Pisan mathematician Fibonacci's legacy of innovation and discovery began in Bougie, where his first foray into the world of Graeco-Arabic mathematics began under the supervision of a Muslim teacher. Fibonacci, son (*filus*) of a merchant named Bonacci, was developing the education necessary to enter the world of commerce, finance, and exchange himself. His education included his use of an abacus and

Figure 5.2 The Arabic-language documents of the Cairo *genizah*, the storeroom of a Cairene synagogue, indicate that shipping vessels from the Italian peninsula had become ubiquitous in the southern Mediterranean by the 1200s. The present-day Italian navy's flag features the coat of arms of each of the most influential maritime republics of the medieval era. Stories from the *genizah* documents, written in Arabic with Hebrew letters (Judeo-Arabic), paint a picture of a vibrant Jewish merchant community linking Europe with the Middle East and North Africa.

Source: https://commons.wikimedia.org/wiki/File:Cairo_Genizah_Fragment.jpg, public domain.

instruction in algebra, including the use of Arabic numerals. This exchange in the twelfth and thirteenth centuries facilitated a growing Pisan literary and material imagination of the *Maghrib* that paralleled Latin–Arabic encounters in the *Mashriq*.

Pisan Commerce across the Levant's Latin–Arabic Frontiers

One of the most multifaceted windows into the increasingly intertwined worlds of the twelfth-century Mediterranean Sea, including the worlds of the Normans and Pisans from Almohad Marrakesh to Fatimid Cairo, is a collection of documents known as the Cairo *genizah* collection. The stories they tell offer a much more intimate look at the lives of merchants, particularly Jewish merchants, and their successes and disappointments as they pursued the complex art of managing trade between Europe, the Middle East, and North Africa. On the margins of these narratives are actors like the Pisans and Genoese, whose ships make an increasingly frequent appearance as vessels of transport both for regional merchants and their commodities. That the Age of Exploration was looming on the horizon in the late fifteenth century indicates something interesting about where these ships fit in history: in advance of the high-speed oar-powered Venetian war galleys and the high-walled tank-like Portuguese transoceanic carracks, the Pisans and Genoese were making advances in their maritime technology that would pave the way for a European shipping revolution in later years. Large sections of this multifaceted picture emerge from the *genizah* collection.

For centuries, the *genizah* (storeroom) of the old Ben Ezra synagogue in Fustat (old Cairo) held some 300,000 complete manuscripts and manuscript fragments written by Jewish congregants in primarily three languages: Arabic, Hebrew, and Aramaic.[9] One of the immediately striking things about the collection is its multilingualism. The ability to either speak or write in multiple languages was a major facet of medieval urban and rural worlds, and Jewish communities like others used language to navigate multiple social and intellectual worlds. Arabic was the primary spoken and written language of Jewish communities throughout the *Maghrib* and *Mashriq*. As the writings of Cordovan physician and philosopher Maimonides (d. 1204) indicate, Arabic was even used for theological commentaries on the Hebrew Bible. As a native speaker of Arabic, Maimonides (Musa b. Maymun) was able to begin his career as a physician in Cordoba and continue in Cairo, where he was the personal physician of Crusader-era Ayyubid sultan Saladin (d. 1193).

Jewish merchants on the Iraqi, Syrian, and Iberian frontiers were sometimes bilingual in Arabic and Persian, Arabic and Greek, or Arabic and Iberian languages like old Portuguese. Other spoken languages like Aramaic, Berber, and Kurdish could also be heard in Jewish circles, especially outside most urban centers of the Middle East and North Africa. That many Jewish intellectuals could write in both classical Arabic and Biblical Hebrew, including Maimonides, spoke to the continued respect that Arabic-speaking Jews accorded to Biblical vocabulary as a medium of communicating sacred ideas. Education in at least the Aramaeo-Hebrew script was commonplace, even if the ability to write Biblical Hebrew was not.[10]

It is for all these reasons that the surviving Arabic documents of the Ben Ezra synagogue's *genizah* (storeroom) had an interesting feature: they were written in a form of the Aramaeo-Hebrew script that, when read out loud, sounds like Arabic. More than reflecting the Jewish authorship of these documents or the sacred value accorded to Hebrew orthography, the script also brought the same benefits that Armenian-speaking Iranian Armenians derived from recording their commerce in Armenian rather than their other native language: Persian. Keeping records in Armenian, with a vocabulary almost entirely distinct from Persian and a radically distinct script, offered a form of privacy or medieval encryption across commercial channels.

One letter, dated 1064, paints a picture of how Arabic-speaking Jewish merchants active throughout Egypt and Tunisia came to be involved in commerce in the Italian peninsula. The letter is the longest one found in the storeroom, and it was contemporary with the era when Roger I was about to become the first Norman ruler of Sicily (1071) and inherit the Sicilian emirate's trade relationship with the Zirids in Tunisia. The letter's author was a certain Salama b. Musa al-Safaqisi, whose name indicates his family's origins: Sfax. While in Mazara (Sicily), Salama wrote to a business partner in Cairo— Yahuda b. Sighmar—hoping to persuade him not to terminate their partnership after a series of mishaps.[11]

The geographical variety of Salama and Yahuda's misfortunes illustrates the wide expanse of these Arabic-speaking Jewish merchants' social and commercial relationships. One mishap in Salama's commercial portfolio occurred in Mahdia near Tunis. There, the previously discussed Zirid emir Tamim (r. 1062–1108)—associate of both the last ruling emir of Palermo and the first Norman ruler Roger I—had just expanded his dominion into the city of Sfax and its environs. In Sfax, the local governor had previously in the 1150s governed independently, only nominally paying homage to Tamim. Salama had worked in the service of this independent governor in Sfax, earning the privilege to collect taxes in a particular district. Immediately prior to Tamim's conquest of Sfax, Salama used this privilege to collect taxes in the environs of Sfax to write up an ambitious business plan. In partnership with Jewish and Muslim associates from Palermo to Cairo, Salama proposed pooling money together and putting it forward to local owners of olive crops and Bedouin in order to secure in advance a large amount of the valuable unharvested olives. Tamim's conquest of Sfax, however, saw a political reappropriation of the olive groves, which was intertwined with restrictions on sales of olive oil. Salama's business plan, in other words, was dealt a financial blow by the realities of the region's unpredictable politics.

Salama's other failed ventures included an attempt to sell indigo from Cairo in Mahdia on behalf of his Cairene business partner Yahuda. A disagreement with business associates in Mahdia, however, led to Salama falling afoul of the same emir Tamim. In the end, he abandoned commerce in Ifriqiya altogether in favor of Sicily, which was about to enter a transitional period between Islamic and Norman rule. Salama decided to settle in Sicily in the final years of its Islamic period and pursue his remaining business ventures there, but he again ran into a series of mishaps with local associates in Palermo. It was there in Mazara, a port city on Sicily's southwestern coast closest to Tunisia, where he wrote his letter to a certain associate in Cairo named Yahuda. Salama indicated that he received Yahuda's letters about wanting to end their partnership and agreed that he himself vowed not to enter another partnership that year.[12]

Interestingly, as the Cairo *genizah* documents move into the twelfth century, new interlocutors appear with greater frequency: "Frankish" (*afrang*) merchants. These were the vernacular Latin-speaking European merchants among whom the Pisans, Genoese, and Venetians numbered, and who lived in lands once controlled by the Frankish kingdom. As the worlds of the Latin and Arabic Mediterranean became increasingly intertwined, merchants from the Italian peninsula increasingly interacted with Egypt and the

Levant's local Muslim, Jewish, and Orthodox (Syrian, Coptic, Armenian) merchants. This change can be seen in reference to the names of business associates. While eleventh-century *genizah* documents largely note Arabic names in reference to these Arabic-speaking merchants, Latin names appear frequently in the twelfth century, particularly in reference to the proprietors of vessels on which Egypt's Jewish merchants traveled. These ships were owned especially by Genoese and Pisans.[13]

By the twelfth century, Pisans and Genoese mariners had begun to move from vessels that sailed close to the coast to larger ships able to traverse the Mediterranean with fewer risks. Arab dhow ships, one of which was recently unearthed deep in Indonesian waters, had a long medieval history of transporting Chinese ceramics and other commodities from coastal China to Iraq's Persian Gulf and Egypt's Red Sea via the Indian Ocean. The fact that the particular ship unearthed in Indonesia was shipwrecked, complete with its cargo of Song-dynasty Chinese porcelain, indicates something about the challenge of crossing the high seas in treacherous weather. Early Crusader-era ships used by the Pisans, Genoese, and Venetians came to be known as coasters due to the captains' predilection of sailing close to shore. This approach, however, meant that a transport of pilgrims, soldiers, or commodities from the Italian peninsula through the Balkans and Anatolia to the Levant via the Adriatic and Aegean seas took weeks.[14]

By the twelfth century, contemporary with developments in the North Sea's Hanseatic nave (*nava*) ships, Pisan and Genoese ships were controlled by multiple masts and equipped with newer varieties of sails and, in place of rows of oars or a steering oar, sternpost-mounted rudders. Arab vessels in the Middle East and Indian Ocean were using sternpost-mounted rudders by the tenth century, while a distinct variety of rudder appeared centuries earlier in Chinese ships.[15] The sternpost-mounted rudders that became ubiquitous among southern and northern European ships in the thirteenth and fourteenth centuries most closely resembled the earlier Arab rudders, pointing to the likelihood of a transfer of technology. Travelers who observed and remarked on European and Middle Eastern shipping technology at the time included Venetian Marco Polo, who described the rudders on ships anchored in Hormuz in 1272, as well as chronicler Friar John of Montecorvino (d. *c.* 1328), who described their features. A contemporary Arabic text called the *Kitab Suwar al-Kawakib* (*Book of Fixed Stars*), written centuries earlier by Abd al-Rahman al-Sufi (d. 986), even includes a detailed picture describing exactly what these rudders looked like and how they functioned.[16]

Twelfth-century European shipbuilders, in sum, began to catch up with their Middle Eastern and Indian Ocean counterparts in moving from coastal vessels to ships able to traverse the open seas, and the Cairo *genizah* collections' frequent references to "Frankish" merchants in the ports of the Arabic Mediterranean correlate with this shift. What also correlates with the increasingly frequent reference in Arabic to Frankish merchants is the previously discussed construction of a sprawling southern Mediterranean trade network by the Pisans, Genoese, and Venetians alike. What appears in these texts in particular, as well as in Arabic texts more broadly, are references to the growing array of warehouse-inns (*funduq, fondaco*) used by these merchants.

The first Arabic-language mention of any warehouse-inn designated specifically for European merchants, as opposed to inns for travelers from other sultanates and emirates, appears in 1154. That year, almost a century after Salama's letter from Mazara and contemporary with the Pisans' diplomatic inroads with the Almohads in the *Maghrib*, Pisan ambassador Ranieri Botacci was in Fatimid Cairo negotiating a trade deal. Less than twenty years after Norman king Roger II was exchanging letters in Arabic with the Fatimid caliph justifying his capture of the Tunisian island of Gerba, the Pisan ambassador was at the Fatimid court in Cairo negotiating in person a renewal of commercial and residency privileges with a certain Abu al-Fadl Abbas b. Abi l-Futuh, vizier of the Fatimid caliph al-Zafir (r. 1149–1154). Caliph al-Zafir was the successor to al-Hafiz (r. 1132–1149), seen earlier in his letter to Roger II (r. 1130–1154).

The increasingly multifaceted role of European shipping vessels in the twelfth-century Arabic Mediterranean appears in the contract itself. The Pisan–Fatimid deal included the right of safe passage for Pisan pilgrims headed east. Pilgrims headed for the Levant not via the coastal Adriatic and Aegean route, but rather the growing trans-Mediterranean Italian–Egyptian routes traversed by the larger nave ships used by the Pisans and Genoese.[17] Safe passage was also guaranteed for Pisan merchants, and the Pisans' inn-warehouse in Alexandria would be rebuilt. In what points to the degree that the Pisans were pioneers in their ability to access the innermost commercial centers of the Arabic Mediterranean, the treaty even promised the construction of an inn-warehouse for Pisans in Cairo. The Fatimid capital was not a Mediterranean or

Red Sea port, and required following one of the Nile's tributaries from Alexandria on the Mediterranean or Port Said and Ismailia on the Red Sea. Fatimid Cairo was built partly in competition with Abbasid Baghdad, both new cities in the eighth and ninth centuries. For European merchants who were able to reach them, the cities and their imports offered privileged access to Asian commodities arriving via Red Sea and Persian Gulf ports. Only the Amalfitans, present in Cairo as early as the 900s, preceded the Pisans in a major way in their presence at the heart of Fatimid politics and commerce.

In what reflected enduring concern over Pisan and Genoese military power, a key stipulation of the Pisan–Fatimid agreement of 1154 was that the Pisans agreed to neither furnish "Frankish" Christians—that is, Christians from Latin Europe—with for Crusader missions nor help them in any attacks on Fatimid Egypt. This last stipulation committing the Pisans to nonaggression during the Crusades tells two political stories. First, although the Pisans participated in the First (1096–1099) and Second (1147–1149) Crusades, and though the Fatimids pushed back against the Crusaders in the Levant, the Fatimids had enough political and economic leverage to push the Pisans to stand down. From another perspective, in what foreshadows the way Italian powers supplied Saladin with arms, the Pisans equally had enough military leverage to secure a favorable trade agreement with the mighty Fatimids.

The second political story this agreement tells is the one previously discussed, namely, that the Pisans were already by the mid twelfth-century in the process of transforming their engagement in the Middle East and North Africa from one of Crusader-like conquest to the kind of merchant diplomacy seen increasingly among their Genoese, Venetian, and later Florentine counterparts.

Put simply, Pisa's twelfth-century commercial enterprise across the *Mashriq* paralleled developments in the *Maghrib*. The Pisans' diplomatic and commercial relationship with the two most powerful empires of the Arabic Mediterranean—the Almohads of Marrakesh (r. 1121–1269) and the Fatimids of Cairo (r. 909–1171)—illustrates the extent that the Pisans pioneered the model of trans-Mediterranean merchant diplomacy that the Genoese, Venetians, and even Florentines would later master moving into the era of the Almohads' and Fatimids' most influential successors in North Africa—namely, the Hafsids (r. 1229–1574) of Tunis and Mamluks (1250–1517) of Cairo. From one perspective, the Pisans gave the impression that they had transformed from Crusaders to militarized merchant diplomats, and their two trips to Tunisia—first as Crusaders in 1087 and fifty years later as merchants—suggested as much. From another perspective, the Pisans' ability to court the Fatimids in Cairo in the mid-1100s with a promise to not arm the Crusaders, suggests a slightly different reality: the Pisans had learned to flex their military muscle in service of their own trade priorities rather than attempt to conquer ports that they could not hold onto.

Their approach foreshadowed aspects of British gunboat diplomacy in China in the 1800s, with the difference here in the 1000s being that the Almohads and Fatimids commanded two of the most powerful navies in the world at the time, with the Pisan and Genoese navies still far from the might of Venetian war galleys built at Venice's Arsenale. As the Fatimids fell to the

Figure 5.3 The *fondaco dei turchi*, a warehouse-inn in Venice for visiting Ottoman subjects, was one of several Venetian inns for merchants from both sides of the Mediterranean. The equivalent of the Venetian *fondaco* was the earlier and architecturally similar Arabic *funduq*, where merchants from the Italian peninsula stayed in ports like Tunis and Alexandria in accordance with trade agreements dating back to the Crusader era. The Pisans were exceptional among the Italian republics for having been able to secure a *funduq* in the inland capital of Cairo during Saladin's reign. In an illustration of the growing sophistication of the Italian republics' shipping and weapons' technology, Saladin—one-time conqueror of the Crusader Kingdom of Jerusalem—wrote a letter to Baghdad remarking on the high quality of weapons he secured from merchants of the Italian peninsula.

Source: https://commons.wikimedia.org/wiki/File:Fondaco_dei_Turchi_%28Venise%29.JPG, public domain.

Ayyubid dynasty's founder Saladin (r. 1174–1193), and as the Crusades carried on along the increasingly complex Latin–Greek–Arabic and increasing Latin–Greek–Turkish–Arabic frontiers of twelfth- and thirteenth-century Levant, this push and pull of Pisan flexing and an emir or sultan's willingness to benefit from a mixed military–commercial Pisan presence became even clearer. By the middle of the thirteenth century, as the Pisan–Genoese rivalry slowly transformed into a Genoese–Venetian rivalry over Mediterranean dominance, the Genoese and Venetians came to master the Pisan art of wearing three hats in the region: Crusade-supporters, anti-Crusade arms dealers, and unarmed merchant civilians.

Crossing Cultures in Saladin's Egypt and Crusader Syria

Across Latin–Arabic Boundaries: Courting Cairo's New Anti-Crusader Sultan

By 1154, Fatimid-era ruling circles accorded the Pisans exceptional access to both Alexandria and Cairo's markets. A *funduq* in Alexandria was a privilege that became commonplace among "Frankish" merchants visiting the port, including the rising Genoese and Venetians. A *funduq* further along the Nile in Cairo, in contrast, was unusual. The Pisans' ability to secure one in 1154 was a testament to their exceptional ability to make inroads on both sides of the Arabic Mediterranean. Pisan–Cairene relations cooled, however, in the lead up to the Third Crusade (1189–1192). By then, the Fatimids had been overthrown by their own army officers, the Levant had become the boundary of an increasingly complex Latin–Greek–Turkish–Arabic frontier, Christian and Muslim powers in the region were divided into a litany of kingdoms with complex political and commercial arrangements, and there was an entirely new Muslim force reaching the Mediterranean from Syria's Anatolian frontier: the Turkish Seljuk sultanate of Anatolia (r. 1077–1308), a principality based in Iconium (Konya) that was an offshoot of the older Seljuk Turks governing Iraq, Iran, and Central Asia. The latter Seljuks famously ruled as sultans in Abbasid Baghdad in the two hundred years (r. 1055–1258) before the Mongols captured the city, subsuming the region into the Mongol Empire's breakaway ilkhanate.

The Pisans, armed with a century of sophisticated diplomacy and military know-how, attempted to tread carefully in this increasingly complex eastern Mediterranean world of Greek, Turkish, Latin, and Arabic political cultures. They were particularly careful in their relationship with powerful anti-Crusades sultan Saladin in Cairo, one-time general of a Seljuk vassal state along the Anatolian–Syrian frontiers.

Pisan–Egyptian relations grew complex during the career of Saladin, the famous sultan who usurped the power of the Fatimid caliphate while vizier in Cairo. About ten years after the Pisans secured a *funduq* in Cairo, Saladin first arrived in the city in 1164 upon being sent from a Turkish-held part of the Levant to work for the caliphate. The Zengid (r. 1127–1250) beys of the Anatolian–Syrian frontier, a Turkish vassal state of the Seljuk sultans of Anatolia, sent him to restore a particular Cairene vizier they were connected with. Saladin's work for the dynasty, including his campaigns against the Crusaders, allowed him to rise up the ranks of Fatimid government, eventually being named vizier himself in 1169.

Over the next two years, Saladin quickly undermined Fatimid authority and established a decidedly global reputation for the first of two enduring legacies. The first was his coup of the Fatimid government in the very imperial capital they built, Cairo, which he then aligned with the administration of its historical rival: the Abbasid caliphs in Baghdad. As mentioned, when these events took place in 1171, the Abbasid caliphate was under the military authority of the same network of Seljuk sultans with authority over Saladin's former Zengid employers in northern Syria. While the rise of the Ottoman sultans (est. 1299) were still more than a century away, the process of the Anatolian–Syrian frontier becoming an increasingly Turkish heartland of the eastern Mediterranean's Greek, Turkish, Latin, and Arabic political boundaries was well underway, which in the short term meant that the Latin Crusader principalities were becoming increasingly squeezed between a crowded field of powerful players. What made the field especially crowded was Saladin himself, founder of Cairo's Ayyubid dynasty and patron of the Mamluk military dynasty that usurped his descendants' authority. Both the Ayyubids and the Mamluks consolidated Cairo's hold over both Egypt and the Levant, and one of the first forays into that was Saladin's demonstration that Crusader Jerusalem was weaker than observers imagined.

More specifically, in what became Saladin's second enduring legacy, he captured Jerusalem in 1187 just prior to the Third Crusade (1189–1192).

His campaign, and especially its conclusion, brought him renown even in Latin and Greek Christendom. In a move that impressed both Latin and Greek European observers, Saladin granted his enemies a kind of amnesty. He allowed the "Franks," that is, Latin Europeans, to remain in the city and left those who wanted to leave free to depart westward. Saladin's abilities as well as his generous forbearance with the defeated Crusaders earned him a reputation in Europe as a kind of chivalrous warrior and shrewd diplomat on a par with Charlemagne.[18]

The Pisans had to tread carefully in all of this activity, which included when they supplied Saladin with arms. Saladin had a mixed perspective that initially saw a cooling of Pisan–Egyptian relations before he warmed to them again. Throughout his thirty-year career based in Cairo, both in service of the Fatimids (1164–1171) and as head of state (1171–1193), Saladin had a position on the Pisans that was multidimensional. He was simultaneously suspicious of the Pisans' presence in Cairo and intrigued by the possibilities of extracting some benefit from them. When he first overthrew the Fatimid dynasty in 1171, he made plans to limit Pisan commerce to Alexandria. At the same time, in anticipation of consolidating his hold over the region, he was in need of arms. Saladin knew from his own experience in the region that the Levantine political arena adjacent to Egypt had become complex, and he sought to make shrewd political calculations that would help him to subsume the litany of small Catholic and Islamic kingdoms into Cairo's centralized authority.

At the height of his reign as sultan in Cairo, Saladin sent a letter to the Abbasid caliph in Baghdad simultaneously celebrating and defending his strategic relationship with Pisan, Genoese, and Venetian merchants: "Among the [enemy] armies were also Venetians, Pisans, and Genoese. They sometimes behaved like invaders, producing a harmful effect and maleficence that were intolerable, and sometimes like travelers, imposing their law on Islam with their imported goods and escaping strict regulation. Yet there is not a single one of them who does not come today to bring us the weapons with which they fought . . ."[19] Interestingly, Saladin's comments point to the three hats worn by the Pisans, like their Genoese and Venetian contemporaries, when engaging Muslim ruling circles: Crusaders, merchants, and supporters of anti-Crusaders.

For the Pisans, navigating the changing alliances of the Crusader Levant was complex and fraught with risks. Their ability to navigate these risks was a testament to how deeply they made inroads across all frontiers despite never actually governing any Crusader territories in the way Roger II's cousin Bohemond of Antioch did. In the case of the Latin–Arabic frontiers, the same Pisan maritime networks arming Saladin in Alexandria were simultaneously involved in the Crusader Kingdom of Jerusalem's naval campaigns against Saladin in Beirut.

In 1182, seven years after Saladin's letter, Pisan vessels were among the ships that breached Saladin's naval siege of Beirut. King Baldwin IV of the Kingdom of Jerusalem requested that Pisan ships anchored in local harbors participate in the operation. The breach was a success, and the Pisans were rewarded with a royal grant and the expansion of their quarter in Acre.[20] Just five years later, Saladin captured Jerusalem during the reign of empress Sybilla, whom Saladin allowed to leave for Acre with her daughters. Conrad of Montferrat, ruler of Tyre, granted Pisan administrators jurisdiction over their own citizens in 1187, including local Pisan residents and ship crews. One of the most remarkable outcomes of this legal framework was the ability of other merchants from southern Europe to naturalize as Pisans in accordance with Pisa's own definition of a Pisan, that is, visitors and residents *qui Pisanorum nomine censentur*.[21] This process of naturalization was one that foreshadowed the process of Genoese and Greek subjects of the Ottoman Empire naturalizing as Venetians via the Venetian *nazione* that lived with its consul (*bailo*) in Istanbul's Pera district. Many of the patterns of political and cultural transfer picked up speed in the first two Crusades, especially with the rise of long-duration states like that of the Levantine Normans around Antioch. In the decades following Bohemond's establishment of a Crusader state in Antioch in 1098 and the rise of the Crusader Kingdom of Jerusalem (1099–1291) a year later, political and social networks of the Italian peninsula began to intertwine both with one another and with those of the eastern Mediterranean to an extent that evoked the interconnected history of the late antique Roman Empire.

In the following century, the Genoese famously straddled these worlds as they reinstalled Greek authority in Crusader-held Constantinople and were rewarded with full autonomous control over the district of Pera and access to the Black Sea. Both the Venetians and Florentines cultivated close commercial relations with the Ottomans despite frequent papal pressures. In certain instances where commercial boundaries between the Italian peninsula and the Ottoman world were most fluid, the cleric seated on the papal throne was a Medici from the Medici family of Florentine merchant governors. The same Medici dynasty, meanwhile, originally attempted to participate in a papal-sponsored attempt to push the Ottomans out of the former Byzantine capital. For the Pisans, straddling these many worlds similarly meant having a hand in all commercial, military, and religious dimensions of the eastern Mediterranean frontiers. Foreshadowing the Florentine hold over the papacy during Medici rule, the Pisans' ability to straddle multiple political and commercial worlds extended into the worlds of clerical administration: the Pisans similarly managed to have their archbishop secure the new Latin Patriarchate of Jerusalem in a demonstration of the variety of inroads they had made in the Crusader-era Middle East.

Across Sacral–Clerical Boundaries: A Pisan in the Latin Patriarchate

By the end of the twelfth century, the Pisans had made inroads across both the Crusader states and the anti-Crusader territories like Saladin's Egypt. As mentioned, Tyre ruler Conrad of Montferrat granted Pisan administrators jurisdiction over their own citizens in 1187, including local Pisan residents and ship crews, and southern European merchants were able to naturalize as Pisans while in the Levant. On a specific level, this phenomenon foreshadowed how the Venetian *nazione* in Ottoman Istanbul absorbed some southern European networks heading east. On a broader level, it foreshadowed the variety of boundaries Italian peninsular powers crossed very deliberately in order to build inroads in the eastern Mediterranean. There were the more obvious confessional and linguistic boundaries of the Greek–Turkish–Latin–Arabic Levant, but there were also boundaries of authority—specifically clerical and sacral authority.

When Sicilian Norman king Roger II's first cousin Bohemond entered Jerusalem in 1099, a certain Pisan cleric named Daimbert (Dagobert) accompanied him. Daimbert was the previously discussed archbishop in Pisa, and he would become the second patriarch of the newly established Latin, that is, Roman Catholic, Patriarchate of Jerusalem in a world where Pisan and Genoese mariners were vying for access and privileges. Part of what allowed Daimbert to step into this role was how well he and a patron, Countess Matilda of Tuscany, navigated Pisa's relationship with the papacy in Rome. In the years before he came to Jerusalem, Daimbert of Pisa was close to Countess Matilda of Tuscany, where Pisa is situated. Matilda, a powerful figure in Tuscan ruling circles, was a major supporter of the papacy at a time when there was conflict between the pope's clerical authority and local sovereigns' sacral authority—that is, a conflict between church and state. There was, in fact, a long history of tension over how local church officials were appointed, and the background of that clash points to how the maritime powers of the Italian peninsula—from the Crusader-era Pisans and Genoese to the Ottoman-era Venetians and Florentines and even the modern Italian republic—simultaneously aligned themselves with the religious authority and popular prestige of the papacy, while frequently breaking away from specific political, military, and economic policies that the pope called for. This push and pull of papal authority in Rome was, in the long run, a major component of what tied the Italian peninsular powers' historical experience together in the lead-up to the *Risorgimento* of the 1800s. It was also a major element in the story of how Italian peninsular powers independently managed their relationships with Middle Eastern and North African administrations.

For the Pisans back in Tuscany, their participation in debates about the papacy's sacred and sacral authority—and specifically support for papal authority—translated into raising the ranks of the Latin patriarchate in the Levant (r. 1099–1107), where the sacred underpinnings of the entire Crusader enterprise meant that high-ranking clergy were major players in Crusader politics. For Daimbert of Pisa, the future Latin Patriarch of Jerusalem, he rose through clerical ranks partly as the beneficiary of having answered an enduring question correctly: should monarchs or the pope select the abbots of local monasteries and the bishops of local cathedrals?

Far from the minutiae tucked away in the dusty annals of clerical administrative history, this question became central to the clashing millennium-long history of the peninsula's complex cultural connections with Rome. On the one hand, Rome became the future republic's capital in the 1900s following hundreds of years of families like the Medicis intermingling with other ruling families in the villas they maintained in the papal capital. On the other hand, across individual Italian duchies, counties, communes, and maritime republics, these same governing circles—complete with their own city's patron saint, whether St. Mark in Venice or St. John in Genoa—maintained their distinct centripetal desires to keep their distance from a single shared sacred center in Rome. One of the key ways for monarchs to maintain this distance was to select for themselves the abbots of local monasteries and the bishops of local cathedrals rather than allowing the pope to do it. In seventeenth-century Florence, where the Medicis were trying to attract Greek mariners and merchants to Pisa's coastal successor Livorno, this independence meant bypassing papal authority when allowing local Greek churches—officially Byzantine-rite Catholics and in practice sometimes ambiguously Orthodox—flexibility in managing their own clerical affairs to the exclusion of the pope's concerns over the proliferation of Greek Orthodox rituals amongst the Tuscan Greeks.

For Daimbert of Pisa in the eleventh century, there were more benefits to taking on the reverse position, that is, aligning himself with papal authority. In this case, it allowed this earlier era of Tuscans, with no Crusader state of their own, key inroads into the governing worlds of the Crusader Levant. The background of Daimbert's rise in the Levant began in the years leading up to his appointment as archbishop of Pisa in 1080, when monarchy–papal tensions reached one of its earliest and most lasting breaking points following a German king's protests against papal authority.

When Saxon king Heinric (Henry) IV became king in 1056 at the age of six, his mother Empress Agnes began her work as de facto regent consolidating the German aristocracy's support for the new government. Just three years later, her sacral authority as a German monarch began to clash with the sacred authority of the pope in Rome. The pope was in the process of consolidating his own authority over the entire clerical administration to the exclusion of monarchs and regional aristocracies, including in regions as far away from Rome as German Saxony. More specifically, in 1075, the office of the papacy issued a compilation of twenty-seven statements known as the *Dictatus Papae*. They claimed papal authority over the appointment of all church officials in Latin Europe. The statements are historically attributed to Pope Gregory VII (1073–1085). While the pope's authorship has been debated, a council was held that year (1075) in the Lateran Palace ascribing the same authorities to the pope. The statements built on a papal bull issued by Pope Nicholas II (r. 1059–1061) in 1059. Known as *In Nomine Domini* (*In the Name of the Lord*), it stipulated that only cardinal-bishops, that is, clerical figures closest to the pope, would be allowed to elect new popes, while minor clergy throughout Latin Europe had authority only to consent to the decision.

In protest of the limitations Rome placed on monarchical authority over local clerical affairs, the now twenty-five-year-old Saxon king Henry IV sent a letter to the pope in 1075 with the heading, "Henry [Heinric], King not through usurpation but through the holy ordination of God, to Hildebrand [in Rome], at present not pope but false monk."[22] By 1076, the pope had excommunicated the Saxon king following their respective appointment of two different bishops of Milan. As the monarchy's tensions with the pope grew, Saxon noblemen already in rebellion against Henry IV around Langensalza took advantage of their opportunity to carve out their autonomy from the Saxon king. The rebellion culminated in the so-called Great Saxon Revolt.

Pope Gregory VII supported the revolt, while Henry responded by appointing an antipope: Clement II. In a surprising escalation of hostilities, and in an equally remarkable convergence of stories around the Italian peninsula, Henry invaded Rome in 1081 only to find that the pope was able to call on his allies in Norman southern Italy—specifically Roger I (r. 1071–1101) based in Sicily. Ever resourceful in managing political alliances, Henry IV secured an alliance with Byzantine emperor Alexios by promising to help push back against Roger's brother Robert Guiscard, who was invading the Byzantine Aegean with his son Bohemond. Bohemond will reemerge shortly as the head of Norman Syria, where Daimbert could be seen serving as a Crusader cleric on the way to becoming Latin Patriarch in Jerusalem. In the meantime, Henry IV's efforts to push into Rome were successful enough that he managed to curate a ceremony in Rome in 1084, when antipope Clement III crowned him Holy Roman Emperor.

It was against this backdrop that Daimbert came onto the scene. Matilda, one-time mediator between Henry IV and Gregory VII, was a supporter of the papacy and recruited Daimbert to the cause. Daimbert was originally associated with the emperor-aligned side of the investiture controversy, and appears to have been ordained originally by Wezilo, archbishop of Mainz (1084–1088). Wezilo was a prominent supporter of Antipope Clement III, and was later excommunicated by a pro-papal synod in Quedlinburg on charges of simony, a practice central to the theological protests of the future ex-Catholic Protestant movement in Germany.[23] At some point between 1085 and 1088, Daimbert came to know Matilda, a supporter of Pope Urban II. In accordance with papal authority, Pope Urban II reordained Daimbert and named him bishop of Pisa. The pope did this despite the protest of other clerical figures like the bishop of Pistoia who were aware of Daimbert's background and position in the investiture controversy. By 1092, after several years of activity in the politics and economy of Pisa, Matilda recommended elevating the see of Pisa to an archbishopric, which in turn raised Daimbert's authority. Pope Urban II (1088–1099) was the pope who called for the Crusades, and by the mid-1090s, Daimbert was preaching the Crusades alongside him.

It was in this context that Daimbert himself sailed eastward together with Bohemond, son of Roger II. Daimbert's enthronement as Latin patriarch at the start of 1100 saw a new episode of controversy over sacral and clerical authority, this time in the Levant. Having previously risen to prominence in Pisan political, economic, and civic life, Daimbert now had the support of Pisan mariners in the Levant. It was this support among Pisan mariners that pressured Baldwin—Lord of Edessa (Urfa) and, since 1100, king of Jerusalem—to confirm Daimbert's position as Latin patriarch. Still, Baldwin himself was resistant to paying homage to the Pisan, even as Bohemond in Antioch and Baldwin's predecessor Godfrey of Bouillon in Jerusalem knelt before Daimbert in order to be invested with sacral authority. What strengthened Baldwin's resistance to the Pisan's expanding authority as Latin patriarch was the inroads made by the Genoese.

With the arrival of a Genoese squadron by 1101, Baldwin's position was strengthened, with Daimbert eventually being pushed by the legate to step down on charges of financial corruption. Daimbert was originally permitted to operate from the Church of St. George. After initially being welcomed by Bohemond's successor Tancred in Antioch, Daimbert faced new charges before a synod under Robert of Paris, who served in 1102 as an apostolic legate to the Crusader states. Daimbert eventually died in Messina (Sicily) in 1105 while on his way back eastward from a trip to Rome to see Pope Paschal (1099–1119), successor to Urban II, whom Daimbert hoped would rectify his standing in the Latin Church.

In the long run, the rise of a Latin patriarchate in Jerusalem—together with the career of Pisan Archbishop Daimbert as Latin patriarch—pointed to two outcomes relevant to the long duration history of how the Italian peninsula became so closely intertwined with European and Middle Eastern history alike. First, Daimbert's career in the Latin patriarchate foreshadowed the extent that political and clerical administrators of the Italian peninsula, including heads of state, came to build much of their careers in the Levant. Ottoman-era merchants and clerics from the Italian peninsula could be seen working in Ottoman Istanbul before returning to govern as head of state or even as pope. Andrea Gritti, doge of Venice for fifteen years (r. 1523–1538), spent twenty-five years of his life living in Istanbul, and—according to contemporaries—spoke Greek and Turkish. Secondly, as much as the Crusader-era rise of a Latin patriarchate pointed to a broader convergence of southern European and Middle Eastern histories, the patriarchate's growing clash with eastern Orthodoxy also pointed to a lasting reality that would emerge during the Age of Exploration and continue into the modern world: a turn away from the Middle East as the primary arena of its evangelism in favor of Asia and the Americas. Some of the factors that shaped this turn were already visible during Daimbert's career. The biggest was the inability of the Roman Catholic Church to force its main eastern counterpart—namely, Eastern Orthodoxy in its Greek-speaking and Arabic-speaking (Melkite) forms—to unite with Roman Catholicism. This was in addition to the inability of the Latin patriarchate to gain a foothold among the region's Muslims, Jews, and older churches. Once the eastern Orthodox Church doubled down on its independence after being subsumed into the Ottoman Empire, where it continued cultivating a Hellenistic project oriented towards other Slavic Christians, and once the Protestant movement among former Catholics gained a foothold in sixteenth-century Germany during an opportune moment of Habsburg–Ottoman rivalry, the Roman Catholic Church turned elsewhere: the Spanish Americas, Spanish Manila, the many Portuguese worlds of the Indian Ocean and South China Sea, China, and Japan.

Under the leadership of new societies—the Jesuits, Dominicans, and Benedictines—Asia and the Americas became the new global arenas for the development of Catholicism. For the Jesuits, whose expertise spanned from astronomy to botany and linguistics, evangelism was part of a two-way process of cultural exchange that saw the Iberians and Dutch develop an insatiable taste for the objects, images, and wonders of these new worlds: Mexican drinking chocolate and red cochineal pigment for velvet, Chinese tea and blue-and-white porcelains, and Indonesian spices. By then, the Pisans had faded into the shadow of two Italian maritime powers that were poised to take full advantage of the Mediterranean's new connection with the Atlantic, Pacific, and Indian Ocean worlds: the Genoese and Venetians.

6

GENOESE COMMERCE ACROSS THE HABSBURG–OTTOMAN MEDITERRANEAN

The Republic of Genoa (r. 1005–1797, 1814–1815) and the Republic of Venice (r. 697–1797) were two of the most culturally and commercially influential powers of the twelfth century. Known in their heyday as "La Superba" (The Superb) and "La Serenissima" (The Most Serene), they were Mediterranean powers that developed wide renown as far west as the North Sea and as far east as the Black and Caspian Seas. In the centuries leading up to the Iberian-led Age of Exploration, Genoese and Venetian merchants commanded sprawling networks linking the Hanseatic League's northern cities—London, Flanders, and others—with Levantine and North African centers. In cities like Alexandria and Tunis, Genoese and Venetian merchants conducted business with Arabic-speaking Muslims, Orthodox Christians, and Jews trading in Chinese and Indian Ocean commodities. Those commodities, in turn, arrived in Red Sea and Persian Gulf ports in vessels that connected ports in present-day Yemen and Iraq with those in coastal India, Southeast Asia, and China. From there, Asian commodities were brought to European markets.

In developing these transcontinental maritime trade routes, Genoese and Venetian merchants inherited the legacy of the Republic of Pisa (r. *c.* 1000–1406). Pisan merchants pioneered the construction of a sprawling network of consulates across North Africa and the Levant in a way that paralleled the Hanseatic League's network in the North and Baltic seas. To Genoa and Venice's benefit, Pisa was absorbed into the rising Florentine republic's dominion in 1406, and it

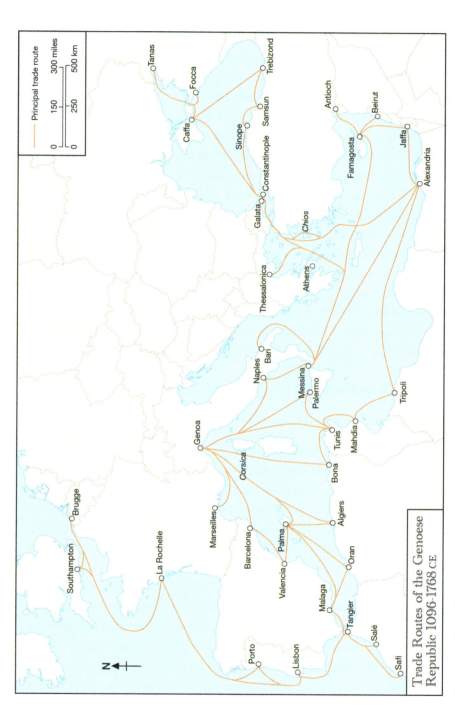

Figure 6.1 Maps of the Italian Republics' territorial holdings, like this map of the Genoese Republic's sprawling and decentralized empire stretching into the Aegean and Black Seas (c. 1300s), illustrate the growing sophistication of the republics' commercial diplomacy, naval might, and ship design on the eve of the Age of Exploration.

would be another century still for Florence's Medici family to cultivate Livorno as a commercial hub evocative of Pisa's old glory.

Genoese and Venetian merchants navigated the politics of England, the frontiers of Spain's Catholic and Islamic kingdoms, the Levant's Crusader–Mamluk frontiers, and the simultaneously Byzantine and Ottoman Aegean. Their ability to do so, moreover, was a function of the same political and economic circumstances that shaped their Pisan predecessors' activities. More specifically, politically active merchant families with close links to overseas commercial ventures drove the Genoese and Venetian economies.[1] Legally, echoing the Pisans' diplomatic abilities, these Genoese and Venetian merchant families built their overseas ventures by negotiating the same kind of legal agreements with foreign powers that the Pisans negotiated, namely, privileges in security, residency, and taxation. The result was not only the formation of a local and overseas culture of global diplomacy, but also the rise of new patterns of legal pluralism and extraterritorial rights in Genoese and Venetian centers abroad. These rights facilitated Italian commercial activity in the Middle East and North Africa, but they were also contentious in times of conflict.

An Italian Republic in the *Maghrib* and *Mashriq*

Navigating the Mediterranean and Black Sea Frontiers

The thirteenth and fourteenth centuries were transformative years in the history of Europe, the Middle East, and Central Asia, and the litany of changes in political arrangements were of central interest to the rising republics of Genoa and Venice. The most transformative changes occurred along the Mediterranean's western and eastern peripheries. Around the western Mediterranean, the mighty Almohad caliphate lost the last of its Iberian domains to the crown of Castile in 1230, ushering in the long and precarious ascendancy of the Nasrid emirs in Granada (r. 1230–1492).[2] For Genoese merchants in the region, the political shuffles were in many ways hardly consequential. The Almohads, Nasrids, and Castilians alike were all interested in cultivating relations with Genoese merchants, whose thirteenth-century foothold in the region paved the way for Genoese activity in fifteenth-century Habsburg-era banking, silk commerce, and transatlantic maritime exploration between Seville and Mexico City.[3]

In the eastern Mediterranean and its frontiers, the thirteenth-century Genoese closely watched several other major political shuffles connected to the future of Ayyubid Cairo, Abbasid Baghdad, and Byzantine Constantinople. In Cairo, a Turkish mercenary dynasty overthrew Saladin's Ayyubid government in 1250, less than a century after Saladin overthrew the mighty Fatimids before them. In Constantinople, the Venetians facilitated a Crusader conquest of the city, making it the capital of a new Latin empire for several decades. In Baghdad, the Mongols marching westward captured the Abbasid empire's legendary capital, ending more than 700 years of Abbasid rule in the city the dynasty founded. In what awarded the Mamluks a degree of military and imperial prestige, the dynasty halted the Mongols' southwestward advance in Syria while welcoming the exiled Abbasid caliphs to Cairo. These developments were in addition to the Mamluks' continued efforts to consolidate power over formerly Crusader-held parts of the Levant.

It was into this mix of political uncertainty that the Genoese inserted themselves, cultivating connections with the surviving Byzantine powers of the Aegean, the Mamluks of Cairo, and the nearest of the Mongol states—namely, the Golden Horde—based in present-day Russia. In what illustrates the Genoese merchants' ability to work across political frontiers, they managed to dominate the Mamluks' supply of mercenary soldiers coming from their newly Mongol-controlled homelands in the northern Black Sea. Genoese access to these regions, in turn, came from their trade relationship with the Golden Horde and with the Byzantines, who rewarded Genoese efforts in ousting the Crusaders from Constantinople with access to Black Sea trade via the Marmara crossing. At the heart of Genoese efforts in all of this was their rivalry with the Venetians, who managed to follow the Genoese into the Crimean Peninsula.

By the time the Ottomans claimed Constantinople as their capital in 1453, however, the Venetians had begun to prevail over Genoese political interests in the eastern Mediterranean through their conquest of various Ionian and Adriatic territories. Still, in the lead-up to Ottoman conquest and the Iberian-led Age of Exploration, the Genoese had far from disappeared. While the Venetians were expanding territorially, competing with the Ottomans over Byzantine territories and the absorption of various trans-Mediterranean trade diasporas, the Genoese were naturalizing as local subjects across the Mediterranean from Habsburg Iberia to the Venetian and Ottoman Aegean.

This distinction between the centripetal force of Venetian subjecthood and the centrifugal force of Genoese naturalization is indicative of the two republics' very different political models. By the fifteenth century, the two powers had developed contrasting modes of governance and expansion that afforded the Genoese—via Ottoman Istanbul and Habsburg Seville—a truly global political and commercial presence despite their territorial losses. That is, despite their long-duration losses to the Venetians in the race for territorial expansion, the Genoese in some ways outlasted their Venetian rivals because of the way Genoa's decentralized political model facilitated the transformation of its nobility into a global trade diaspora well into the modern period.

The Cog and the Arsenal: Genoese and Venetian Shipping Westward

A comparison between Genoese and Venetian ventures into English markets offers a contrast of shipping technology, trade routes, and merchant networks illustrative of how Genoa and Venice diverged sharply in the political dimensions of their commercial activities around the North Sea, Mediterranean Sea, and Black Sea. In 1304, when Genoese merchants had already begun to arrive in the North Sea and English Channel, Florentine chronicler Giovanni Villani wrote that Mediterranean shipwrights were beginning to emulate the ships that Basque mariners sailed into the Mediterranean. Villani identified this ship as the *cocha*, most likely in reference to the high-sided roundships that were ubiquitous along the coasts of northern Europe, including in the North and Baltic seas.[4] In those northern European regions in the twelfth century, the most influential merchants were not those of the Italian peninsula, but rather the Low German merchants whose guilds made up the Hanseatic League.

Connecting the North Sea and English Channel with the Baltic Sea, the League's foreign outposts stretched from present-day England and Norway to Russia, and were located in London, Bruges (Flanders), Bergen (Bjørgvin), and Novgorod. Commodities like wool that were exported from London to eastern and southern European cities were taken by Hanseatic merchants across the North and Baltic seas, where they were carried most commonly in round ships with high, clinker-built sides. Known as the cog, and most likely identical to what Villani referred to as the *cocha* among the Basque, these ships allowed large cargos to be carried at high speeds, and their height additionally offered

Hansa merchants a degree of defense from pirates and combat advantage in times of war.

If southern Europe was the final destination, these cargoes were transferred to barges that sailed up the Rhine from northern Europe to cities like Florence, Genoa, and Venice. These Hanseatic cogs contrasted to the kind of galleys used by the Genoese and Venetians for both commerce and war in the eleventh and twelfth centuries. By the thirteenth century, as suggested by Villani, there were major changes in Genoese shipping methods that appear to have drawn on Hanseatic models.

By the time Genoa pursued a new coastal Atlantic trade route connecting the Mediterranean to the North Sea in the thirteenth century, the republic was in the process of pursuing a trajectory of shipbuilding technology distinct from that of Venice with a distinct program of long-distance trade. Genoese merchants who came to England in the fourteenth century began to use a new modified cog that abandoned the ribbed clinker-based hull and adopted the carvel-based structure common in low-sided Mediterranean galley ships.[5] The Genoese cog–galley hybrid, combining the high sides of the cog and the strong skeleton of the galley, allowed Genoese merchants to travel with larger cargoes, smaller crews, and could be used in defense. The shipments brought in were often not part of official Genoese convoys, but privately chartered.

Alum, the key commodity among these shipments, offers one example of how expansive Genoese commercial networks were in the 1300s. Alum came from the Aegean island of Fokaia. The island was officially under Byzantine suzerainty but controlled in practice by the Genoese Benadetti family. Having privately controlled the profits of alum, the Benadetti family chartered ships to Flanders for its export. A shipment came from Majorca to London in 1281 to load 267 sacks of wool and bundled woodfells, and another arrived in Sandwich in 1287. A shipment in 1311 from Catalonia brought to Southampton almonds, quicksilver, leather, and iron.[6] The Genoese slowly abandoned the use of galleys for commerce in the 1300s as their activities became more centered on the western Mediterranean and Atlantic coast. Those galleys that remained were used for military purposes.

Venice, meanwhile, moved in a very different direction in terms of shipping technology and the political entanglement of its trade routes. The Venetians' participation in English trade in the 1300s occurred against the technological backdrop of a repeated enlargement of their galleys into what became the so-called "great galleys," which were some three times as large as the earliest Venetian galleys.[7] In 1290, 200 crew members were required for fifty tons. By 1314, the Venetian galley was again enlarged specifically for voyages to Flanders. In 1344, they could carry 150 tons of cargo. By 1400, they were built even bigger.[8] The enlargement of the galleys went hand in hand with the expansion of the official state-sponsored trade routes, the *mude*, which included systematic stops at Tunis, Annaba, Béjaïa (Bougie), Algiers, Oran, Honein, Cádiz, Valencia, Barcelona, and finally returning to Venice via Sicily, Djerba, and Tripoli.

When Venice's great galleys did begin to arrive in Flanders, London, and Southampton, spectators remarked on the novelty of them and their distinction from earlier Genoese and Hanseatic ships. In Southampton, for example, Venetian galleys began to arrive in 1319 in pursuit of English raw wool and cloth. They came to be known locally as the Flanders galleys, and their arrival was met with disputes with the Venetian crews that turned violent.[9]

From the perspective of the long-term trajectory of Genoese and Venetian trade in northern Europe, these distinctions in the political dimensions of shipping technology and trade routes pointed to an enduring difference in the realm of political boundaries with the English. The Genoese had a much deeper level of engagement with English political and civic life than the Venetians to the point where they even naturalized. The rights of traders, retailers, and shopkeepers in the early 1100s were recorded in the *Libertas Londoniensis*, an extant legal charter.[10] Prior to the arrival of the Genoese, merchants were not allowed to remain for more than forty days in accordance with the interests of urban burgesses.

Southampton, on the southern coast, was where economic circumstances were conducive to greater privileges for the Genoese. Genoese were able to rent homes and cellars for storing their merchandise, and could even participate in English civic life by being elected in town offices. By the 1330s, the Genoese merchant Niccholino Fieschi was named state councilor. Genoese commercial rights were guaranteed unprecedented freedom of trade in England in Edward III's Acts of 1335 and 1351.[11] An Act of Parliament in 1378 similarly allowed Genoese merchants to unload and load goods in Southampton for the same customs payment that they paid at Calais, which was their more regular destination. By the late 1400s, the decline of Florentine consumption of English wool as well as the loss of Genoese "primacy" in alum meant a decline in Genoese shipping in England. Still, Genoese residents in Southampton like Benedetto Spinola remained and applied for naturalization. Spinola was not the only one. A century later, a prominent businessman named Sir Horatio Palavicino was knighted by the queen. Born Orazio Palavicino in the Republic of Genoa, Sir Horatio and his family managed the papal alum monopoly from 1566.[12]

Venetian commercial expansion in Southampton, which was coterminous with Genoa's, was markedly different from Genoese merchants' broad participation in English civic and commercial life. In the fifteenth century, the Venetians chose to have a Genoese representative as their consul in Southampton, while they worked with Florentine merchants in London as their agents.[13] The Venetians were also distinguished by their specialization in luxury trade in an era when alum and wool continued to be the main trading commodities in Anglo-Genoese commercial exchange. The *Libelle of Englyshe Polycye* (c. 1436–1438) singled out the Genoese among merchants from the Italian peninsula as having brought commodities useful to the English textile industry, while the Florentines and Venetians were criticized for various luxury imports that reduced local textile market share and that included marmosets.

As late as the eighteenth century, English economists singled out Anglo-Genoese trade as having been favorable, in contrast to Anglo-Venetian trade.[14] The history of state sponsorship of Venetian trade expeditions appears to have had the unintended consequence of limiting the spectrum of commercial and civic engagement with England seen among the Genoese. Other factors were at play in this process, including Genoese losses in the political conflict with Venice in the eastern Mediterranean, but the greater privatization of Genoese commerce fit into a larger pattern that correlated with more porous political boundaries between English and Genoese commerce throughout these centuries. The case of Anglo-Genoese commercial relations paralleled that of Ibero-Genoese relations, where the Genoese straddled their roles. This was especially true in the way the Genoese transcended Muslim–Catholic political divides in Iberia and North Africa.

Figure 6.2 Quinto Cenni's fourteenth-century representation of the Genoese navy captures the Genoese Republic's use of high-sided armed merchant cogs alongside a variety of high-speed oar-powered galleys. The Venetians developed the merchant galley further for wartime purposes and lucrative commercial convoys. Genoa's turn to the western Mediterranean at a time when the Venetians doubled down on the eastern Mediterranean coincided with the rise of a global Habsburg–Ottoman rivalry during the Age of Exploration. By then, with large swathes of Genoese merchant families naturalizing as Habsburg Iberian subjects and pursuing business opportunities in the Spanish and Portuguese New World, a variety of the cog came to dominate transatlantic and trans-Pacific trade routes that brought the Spanish and Portuguese to the South China Sea.

Source: https://en.wikipedia.org/wiki/Genoese_Navy#/media/File:The_port_and_fleet_of_Genoa,_early_14th_century.jpg, public domain.

Genoese Settlement around the North and Mediterranean Seas

Between Diplomacy and War in the Balearics and Iberia

The Balearic Islands were strategically positioned at the crossroads of Provence and the Ligurian coast on the one side, and the *Maghrib*, that is, North Africa, on the other. Genoa's relations with local rulers in the Balearics saw a similar pattern of Genoese merchants securing commercial and residency privileges in a manner that contrasted to Venice's state-oriented policy of pursuing limited engagement with these regions in favor of the *mude* traffic system. Genoa's activities in the Balearics date back to the twelfth century, when Genoa's competition in the region was not Venice but rather other Roman Catholic naval powers eager to expand Crusader expeditions westward: the Pisans, the Normans, and, most importantly, the Catalans of Barcelona and Crown of Aragon.

The Pisans and Genoese previously crossed paths in North Africa in the lead-up to the First Crusade (1095–1099), when both powers competed with the Normans of Sicily over territories in North Africa. Genoa participated specifically in Pisa's attack in 1087 on Mahdia, which subsequently developed a long-term relationship with the Normans. By 1114, however, Genoa did not participate in Pisa's attack on Majorca as it began to navigate Iberia's increasingly complex political world. Most important among these changes was the rise of the Catalans, the major Roman Catholic naval power in the region that was in a better position to advance on the Balearics than any Italian power. The consequence of this mix of powers in the western Mediterranean was that while Genoese military expansion westward was an enduring possibility, it was only a sporadic reality from the start because it was not militarily sustainable. In the lead-up to the Second Crusade (1147–1149), the Genoese concluded an agreement with the Castilians in 1146 to carry out an expedition against Almoravid-held Almeria. The siege took place in 1147, the same year as the start of the Second Crusade (1147–1149), while in 1148, the Genoese had participated in Barcelona's siege of Tortosa. In both cases, the long-term rewards belonged to the Castilians and Catalans.

The outcome of Castilian and Catalan power over the Genoese in the western Mediterranean was the readiness of the Genoese to scale down military activity in the region and, instead, secure commercial connections on both sides of the Catholic–Islamic frontiers of Iberia and the Balearic Islands. As early as the Second Crusade, the Genoese began building a complex web of trade agreements that guaranteed them a core privilege: settlement rights for participation in local trade. More specifically, in what points to the extent that the Genoese began to resemble a trade diaspora several centuries before they numbered among Habsburg Seville and Ottoman Istanbul's elite trading families, the Genoese secured guarantees of a *fondaco*—together with a bathhouse, oven, and garden—from Castilian king Alfonso VII and Barcelona count Ramon Berenguer IV in return for naval support in their capture of Muslim-held Almeria.[15] Genoese merchants simultaneously accelerated their commercial activity in Muslim-held regions of southern Iberia, and were likewise much more judicious than the Catalans and Castilians when flexing military power against Muslim rulers in accordance with a commitment to securing commercial privileges.

This Genoese preference for armed diplomacy over conquest could be seen in 1149. That year, the Genoese concluded a ten-year peace agreement with Ibn Mardanish, the ruler of Iberia's eastern coast around Valencia and part of the Balearics. Ibn Mardanish was forced to pay a financial tribute to the Genoese and offer various trade-related concessions in return for a commitment to stop raiding. The Genoese were granted the use of a bathhouse once per week and two *fondaco*s in Valencia and Denia, respectively.[16] By the following year in 1150, the Pisans received similar concessions.[17] In Seville, likewise, Genoese commercial contracts provide evidence of Genoese trading activity in the 1160s.[18]

Both the Genoese and Pisans were simultaneously in negotiation with the Majorcan Banu Ghaniya dynasty, Almoravid governors who outlasted the collapse of the Almoravids during the Almohad conquests of the 1150s.[19] Pisan envoys visited in 1161, most likely to sign the first of several peace treaties. Agreements were renewed in 1173 and 1184. In surviving Arabic and Latin texts about Genoa's agreement in 1184 and Pisa's agreement in 1181, all parties agreed to refrain from attacking each other's subjects both in their respective territories and at sea.[20] Moreover, against the backdrop of the continuing Catalan threat of conquests in the Balearics, the Genoese managed to find another way to protect their interests in the *Maghrib*: agreements with other naval powers that competed with Barcelona, including the Holy Roman Empire and the mighty Almohads themselves.

More specifically, the German monarch Frederick I Barbarossa had set his sights on the islands by the 1160s. In what illustrated Genoa's ability to navigate the rapidly shifting naval landscape of the western Mediterranean, the Genoese concluded a peace agreement with Frederick I Barbarossa in 1162 with an intriguing military element: naval assistance in his capture of the Balearics. In theory, the deal looked as though Genoa was finally ready to close in on the Balearics' Muslim rulers. In practice, the deal served more to challenge Catalan attempts to conquer the islands, as the Genoese simultaneously renewed agreements with Ibn Mardanish of Valencia and Banu Ghaniya of Majorca. Interestingly, the Genoese were even involved in trade agreements with the Almohads at this time.

As in the case of Genoese activity in Iberia and the Balearics, Genoa's decentralized commercial activity in North Africa was not conditioned by any specific state-centered diplomatic arrangements seen in contemporary Venetian diplomacy in the region. When the Almohad caliph Abd al-Mu'min signed an agreement with the Genoese in 1161, the arrangement came with no expectations of a consul with independent legal jurisdiction that the Venetians frequently sought in North African ports. It simply guaranteed Genoese settlement and property rights in various *fondaco*s as well as a reduction by 2 percent of the 10 percent customs fee together with the ability to travel without harm.[21] The agreements were renewed every fifteen years and were echoed in similar agreements with the Pisans.

In contrast, from Tunis to Constantinople, Venice frequently secured the right to install consuls with legal authority over Venetian merchants. The Venetians negotiated the construction of a *fondaco* in Tunis in 1231, just eight years after the Genoese secured one.[22] Their negotiation for a customs house (*dogana*) and a consul to administer justice was indicative of Venice's enduring state-centered policy of expanding its territorial acquisitions in a manner that expanded the hierarchical legal authority of the Venetian Senate. Even more state-oriented was the Catalan arrangement. In contrast to local government ownership and administration of foreign *fondaco*s throughout the Arabic Mediterranean, the ownership and administration of Catalan *fondaco*s in Tunis and Bougie belonged to King James I as his own royal property (*fondaci nostri*) in accordance with the practices of his own *fondaco*s for foreign merchants Valencia and Catalonia.[23]

Following the transfer of Almohad domains to various successor Catholic and Muslim principalities, the Genoese negotiated pacts that laid the groundwork for their long-term role in the early modern Spanish aristocracy both in Iberia and, across the Atlantic via Seville, in the Americas. The Genoese concluded an agreement with Seville's Muslim emir by 1231 and, after the Castilian conquest of Seville in 1248, with Seville's later Castilian ruler Ferdinand III that extended Genoese trading privileges throughout Castile. By 1278, the Nasrids of Granada granted the Genoese the right to trade inland, the use of a *fondaco*, a church, and exemption from certain port duties. The Genoese presence had become so commonplace in Nasrid-controlled Granada by the fourteenth century that it included inland residency privileges.

The Genoese portfolio, in sum, was a broad one, and its presence across Catholic and Islamic political divides throughout the western Mediterranean foreshadowed the rise of a Genoese subaltern cultural presence within

Habsburg Spain and Portugal that included military noble families descended from Christopher Columbus' son Diego. On the eastern Mediterranean, similarly, the commercial activity and settlement of Genoese merchants across Roman Catholic, Greek, and Islamic political divides foreshadowed their naturalization as Ottoman subjects.

Egypt and the Crusader Levant

In Egypt and the Levant, Genoese navigation of local politics ran parallel with the western Mediterranean against a backdrop of similar competition between various Latin Crusader kingdoms, several Islamic polities, and Greek Byzantium. In what illustrated the continuity of a Genoese presence in the region, Genoese families were simultaneously intertwined with Crusader political and naval power even as they facilitated the removal of Crusader power from Constantinople and the reinstallation of the Byzantines in 1267. The Genoese likewise made sure to protect their interests in Muslim-held regions in Egypt and the Levant under its Fatimid rulers and later Ayyubid and Mamluk successors.

The Genoese presence in Egypt dates back to the Fatimid period. Long before the Ayyubid and Mamluk eras, when the Mediterranean port city of Alexandria became the primary transit point for trade between the Roman Catholic and Islamic worlds, the Fatimid period saw merchants from the Italian peninsula take up residence further inland in Cairo. The presence of Genoese in Cairo echoed the legacy of the Amalfitans and Pisans before them. Prior to the Crusader period, merchants from Amalfi resided in Cairo in a residential complex, while Pisan merchants established a residential complex in both Cairo and Alexandria. With the rise of the Crusades, this relationship became contentious. Pisan merchants were arrested following the Crusader conquest of Asqalan (Ascalon), but were released a year later.[24] That event foretold some of the complexities to come for Venice and Genoa as they attempted to navigate Crusader–Islamic politics.

Bohemond of Taranto, the son of the Norman adventurer Robert Guiscard, agreed to offer the Genoese a *fondaco* in 1098.[25] Bohemond was the nephew of Roger I of Sicily, the patriarch of the famously Arabic-speaking line of Norman kings that embraced both Byzantine and Islamic court culture until the end of Frederick II's reign. Like the Norman kings of Sicily, who were often more interested in securing commercial gains in North Africa than pouring resources into new crusades throughout the Levant, various

Crusader dynasties sought to profit off their locations in the Levant along the trade routes to North Africa and Iraq by granting Italian merchants commercial lodges. For the Genoese, Bohemond's agreement included not only a *fondaco* and church but also houses and a plaza. Bohemond II reconfirmed these privileges in 1128, offering the Genoese an additional *fondaco* and street in Latakia. The Venetians likewise were granted similar privileges including, in keeping with their state-centered territorial expansionism practices, an explicit self-jurisdiction.

In Acre, Genoese and Venetians likewise lived in houses within quarters while still having access to *fondaco*s. The consul in Acre was more central throughout the Levant. The *Pactum Warmundi* signed with Venice represented the classic example of the kind of privileges offered to Italian merchant communities.[26] It offered them a third of Tyre and extensive space in Acre, including streets, plazas, access to their own weights and measures, and distinct tax status inside and outside of their community. Baldwin I guaranteed the Genoese privileges following the Crusader conquest of the city in return for Genoese naval assistance. Decades later, Conrad of Montferrat reconfirmed these privileges following the reconquest of the city in 1192 from the Ayyubids. Conrad of Montferrat also confirmed Genoese *fondaco*s in 1187 in both Tyre and Jaffa.

Venice's more extensive privileges in cities like Beirut, which included tax-free sales of goods inside the *fondaco* and tax free exports from the *fondaco*, points to the comparative commercial and political advantages that Venice was able to garner after the Fourth Crusade. At the same time, however, with the spread of Cairenese authority eastward under Saladin and the Genoese restoration of Byzantine rule in Constantinople, Venice would discover that these privileges were tied to the waxing and waning of Crusader fortunes.

Saladin and the Ayyubids

The rapidly changing dimensions of Italian–Egyptian commercial connections throughout the 1100s and 1200s illustrates how Genoese merchants, like the Pisans before them, were willing to work with any group in the region despite their own connections with the Crusaders as far as shared military ventures and papal sponsorship. While Pisa initially helped the Crusaders fight Egypt in return for a position in Tyre and the promise of returns in Crusader-held parts of Egypt, the Pisans quickly came to an agreement with Saladin once he fought off the Crusaders in 1170.

With the rise of Saladin and the spread of Cairene authority over Crusader-held Levantinese territories, the Genoese managed to stay in place. In the lead-up to Saladin's reign in Cairo, Pisa and Genoa had already been afforded trade privileges and security in Alexandria. A surviving Pisan treaty and Venetian notarial contracts refer to the existence of residential complexes in 1173. By 1177, as Saladin headed off to Jerusalem, Genoese ambassador Rosso della Volta met with him to establish a peace agreement between the Genoese and Egypt.[27]

Saladin wrote to the Abbasids in Baghdad indicating that the Genoese, Venetians, and Pisans provided Egypt materials for arms and other imports. Indeed, timber and metal were the most significant imports that were used in arms. Nile ports also received, iron, coral, oil, saffron, and clothes from Lombardy and Flanders. For Italian merchants, Egypt was a source of alum, flax, as well as spices such as caraway, cumin, and coriander. Italian–Egyptian exchange occurred despite increasingly vocal papal criticism of Italian commerce with the Ayyubids and with the later Mamluks. This critique culminated in an official papal embargo that the Venetians were more publicly respectful of than the Genoese and Pisans.[28] Still, with the rise of the Mamluks, Venetian privileges of the Ayyubid period continued.[29] Genoese negotiations with Cairo likely took place around the same time, as an agreement in 1290 between the Genoese and Sultan Qalawun reaffirmed previously established privileges in Alexandria.

The Genoese negotiations of 1290 were carried out by Alberto Spinola specifically and point to the increasing leverage of Genoese merchants in eastern Mediterranean commerce in the years following both their reestablishment of Byzantine rule and their governance of Pera as a distinct Genoese port city. According to Italian sources, Spinola secured from Sultan Qalawun the privilege of maintaining the Church of Saint Mary in Alexandria—allowing Genoese officials in Alexandria to hear cases against Genoese—and the right to fixed commodity taxes and customs duties.[30] From the Arabic sources' perspective, the agreement ensured that the Genoese would restrict piracy activities and respect the persons and property of Muslims traveling by land and sea.

The immediate context of the agreement was a series of events linked with Genoese activity in both Egypt and the Crusader states that ultimately harmed Genoese–Egyptian relations. More specifically, Benedetto Zaccaria had previously secured Genoese possession of a third of Crusader Tyre, which other Genoese found to be an ill-fated expenditure of resources given Tyre's imminent fall to Egypt. Zaccaria ended up "seizing Egyptian shipping" with the help of several galleys sent by the Genoese consul in the Black Sea port of Caffa, namely, Paolina Doria.[31] The move ended up harming Genoese commercial interests in Egypt, with the agreement between Benedetto and Qalawun helping to thaw relations.

In sum, Genoese trade in Egypt and the Levant saw a steady ebb and flow in trade relations with Islamic polities in partial accordance with Genoa's changing relationship with the Crusader states and Byzantine powers. But there was another power in the mix: the Mongols, with whom the Genoese were in direct contact in Caffa. During the Genoese fallout with Egypt following the Fatimid conquest of Crusader Tyre, Caffa-based Genoese consul Paolina

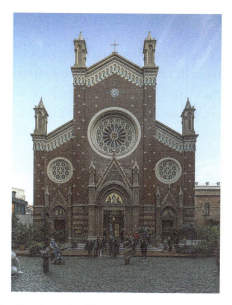

Figure 6.3 The Church of San Antonio di Padova, located on Istiklal Avenue in Istanbul's Pera district, is the largest Catholic Church in Istanbul and was built between 1906 and 1912 by the city's Roman Catholic community. It was built on the site of an earlier Catholic church of the same name built in 1725. Much of Istanbul's Roman Catholic community moved to Italy, other parts of Europe, and the United States in the 1900s and traced their origins to Venetian and Genoese families and more recent arrivals of the *Risorgimento* era. In the lead-up to the Ottoman era, Genoese-held Pera was home to the mansion of the Genoese *podestà*, where it still stands in walking distance of the Genoese tower (*Galata külesi*). Its Venetian counterpart, the palace of the Venetian *bailo*, serves as the current Italian consulate.

Source: https://en.wikipedia.org/wiki/Beyo%C4%9Flu#/media/File:Istanbul_asv2021-11_img71_StAnthony_of_Padua_Church.jpg, public domain.

Doria's participation in a campaign against Egypt points to thirteenth-century Genoa's ability to straddle not only the North Sea and Mediterranean Sea, but also the Black Sea around present-day Ukraine and Russia.

Between the Byzantine and Ottoman Worlds

The Chios–Pera–Caffa Route

The alum brought to London from the island of Chios came from Genoa's Chios–Pera–Caffa trade route, which was the Genoese Republic's eastern Mediterranean circuit during the reign of the Byzantine emperor Michael VIII Palaiologos (1259–1282). In return for Genoa's support of his claim over the Crusaders to the throne in Constantinople, Michael VIII granted the Genoese trading privileges around the Aegean as well as greater access to the Black Sea.

There were three Genoese settlements in the Aegean and Black seas that were critical to Genoese interests in eastern commerce. The first was Pera across the Golden Horn from Constantinople. Pera, which was subsumed into early Ottoman Constantinople (Qustantiniyya), was independently governed by the Genoese during the late Byzantine period. The second was Genoese Chios in the Aegean, which was close to the Sea of Marmara and linked the Mediterranean with the Black Sea. The third was Caffa in the Black Sea's Crimean peninsula. The strategic location of Chios, sitting at the crossroads of the Mediterranean and Black seas and at a slight distance from Constantinople, made it an ideal intermediary point connecting Genoa's European trade with its interests in Central Asia.[32]

In the Aegean, the republic governed islands like Fokaia and Chios as a formal part of Genoese dominion, but in practice they were run under the direction of particular families under whom were either semi-fiefdoms or units within Genoa's oligarchic thalassocracy. The island was first subsumed into Genoese rule following the Paleologian restoration as part of the Treaty of Nymphaeum, which promised the Genoese Republic a variety of trade-related concessions in return for Genoese naval assistance. The Zaccaria family formally acquired Chios during the reign of Andronicus II Palaeologos (r. 1282–1328), who initially requested Admiral Benedetto I Zaccaria's (1304) assistance in protecting the island against Catalan and growing Turkish interests.

Benedetto took over the island and turned it into a kind of fiefdom, semi-independent of both the Genoese Republic and the Byzantines, even as much of local power and authority remained in the hands of Greek landlords. Still, Benedetto secured official Byzantine rights over it in accordance with ten-year lease-like intervals that became five years. During Zaccaria's vassal-like dominion over the island from 1304 to 1329, the family additionally acquired neighboring Aegean islands including Fokaia. The reign of Andronikos III Palaiologos saw renewed Byzantine interest in taking the island back, particularly after Chian noble Leo Kalothetos met with Andronikos and encouraged a recapture of the island.

By 1346, Simone Vignoso's expedition from Genoa captured both Chios and the two ports of Phokaia. The commune mortgaged Chios to the investors who paid for the warships until it could repay the debt, which it could not, resulting in Chios and New Fokaia being run as a corporation of those investors. The old Mahona, that corporation, ultimately leased it to the new Mahona who ran it.

The island of Chios, in particular, was closely linked to Genoese politics after it was given to the families who loaned the government large sums that formed the Banco di San Giorgio. Chios was initially run almost as a fiefdom by the Zaccaria family, who had to negotiate simultaneously with the papacy, the Byzantines, and the rising Turkish principalities.[33] The Zaccaria family's political and commercial activities in the early 1300s extended from the English Channel to the Black Sea, where Genoese merchants were active in Caffa in the Crimean Peninsula. By the 1300s, when Genoa entered a period of internal discord and ran low on finances, the Justiniani family (Giustiniani) emerged as the most powerful figures on the island. The Justiniani family comprised most of the nine families who loaned the government finances, and who were promised Chios in return. Members of the family moved to Chios in 1365, and in a remarkable illustration of the political connections tying Genoa with its distant port cities, the Justiniani family produced the doge of Genoa in 1393, namely, Francesco Justiniani di Garibaldi.

After the Genoese restored the Byzantines, they also established relations with the Golden Horde and Ilkhanid khanates, two of the four successor states to the original Mongol empire. By 1280, they had arrived in Tabriz, Caffa in 1281, and, by 1282, the first consul is recorded as Luchetto Gambono.[34] The

Genoese eventually secured settlements in Sinope, Trebizon, Sebastopolis, Licostomo, Maurocastro, and Caffa.

With such broad access to the Black Sea, how could the Venetians compete? Venice did what was obvious through the use of their galleys. They went out to Crimea as well and claimed Tanais, now Azoff. The Venetians, in other words, followed closely behind the Genoese throughout the final years of the 1200s, and by the start of the 1300s, the Pisans had fallen behind in what had become a three-way competition.

While Venice's control of Crete in the Aegean and Tanas in the Black Sea paralleled Genoa's hold over Chios and Caffa in the same seas, there were key differences illustrative of the two republics' divergent political cultures and approaches to building an empire. As mentioned, while the Venetians grew their presence through a centralized, centripetal pull that brought territories and peoples into its cultural and legal center of gravity, the Genoese became more of a powerful and enduring trade diaspora. Venetian Crete (1205–1669), for example, was characterized by a Latinization in the language and religion of Cretan public space that was directed in a centralized manner from Venice itself.[35] In terms of centralized governance, Caffa was likewise under the revolving control of specific Venice-appointed consuls.

In contrast, both Genoese Chios and Caffa were under the independent control of families to whom the republic leased the islands. Among the more interesting outcomes was a kind of cultural convergence marked by the Genoese ruling family's Hellenization in Chios that contrasted to the Latinization of Cretan ruling circles. More broadly, Genoa's presence in the Aegean islands was marked by a combination of the islands' political independence of Genoa's political authority, the legal ambiguity of Genoese settlers between Genoese and Byzantine authority, and these patterns of Greek language-oriented cultural convergence. This was in direct contrast to the situation of Venice in Crete and Tanas, which were wholly subsumed into Venetian governance and culture. Remarkably, the Genoese capital still profited from these ventures despite the distance, and Genoa was likewise connected to politics and society in the various ports. Genoa, in other words, resembled the center of a trade diaspora of the kind seen among the Iranian Armenians based in Isfahan's New Julfa district.[36] Venice was the capital of a sprawling maritime empire.

As for Caffa, the other key port critical to Genoese eastern commerce, Genoa acquired trading and settlement rights there at least by 1281 through negotiations with Mongol newcomers. The Golden Horde (r. 1240s–1502), the northwestern most dynasty of the four Mongol khanates, encouraged trade with Italian merchants and allowed the Genoese to operate in Caffa. The Golden Horde's chief rival, the Ilkhanids, competed over these shipping routes and likewise offered the Genoese commercial privileges at their capital, Tabriz. Genoese merchants in Pera report of their business dealings in Caffa in 1281, and by 1282, the first consul is recorded as Luchetto Gambono.[37] By 1280, they had arrived in Tabriz. The Genoese were as equally adept in the Black Sea as they were in the Mediterranean in navigating local rivalries to their commercial benefit. Just as they negotiated in the Mediterranean with the Crusaders, the Byzantines, the Anatolian *beyliks*, and the Mamluk sultans, they likewise offered their services to both the Golden Horde and the Ilkhanids.

Pera was at the center of this Aegean and Black Sea branch. Far beyond the *fondaco* and quarters that the Genoese negotiated in Crusader cities, Constantinople offered an entire district: Pera. The district, in turn, became its own city. In contrast to the later Genoese of the Ottoman era, many of whom naturalized as Ottoman subjects, the Genoese of the Byzantine era were wholly independent while still often working in Byzantine service.

In Byzantine Constantinople, specifically in the district of Pera, the Genoese exercised significant political power as a legally semi-autonomous settlement with a political administrator (*podestà*). In the Black Sea, specifically in Caffa, the Genoese were geographically and institutionally further from political power in Genoa. They controlled the port and the interior countryside, employing a fortress. The Genoese presence was so embedded in the late Byzantine world of the eastern Mediterranean and Black Sea, in fact, that upon the arrival of the Ottomans, they largely naturalized as subjects of the Ottoman sultan in Pera.

Becoming Ottomans

Genoese notarial documents indicate that the naturalization of Genoese residents in Byzantine Constantinople as Ottoman subjects after 1453 was a complex and sudden change of circumstances that, nonetheless, had key parallels in other nodes of Genoese Mediterranean commerce.[38] When Byzantine Constantinople became the new Ottoman capital in 1453, the district of

Pera across the Golden Horn had been under independent Genoese control since 1273. The *podestà*, whose residence still stands in ruins within walking distance of the former Venetian embassy and current Italian consulate, functioned as the district's mayor. By 1453, the Genoese Perots had become linguistically Hellenized and were typically bilingual, even as they remained generally beyond the boundaries of Byzantine subjecthood.[39] More surprising was the fact that their political and commercial relations with the Ottomans were already more than a century old. Despite having restored the Byzantine family to the crown in Constantinople after a long period of Venetian-allied Crusader rule (r. 1204–1260), the Byzantines allied themselves with the Venetians in 1350 during the five-year Venetian–Genoese war in the Aegean and Black seas. The Ottomans, based in Bursa, were the surprising entry into the war, and they helped to secure Genoese power in Pera. In return, they were rewarded with key trading privileges.[40] Among the Ottoman agents who helped to secure those privileges, paradoxically, were two Genoese men who worked for Sultan Orhan (r. 1323–1362).

Filippo Demerode and Bonifacio da Sori were originally Genoese ambassadors from Pera who were sent to negotiate a trade agreement with Orhan after the Genoese–Byzantine conflict of 1350. By 1355, they were working as agents in service of the Ottoman sultan. The Genoese document describes them as Orhan's "friends and servants," even as they were originally Genoese ambassadors sent to Orhan five years earlier.[41] In what reflects the early blending of political boundaries between Genoese Pera and Ottoman Bursa, the sultan successfully requested from the Genoese that these two be granted tax immunity during their time back in Pera conducting the sultan's business. While Christians had worked in political positions for sultans, caliphs, and emirs since the seventh century, they were typically local Christian subjects—whether Armenian, Greek Orthodox, Syrian Orthodox, or Coptic—already residing within the original Umayyad and Abbasid domains. That is, with the exception of Andalusi Christians, Christian subjects of an Islamic polity were typically not Roman Catholic Christians from Latin "Frankish" domains. In the unusual case of a married Florentine couple working in Mamluk political service in Cairo as interpreters, the European visitors who met them discovered that they were unsurprisingly Muslim Florentines who presumably converted some years prior.[42] The case of Filippo Demerode and Bonifacio da Sori as Genoese agents in service of the Ottoman sultan Orhan in 1355, in other words, foreshadowed a cultural shift that had certain precedents in Muslim–Crusader frontier lands. Latin Christians naturalized as subjects of an Islamic polity as though the Latin Church were among the various Orthodox churches of the late antique Near East. In another prelude to naturalization, Genoese and Venetian families were allowed residencies in early fifteenth-century Ottoman Bursa to facilitate their trade in Iranian silks. Among the key families who flourished in this market were the Genoese Spinolas, one of whom participated in the negotiations of 1453 and 1454.

When negotiations began in 1453 between the Genoese of Pera and the Ottomans, some families had already left for nearby Genoese-held domains such as the island of Chios, while others remained or returned. The agreement between the Ottomans and Genoese allowed the Genoese to remain in Pera on the condition that they pay the *haraç* tax "like the other non-Muslims."[43] That is, the Genoese were to be subsumed into Ottoman Latin-rite subjecthood like the other churches, thus becoming the foundation of the Ottoman Latin-rite Perot community that eventually included naturalized Venetians. One member of the Spinola family, Luciano Spinola, together with the former *podestà* of Pera, Baldassare Marufo, attempted to secure the return of Genoese independence in Pera under the authority of the office of the podestà—that is, a return to the Byzantine-era arrangement that the Ottomans had helped the Genoese to maintain after the Byzantine–Genoese conflict of 1350–1355. Mehmed II denied the request, and the foundation was laid for the growth of a new Ottoman Latin-rite community. This community theoretically and practically differed from non-resident Genoese and Venetian visitors in terms of laws surrounding property leasing, movement around the empire, and taxation.

From the perspective of residence and movement, what was notable about the naturalization of Genoese merchants as Ottoman subjects was a phenomenon that was seen less in Mamluk Egypt and more in Mamluk Syria in earlier centuries: the free movement and residence of Latin "Frankish" Christian merchants inland within Islamic polities beyond ports such as Alexandria and beyond the lodges or hostelries (*fondaco, funduq*) that were built there for foreigners. Echoing the way Venetian and Genoese merchants in Southampton operated from the port as opposed to buying and selling inland, Venetian and Genoese merchants were previously limited in travel to the ports of the Middle East and North Africa and required special diplomatic accompaniment or pilgrim status to move more freely in inland cities like Mamluk Cairo. Still, there were some precedents to Venetian and Genoese movement throughout the Ottoman capital as they moved freely in Mamluk Syria.[44] In either case, upon naturalization as Ottoman subjects, Genoese merchants secured travel and long-term residency privileges akin to local Christian groups like Ottoman Armenians as well as all other Ottoman subjects traveling along overland and maritime trade routes from the Ottomans' Balkans and Middle Eastern provinces to port cities throughout and beyond the Black Sea and Indian Ocean.

The Gagliano brothers were among the most widely influential Genoese merchants who were naturalized as Ottoman subjects and secured this flexibility in travel for commerce. The Gagliano brothers' trade activities connected Ottoman commerce with Poland–Lithuania, the Venetian republic, and the Republic of Ragusa.[45] The fact that their activities extended to include the Ottoman–Polish frontier illustrates the early modern advantages of Ottoman naturalization in comparison with the more limited privileges afforded by capitulation agreements (*ahidname*). Capitulation agreements with foreign powers guaranteed visiting merchants both security and movement in Ottoman territory, but they did not guarantee foreign Venetian and Genoese merchants the ability to operate and traverse all Ottoman frontiers with the same facility as naturalized Ottoman subjects of Venetian and Genoese heritage. This made Genoese naturalization as Ottomans a clear advantage. In a capitulation agreement with Polish king Sigismund III in 1597, the Ottomans agreed that "The *beys* of the *sanjacks* of Silistra and Akkerman [present-day Bilhorod-Dnistrovskyi, Ukraine], the harbor masters, and the tax collectors, may not permit anyone to enter Poland across the river Dniester except the servants of my felicitous [Ottoman] threshold and the merchants of both sides."[46] The Ottoman–Polish borders reflected the fact that while territorial borders were porous and saw the rise of frontier societies, they were neither theoretical nor imagined. The administrative oversight over merchant ships calling at ports and over pilgrims departing on merchant galleys throughout the Aegean illustrates that maritime borders, like land borders, were real in the early modern world, even as they were only as real as the state's ability patrol them.

These kind of restrictions in movement were intended, among other reasons, to prevent the kind of two-way movement of fugitives and corsairs seen in the Venetian–Ottoman maritime frontier, which compromised the ability of the Republic of Venice and Ottoman sultanate to project a reputation of protecting trade and attracting commerce. The existence of transimperial fugitives and corsairs, furthermore, pointed to the fact that there were cases when it was advantageous to have recourse to Ottoman justice and restitution following an attack on either one's person or property, just as there were other cases when it was preferable to claim foreign subjecthood and immunity. Those with the most movement and advantage, then, were able to claim subjecthood in multiple domains. In the case of the Gagliano brothers, Venice offered them help during a property dispute while acknowledging that they were "*haraçgüzar*s," that is, *haraç*-paying Ottoman subject.[47] In a reflection of their transimperial subjecthood, they were able to appeal to both the Venetian *bailo* resident in Pera as well as the Muslim chief judge (*qadi*) of Pera (Galata).

Beyond border control and questions of jurisdiction for property disputes and criminal cases, customs duties were a key reason that made Ottoman subjecthood sometimes preferable to claiming foreign status in the fifteenth and sixteenth centuries. In the late Byzantine era, prior to the absorption of Genoese-held Pera into Ottoman domain, Genoese–Ottoman trade relations were so strong that the Ottomans lifted customs duties for Genoese goods coming into Ottoman territory.[48] In effect, Genoese Perots operating in Bursa—the key transit point to Europe of Iranian silks—traded as though they were traveling as Ottoman subjects within one Ottoman customs zone. With the absorption of Pera into Ottoman domain after 1453, Ottoman subjecthood was codified with the payment of the *haraç* tax. In return for this payment, the law reads, "I [the sultan] agree that those who trade can [trade] in other parts of my dominion and can travel by sea and by land without hindrance or disturbance."[49] As for Genoese citizens who resided temporarily, the statement read, "I agree that those Genoese merchants who come and go by land and sea must pay customs duties as required in the law, and that they may not be attacked."[50] In this way, many Genoese Perots active in the late fifteenth century in previously Genoese-held territories, including Pera and Phokaia (Foça), took on Ottoman subjecthood rather than emigrate westward with the initial group that fled in 1453. As Ottoman territories eventually expanded into an assortment of customs zones with distinct customs agreements with different neighboring polities, choices became more complex. This complexity correlated with Genoese-origin Ottoman Latin-rite subjects and Ottoman Greeks becoming subjects of the Venetian republic, that is, becoming foreigners again. The comparative advantages of Ottoman and Venetian subjecthood, in effect, became a moving target over time.

The complexity of customs duties, and the growing ambiguity as to whether it was preferable to be a foreigner or Ottoman subject when trading between Ottoman and Italian peninsular domains, can be seen in a treaty signed between Venice and the Ottoman Empire in 1502. The treaty stipulated that Venetians resident in Istanbul for more than one year had to pay the *haraç* tax paid by Ottoman subjects. That is, like the Genoese of Pera before them, they effectively had to naturalize as subjects. As in the case of the Genoese who naturalized, the benefit was that Ottoman subjects involved in Ottoman–Venetian trade paid more favorable customs duties than their Venetian counterparts, who also paid Venetian customs duties (*cottimi*) when they came to and from the city. The result was that Greek Orthodox subjects of the Venetian republic residing in Istanbul, many of whom were Cretans, tended towards becoming Ottoman subjects after 1502.[51] What made this problematic, however, was that their Venetian Greek co-religionists continued to have privileged access to specific Venetian institutions in Istanbul that included a particular hospital in Galata as well as the Venetian chancery, where Venetian Greeks registered wills, testaments, and property sales.

Likewise, for the Genoese Latin-rite subjects in Istanbul, careers in diplomacy represented the key arena where the choice between maintaining a foreign status attached to the Genoese or Venetian republic, naturalizing as an Ottoman Latin-rite subject, or attempting to straddle both subjecthoods carried the greatest political benefits and risked the most uncertainties. Ottoman Latin-rite subjects worked in service of the Ottoman sultan as interpreters and diplomatic go-betweens in negotiations with the resident Venetians. While technically working in service of the sultan, they were employed by the Venetian *bailo* and were often issued *berat* status. This *berat* status offered them the same privileges of foreign criminal jurisdiction and tax privileges garnered by Venetian foreigners resident in Istanbul.[52] Those privileges were not necessarily advantageous in various scenarios, particularly in times of conflict, diplomatic spats, criminal cases, or investigations of espionage. The result was the kind of oscillation of subjecthoods between Ottoman and Venetian domains which was seen previously among merchants, fugitives, and corsairs. Notably, even this movement between subjecthoods became an arena where both the Venetians and Ottomans intervened to keep those associated with their diplomatic machinery within their own political boundaries.

More specifically, with the rise of large numbers of *berat* holders among Latin-rite Christians by the end of the sixteenth century, new-found Ottoman imperial concerns about the Ottoman Latin-rite Christians' transimperial mobility between distinct legal jurisdictions became part of a larger set of Ottoman legal reforms oriented around restricting the number of residents in Istanbul who could claim extraterritorial privileges or exemptions from Ottoman fiscal legislation.[53] The broader Ottoman administrative attempt in the seventeenth century to begin restricting how many *berat*s were associated with each foreign embassy was partly connected to the way some Ottoman Latin-rite Christian families simultaneously claimed foreign tax status, based on a Venetian husband's foreign privileges, and acquired local residential properties, based on an Ottoman Latin-rite Christian wife's local privileges.[54]

The effect of these seventeenth-century Ottoman reforms of boundaries in legal jurisdictions on the political mobility of Latin-rite Catholics ran parallel with seventeenth-century Venetian reforms in Istanbul related to hiring practices of Ottoman Latin-rite Christians. As in the case of concerns in the Italian peninsula about Sephardic Jewish diplomats straddling the information networks of multiple empires, Venetian administrators sought to keep Ottoman Latin-rite Christians dragomans who worked in Venetian service on the payroll well into retirement age for fear that they might move to another embassy and share information.[55] By the eighteenth century, with the diminishing of the Ottoman–Venetian trade route, European powers passed over Latin-rite Christians entirely when hiring Ottoman non-Muslim subjects for diplomatic service.

In sum, the draw of Ottoman and Venetian forms of naturalization in the 1400s, together with the push and pull of residency and subjecthood privileges in either domain according to political and economic circumstances, meant that Genoese trade networks in the eastern Mediterranean would flourish long after the Genoese republic's withdrawal from the region. In the long run, with the Venetians' and rising Florentines' cultivation of a privileged trade connection with the Ottomans in the 1500s, the Genoese model of commercial expansion through naturalization abroad would come in handy as they turned their attention to the Ottomans' adversaries: the Habsburgs in northern Europe and Iberia. With the Genoese out of the way, sixteenth-century Italian commerce in the eastern Mediterranean would be the story of the Republic of Venice.

7

THE VENETIAN REPUBLIC TURNS GLOBAL

Figure 7.1 Istanbul's Fener district, one of the city's principal Greek neighborhoods as recently as the 1950s, was the home of several politically influential Ottoman Greek families who served as governors in Wallachia and Moldavia as well as Grand Dragoman and Dragoman of the Fleet. The last position was a central part of the administration of the Ottoman Aegean islands in the lead-up to the nineteenth-century nationalism debates between Hellenic Greeks and Ottoman Greeks.
Source: https://pixabay.com/photos/balat-istanbul-patriarchate-4634367, public domain.

In April 1454, just one year after the Ottoman conquest of Byzantine Constantinople, the Republic of Venice signed a treaty with the Ottoman dynasty guaranteeing the right of the Venetians to maintain a *bailo*, or ambassador, in the district of Pera. This *bailo* would be responsible for the free movement of Venetian merchants in and out of Ottoman territory, and would exercise certain legal authority over them. The arrangement was nothing new for the Venetians and Ottomans. It was a renewal of an earlier agreement signed in 1408. As far back as 1388, when the Ottoman capital was still in Edirne, the Venetians had already signed agreements with the Ottomans establishing various trading privileges in the eastern Mediterranean. These events took place before western European kingdoms like the Portuguese pursued a western passageway to Asia through the southern Atlantic and Indian Ocean in the sixteenth century.

Back in the fourteenth and fifteenth centuries, the Ottomans provided the Venetians privileged access to a lucrative Asian market, while the Venetians provided the Ottomans access to a profitable European market. One of the formative dimensions of this exchange was the competition that developed between the Venetians and Ottomans over Constantinople's former islands and over the legal jurisdiction of Aegean mercantile exchange in centers like Crete, Cyprus, and even the Venetian and Ottoman capitals themselves. The outcome was that, like the Genoese before them and Sephardic Jewish and Jewish-heritage Iberians (*conversos*) after them, the Greeks—including Ottoman Greek subjects doing business in Venetian territories and Venetian Greeks active in the Ottoman capital—became part of the juridically intertwined worlds of the two powers. Both the Ottomans and Venetians sought to simultaneously expand their territorial holdings and centripetally absorb the Mediterranean's many trade diasporas for commercial benefits. With the Age of Exploration-era expansion of Iberian commerce into the Mediterranean and Indian Ocean worlds, Sephardic Jewish and *converso* networks in the Spanish New World could be seen exporting red cochineal pigment that would be combined with the Iranian Armenian-trade silks of the Ottoman–Safavid frontiers to make one of Venice's most prized commodities: Venetian red velvet.

One of the lesser-known outcomes of this Venetian–Ottoman exchange was a shared legacy in cultivating Renaissance-era Hellenistic learning through their shared patronage of the Greek intellectual network. This patronage, in turn, was intertwined with the way both ruling circles actively co-opted the Roman past. On the Venetian side, the Senate's rising self-representation as Roman Catholic patrons of the Greeks—albeit, Greek Orthodox-turned-Catholics (Byzantine-rite Catholics) eligible to move beyond subjecthood and become Venetian citizens (*cittadini*)—facilitated the Venetians' goal of further cultivating their image as a global holy city. That is, in the aftermath of the Ottoman conquest, the Venetians could claim that their own city of St. Mark—built as a new Alexandria—was now a new Constantinople on a par with Rome. In the Ottoman case, the Ottoman sultan represented himself as a new Roman emperor (Turkish: *kayser-i rum*) in accordance with the still resident Orthodox patriarch's ceremonial investiture and in accordance with the court's eclectic patronage of philosopher-scientists, cartographers, and painters from the Italian peninsula. By the start of the Age of Exploration, in other words, both powers had doubled down on the Mediterranean's Roman past and increasingly global future, while neighboring powers like the Genoese Republic and Papal State were beginning to consider new opportunities along the Iberian trade routes to Acapulco, Manila, and even China.

Greeks between Venice and Istanbul

Venice as a New Constantinople

The doges of Venice and the Venetian Senate faced a major challenge with the demographic reality that their subjects in the 1400s included a growing number of Greek Orthodox communities throughout the Adriatic and Aegean.[1] Since the Catholic–Orthodox schism, and also since the Fourth Crusade that sacked Constantinople, many of the Greek Orthodox communities throughout the eastern Mediterranean had become highly resistant to the implications of Catholic rule. They were specifically resistant to the pope's unwavering demand that the Greek Orthodox Church join the Latin-rite Catholics under his authority. This was the theological position known as unionism. Being conquered by Catholics would risk forcing Greeks into a Catholic-dominated unionist position, which the Venetians themselves were favorable towards, though not as zealously as the Papal States had been. Greek monks and nuns in particular had grown so concerned over the implications of an imminent Venetian conquest for Greek ecclesiastical authority that many preferred the prospect of cities officially submitting to Ottoman rule in order to secure Ottoman support of the Greek rite, a prospect that became a reality for Ottoman Greeks in the early Ottoman capital of Edirne (Andrianopolis).[2]

Against this historical backdrop, the Venetian doge and Senate developed an aspiration to transform their capital into a Roman Catholic imperial patron of Greek intellectual and religious culture. In this manner, Venice, the city of St. Mark that was already a new Alexandria, would simultaneously become a new Constantinople and a home not only for Roman Catholics but also Greeks.[3] One outcome of this political patronage was the attraction of both Greek mercantile and intellectual communities to the lagoon. From the Senate's perspective, the activities in Venice of select Greek clergy like Cardinal Basilios Bessarion (d. 1472) could facilitate this process. Unlike the Greek clergy of the Ottoman domains, who were in large part fiercely resistant to unionism and therefore suspicious of Venetian rule, Bessarion was a Greek-speaking cardinal and unionist who left the Ottoman world to become a Byzantine-rite (Greek-rite) Catholic and Venetian citizen. The cardinal's most famous and public act in Venice was the gift of his collection of 452 Greek manuscripts to the city as the founding collection of the new Biblioteca Marciana. In the dedication of his works to the city, he called Venice "another Byzantium." Specifically, in the letter that accompanied the deed of donation, he explains why he chose Venice:

> I came to understand that I could not select a place more suitable and convenient to men of my own Greek background. Though nations from almost all over the earth flock in vast numbers to your city, the Greeks are most numerous of all: as they sail in from their own regions they make their first landfall in Venice, and have such a tie with you that when they are put into your city they feel they are entering another Byzantium.[4]

The cardinal's words point not just to Venice's aspirational transformation into a cultural center of classical Greek and contemporary eastern Roman (Byzantine) learning, but also to the reality that Venice in the 1400s was indeed in the midst of the second episode of its historically two-step process of deepening its religious claim to being a new Christian holy city on a par with Rome. The first step, Venice becoming a new Alexandria, occurred between the 800s and the 1100s. In 828, the Doge Giustiniano Participazio ordered the capture or theft of the remains of St. Mark from Alexandria in Egypt, where Venetians originally used to travel for pilgrimage, and the transfer of the remains to the heart of Venice's political center in the new church of St. Mark next to the doge's palace.[5] This event was followed centuries later by the public rediscovery of St. Mark's remains in 1094 by the Doge Vitale Faliero in Venice after their temporary loss. With the fall of eastern Roman domains to both the Venetian republic and Ottoman sultanate, Venice's absorption of Greek learning was part of the second step in the historical bolstering of its Christian legitimacy. In effect, projects like the completion of the Biblioteca Marciana added a contemporary Greek religious dimension to its wider Renaissance-era patronage of the Mediterranean's Graeco-Roman past.

The case of the Aldine Press likewise highlights the extent to which political patronage of Greek learning went hand in hand with cultivating the loyalty of formerly Byzantine newly Venetian Greek Orthodox communities. The Aldine Press was the most famous Greek publishing house of the early modern world, and it was founded in Venice.[6] People with a consummate knowledge of the Greek language were needed for the press to grow, and the Greek communities were a natural fit. By the 1500s, large numbers of Greeks throughout the Mediterranean who moved to Venice from newly Venetian- and Ottoman-held islands could be seen working as scribes of Greek manuscripts, bookbinders, and editors.

Venice's patronage of the Greek past and present, in other words, saw a kind of Renaissance-era fusion of the ancient Greco-Roman Hellenistic intellectual culture with contemporary Greek Orthodox and Byzantine-rite Catholic socioreligious heritage.[7] That fusion, in turn, became an interesting precursor to a similar mix that reappeared with the rise of Greek nationalism in the 1800s. Notably, Greek nationalism's key players included Greeks still resident in cities like Venice and Livorno. Back in the 1500s, as an increasingly global metropolis with privileged access to the Ottoman domains, the Venetians were content to secure their place as the central patron of not only Roman Catholic pilgrims visiting St. Mark on the way to the holy cities, but also Greek Orthodox and Greek Catholic pilgrims visiting the many sacred sites that dotted the lucrative Venetian–Ottoman trade routes through centers like Split (Spalato), Dubrovnik, and the Aegean.[8]

In sum, in a world where the Italian republics played a balancing act of honoring the papacy in Rome while pursuing their own political and commercial interests, the doges of Venice and the Venetian Senate ensured that their close connections with the Ottoman world would help Venice emerge as a new

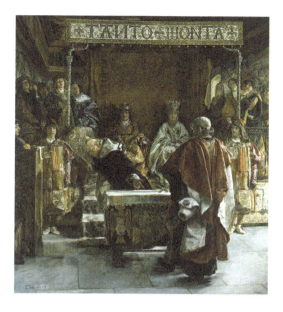

Figure 7.2 The Alhambra Decree of Granada (1492), depicted for centuries in Spanish paintings such as the one pictured above (Emilio Sala y Frances, 1866), saw the newly united Castilian and Aragonese kingdoms stipulate the expulsion of Jewish communities from all Catholic and Muslim-held Iberian lands. The edict, which marked the escalation of the Spanish Inquisition, was issued shortly after monarchs Ferdinand and Isabella negotiated the conquest of the peninsula's last Muslim emirate in Granada. Large segments of Iberia's Muslims and Jews, scattered throughout the Iberian kingdoms since the 1000s, were baptized as Roman Catholics, while many others left for cities like Venice, Ottoman Istanbul, and the Spanish New World. Among those who left in later decades were members of the so-called *morisco* and *converso* communities, Roman Catholics with family names illustrative of their Muslim and Jewish parentage. The memory of these communities' multi-episodal departure was closely preserved well into the twentieth century among Sephardic Jewish communities living in the Italian Peninsula and Ottoman Istanbul, where parallel edicts allowed the settlement of Iberian Jewish exiles.

Source: https://en.wikipedia.org/wiki/Alhambra_Decree#/media/File:Expulsi%C3%B3n_de_los_jud%C3%ADos.jpg, public domain.

type of commercial and cultural capital, the city of Alexandria of St. Mark that could also be a new Constantinople on a par with Rome. Where these increasingly multicultural underpinnings of Venetian political and cultural life took on truly global dimensions was in the city's assimilation of another itinerant mercantile community: Sephardic Jewish exiles from Iberia.

Doña Gracia, the Spanish Inquisition, and the Sephardic Exiles of Venice

The case of Sephardic merchants in Ottoman domains in the fifteenth century represented a similar pattern where a Mediterranean merchant network that was naturalized into Ottoman subjecthood began to move between Ottoman and Italian forms of subjecthood in accordance with changes in laws on residency, travel across certain borders, and customs duties. These merchants had their origins in Iberia on both sides of the Catholic–Islamic frontiers, but by 1492, the Alhambra Decree issued by Castilian Queen Isabella and Aragonese King Ferdinand stipulated that those who had not already left Castilian and Aragonese domains were to choose baptism or expulsion. The aftermath of the expulsion, which was followed by a similar edict in Portugal in 1497, saw two major demographic trends: the overnight expansion in Iberia of Christians with Jewish heritage, known in contemporary Iberia as *conversos*, and the growth of both *conversos* and openly Jewish "Sephardic" communities throughout cities linked to Mediterranean trade.[9] From the later perspective of global trade networks in the sixteenth and seventeenth centuries, the most significant destinations of Iberian Jewish exiles were the northern coastal cities of the Dutch Low Countries, the Italian peninsula, the Ottoman Aegean, and late Mamluk Egypt and Syria. A closer look at the legal fortunes of eminent Sephardic families across these geographies highlights the political and economic advantages of residency in Italian and Ottoman cities, where the practice of Judaism was legally permitted.

The case of the *converso* Diogo Mendes Benveniste, who was among the first in his family to travel from Portugal to Habsburg-controlled Antwerp in 1512, highlights the complexities of residency and commercial life for *conversos* in cities where Inquisition offices were active and were intertwined with governance. A merchant in precious stones and spices, Diogo Mendes was arrested in 1532 on a number of counts, including being a "Judaizing" Christian (*Heresie en Judaïsering*), helping Portuguese *conversos* flee for Ottoman lands, and monopolizing the trade of spice commodities to the detriment of local merchants. According to extant records of the case preserved in the Antwerp Municipal Archives, Diogo Mendes was sentenced to prison but was soon released upon granting Charles V an interest-free loan of 50,000 ducats.[10] This arrangement was not the first or last of its type. Philip III in

1602 secured some 1,860,000 ducats from Portuguese businessmen in return for securing a papal bull that pardoned 6,000 Portuguese *converso* families for any past so-called heresies.[11] In the 1540s, Diogo Mendes' sister-in-law Doña Gracia Nasi and nephew João—that is, the later Ottoman diplomat Joseph Nasi—fled the Low Countries for the Italian peninsula and Ottoman domains after becoming entangled in legal difficulties. In Doña Gracia's case, her legal woes likewise propelled her to offer the cash-strapped government a private loan, but her family's properties were ultimately confiscated anyway in absentia.[12] How Doña Gracia and Joseph Nasi became, respectively, a politically influential philanthropist and a chief advisor to Sultan Selim II (r. 1566–1574) is a story that can be fully contextualized only against the backdrop of Jewish political and commercial life in Medici-era Tuscany, the Ottoman Aegean, and late Mamluk Egypt and Syria during the years when Mamluk territory was subsumed into Ottoman dominion.

Lorenzo "The Magnificent" de' Medici

Lorenzo "The Magnificent" de' Medici, the de facto ruler of the rising Florentine Republic (r. 1469–1492), had an unusual connection with two popes who attempted to protect *conversos* from the offices of the Inquisition. Pope Leo X (r. 1513–1521), the first of the two Medici popes, was Lorenzo's second son Giovanni di Lorenzo de Medici. Pope Clement VII (r. 1523–1534), the second, was Lorenzo's nephew Giulio di Giuliano de' Medici. As the Medici popes rose through the ranks of the Church and reigned almost continuously from 1513 to 1534, they developed the same awareness that Lorenzo and his descendants had of how lucrative Sephardic trade networks were for Italian commerce throughout the Atlantic, Mediterranean, and even Indian Ocean worlds. Both Medici popes developed a reputation for protecting Portuguese *conversos* in the Italian peninsula from the jurisdiction of Charles V, the Habsburg monarch and Holy Roman Emperor. The second of the two Medici popes in particular, Clement VII (r. 1478–1534), famously issued the Bull of Pardon (*Bulla de Perdão*) for Portuguese *conversos* in 1533 that pardoned past offenses for those accused of "Judaizing" heresies. By 1536, however, Charles V had officially instituted an office of the Inquisition in Portugal (*Conselho Geral do Santo Ofício*) based on the model of Spain's office (*Tribunal del Santo Oficio de la Inquisición*), which was established in 1478. That is, while both Spain and

Portugal saw nearly simultaneous campaigns of mass baptisms and expulsions, Portuguese *converso* communities that included Spanish *converso* exiles had an almost fifty-year respite before being pursued for "Judaizing" heresies. Spanish *conversos* were able to escape tribunals in Mexico, as the office of the Spanish Inquisition waited until 1571 to establish a branch in the Americas. In Oaxaca, Spanish *conversos* participated in the wholesale export of red cochineal pigment that, beginning in the 1540s, began to compete with Iranian *qermez* in the Italian silk industry, particularly in the production of Venetian red velvet. By the end of the century, *converso* networks linking the Americas and Iberia with the Dutch Low Countries and the eastern Mediterranean saw the movement of merchants who were simultaneously navigating the changing dynamics of the Inquisition offices and trading in wholesale precious commodities like cochineal. Along with those commodities came the news that Istanbul and Cairo, which were now connected to Europe through the Ancona–Ragusa–Istanbul route and the Venice–Spalato–Istanbul route, saw the widespread presence of openly Jewish Iberians in Islamic political dominion.

While the second of the Medici popes, Clement VII (r. 1478–1534), was only able to offer *conversos* in Portugal a three-year respite from political pressures with the issuance of the Bull of Pardon in 1533, his defense of *conversos* played a role in the continuity of Jewish commerce in the port city of Ancona upon its absorption into papal control in 1532. It was during Clement VII's administration when Ancona began to attract Sephardic merchants who had settled decades earlier in the Islamic world, and ultimately the Venetian Senate responded quickly by allowing long-term residency permits for Jewish merchants from Portugal and the Ottoman world.

The Venetian and Anconan policies towards Jewish settlement developed in parallel. Specifically, the government of Ancona issued a series of decrees, beginning in 1499, lowering customs duties to encourage business with merchants from Ragusa, Lucca, and Florence, ultimately offering the same privileges to all Ottoman subjects—including Jewish merchants—in 1518.[13] The Venetian Senate responded swiftly and deliberately to the movement of the Genoese westward and to the ascendancy of Ancona in the increasingly Ottoman-dominated Adriatic. Partly due to pressure from Venetian businessmen, the Senate decided in 1541 to allow the settlement of Jewish merchants for long periods as part of a larger move away from a strictly protectionist approach to the local silk industry and as part of a simultaneous aspiration to control the Adriatic silk trade.[14] This move was part of a longer post-Byzantine process that saw the Venetian Senate attempt to transform Venice not only into a belated Catholic patron of the Greek Orthodox Aegean, but also a commercial gateway to the expanding silk and spice routes further east.[15]

The Pull of Ottoman Subjecthood

Residency privileges in Ancona and Venice were still problematic for Sephardic merchants, particularly Ottoman subjects who had already established residence in the Ottoman Aegean. In Ancona, residency privileges were unpredictable in a manner evocative of Sephardic experiences in Portugal, Spain, and the Dutch Low Countries. Specifically, the first pope who came to power following the Medici popes withdrew the right of Jews to reside in Ancona, resulting in a return to Istanbul. In Venice, which saw greater continuity in Jewish residency privileges, movement remained officially restricted, and petitions of exception were granted with uneven frequency.

More specifically, the decree of the Venetian Senate that allowed Portuguese and Levantine Jews to settle in the city, issued in 1541, was issued partly as a result of local complaints among Venetian merchants about the government's protectionist approach towards local silk industries.[16] That is, the sumptuary laws oriented around specific conceptions of Catholic ethics in public space was in contrast to the state of affairs in nearby cities like Livorno and Lucca, where the presence of Sephardic merchants helped silk commerce take on global dimensions. In the case of cochineal, the earlier protectionist approach meant that Venetian merchants had little access to this simultaneously lower cost and high quality Mexican alternative to Persian crimson (*qermez*) in the production of red velvet.[17] Once the decree was issued, however, restrictions on movement remained in the form of the enduring and politically complex phenomenon: the *ghetto vecchio*.

The rise of the *ghetto vecchio*, an urban space for "Ponentine" (Portuguese) and "Levantine" (Ottoman) Jews that officially restricted their movement at night, can be read in the context of this clash between, on the one hand, much of the Venetian Senate's resistance to the absorption of Jews in Venetian civic life and, on the other hand, individual senators' and businessmen's shared vision of turning Venetian commerce global in competition with Ancona. The application of a night curfew and restrictions on certain types of commerce at the Rialto market was somewhat haphazard, as influential Jewish merchants were able to secure exceptions.[18] While this haphazardness has been read as the halting tolerance of Venetian governance, it can also be read in a legal context as that aspect of Venetian conceptions of residency and subjecthood that made the city only partly able to pull the Ottoman world's global commerce to the westernmost point of the Venice–Spalato–Istanbul trade route. In a parallel manner, the change of papal policies on Jewish residency in Ancona reflects a similar weakness in the attraction of Ancona for Sephardic Jews and their business associates along the Ancona–Ragusa–Istanbul route.

What Ottoman domains offered, in contrast, were wide-ranging residency and movement privileges that gave Sephardic merchants access to Middle Eastern trade networks in the Levant, which included Arabic-speaking Jewish networks trading in Iranian silks. As part of a specific approach to urban planning and empire construction, one that oriented the centripetal pull of Ottoman subjecthood and its economic outcomes, Ottoman administrators developed an interest in the long-term settlement of Sephardic merchants in Istanbul and around the Balkans. Under Beyazid II in the late fifteenth century, Sephardic exiles played a major role in interimperial commerce both with neighbors in the Italian peninsula and with centers in the Islamic world like Mamluk Cairo. In the Ottoman context, this rise of Ottoman Sephardic subjecthood developed in tandem with the dynamics of Ottoman Latin-rite subjects.[19]

As in the case of Ottoman Latin-rite subjects, diplomacy was a key arena that saw the political mobility of Sephardic Jews moving within Ottoman governing circles and across Italian–Ottoman political boundaries. Jewish diplomats working in Ottoman service were found within and outside Ottoman lands throughout the Adriatic in places where merchant communities existed.[20] Interimperial diplomacy was a natural fit for these merchants given how Sephardic Jewish commercial networks of the late sixteenth century connected the Italian and Ottoman eastern Mediterranean with places as far afield as Mexico in the Spanish Atlantic.[21] The Ottomans were keen to benefit from the service of such entrepreneurs with their far-flung family networks, but the decision to work in Ottoman service abroad was often a precarious one in according with the fickle nature of trade relations and wars.

One of the most well-known examples of this complexity is the career of Joseph Nasi, mentioned previously. João Nasi was also known as João Michel and Giovanni Miguel. His multiple aliases are indicative not only of the complexity of identity among transimperial subjects straddling the porous Mediterranean political worlds, but also the surprising interconnectedness that existed at the level of imperial intelligence gathering.[22] On the one hand, Nasi's activity in multiple empires points to the fact that interimperial diplomatic activity facilitated the sharing of information for administrations that were in alliance. On the other hand, Nasi's straddling of multiple information networks points to a key concern among ruling circles and these transimperial subjects: accusations, both false and substantiated, of espionage that could come from either side of these diplomatic and commercial networks.

The fact that Sephardic diplomatic and mercantile activities throughout the Mediterranean extended into the realm of information networks should be read as a phenomenon illustrative of how transimperial identities and cultural literacy could be as much a source of political and economic advancement as they were a potential political disadvantage. In the case of accusations of espionage, the precariousness of careers in interimperial diplomacy or the repercussions of unpredictable political scenarios was often clearer on the side of Italian city-states. In an era when politicians from Sephardic families such as Sinan Reis could be seen fighting under the Ottoman flag against the Spanish Habsburgs, two Jewish subjects in the Kingdom of Naples were prosecuted for passing Habsburg information to the Ottomans through contacts in Ottoman Thessaloníki.[23] Likewise, during the Ottoman–Venetian war over Cyprus from 1570 to 1573, Sephardic merchants in Venice faced accusations of helping the Ottomans. The outcome was that their mercantile and political status was frequently unstable within the Venetian Republic.[24]

How Sephardic merchants and diplomats navigated these interimperial political conflicts was in part a function of the fluid and, in practice, often unclear legal distinctions throughout the eastern Mediterranean that delineated the civic and commercial status of local subjects and long-term foreign residents. From the perspective of citizenship and subjecthood, Venice, in principle, strictly distinguished between nobles, citizens, subjects, and foreign residents. The existence of sumptuary laws in Venice, which were an extension of this civic hierarchy, governed social practices of dress and the mixing of classes to an extent that reflected a theoretically strict but practically fluid understanding of Venetian society and ethics.[25] Many Sephardic Jews in sixteenth-century Venice were considered long-term resident foreigners, specifically as subjects of the Ottomans. It was, therefore, as Ottoman subjects, not as Venetians, that many conducted much of their transimperial mercantile business dealings throughout much of early modern Venetian history. Their trading connections, especially with Ottoman elites, coupled with a lack of access to many other professions in Venice beyond brokers in sixteenth- and seventeenth-century Venetian law, helps to explain why the Ottoman side of these dangers was often the safer one.[26]

In other words, even the precarious circumstances of being potentially accused of espionage saw the same centripetal forces that drew many Genoese and Sephardic merchants more closely into Ottoman subjecthood than Venetian subjecthood. More specifically, Ottoman governing circles in many cases

Figure 7.3 The arrival of Sephardic Jewish exiles throughout the Adriatic and Aegean during the height of Venetian–Ottoman commercial exchange saw Spanish-speaking Jewish communities live alongside older Greek-speaking Romaniote Jewish families (pictured here in early twentieth-century Greece). The outcome of the communities' distinct varieties of bilingualism meant that Sephardic subjects of the Venetians and Ottomans, typically fluent in Spanish or Portuguese well into the twentieth century, could serve in various interimperial diplomatic roles linking the eastern Mediterranean with the Habsburg world.

Sources: https://en.wikipedia.org/wiki/Romaniote_Jews#/media/File:Mordechai_Frizis_Romaniote_Greek_Jew.JPG, public domain; https://en.wikipedia.org/wiki/Romaniote_Jews#/media/File:Greek_Romaniote_Jews_Volos_Greece.JPG, public domain.

protected these transimperial diplomatic figures in a way that made Ottoman diplomacy a more politically secure option for transimperial subjects. This trend is particularly clear in the example of Hayyim Saruq, whose story rounds out this picture of the Venetians and Ottomans simultaneously absorbing the region's trade diasporas while also constructing imperial boundaries.

The Case of the Ottoman Sephardi Subject Hayyim Saruq

Hayyim Saruq's career illustrates the role of Sephardic Jewish merchants in the era of close Ottoman–Venetian political, commercial, and diplomatic relations. Hayyim offers an illustrative example of the multifaceted importance of Jewish merchants in early modern Mediterranean trade between centers in the Italian peninsula, the Balkans, Egypt, Syria, and the Ottoman Aegean.[27] Hayyim was an Ottoman subject from the Sephardi community of Thessalonica.[28] He appears in Venetian notarial records as early as 1561 and was connected to prominent Ottoman Jewish families like the Segura family, who operated in centers including Istanbul, Venice, Ferrara, and Ancona.[29] Apart from involvement in the transfer of Ottoman exports, credit operations, and the acquisition of shipping vessels, Hayyim was also a patron of Talmudic literature in Venice.[30]

Hayyim, in other words, was an Ottoman subject able to build connections between a variety of Sephardic and non-Sephardic Jewish communities in the eastern Mediterranean, as well as connections between Jewish merchants and the various Muslim and Christian communities in Italian and Ottoman lands. Politically speaking, his negotiations with Venetian authorities on behalf of Thessaloníki's Jewish community are particularly illustrative of the many hats he wore. In the context of a communal commercial dispute, an extant responsum of Rabbi Samuel de Medina of Thessaloníki indicates that Hayyim was asked to appeal to the Venetian authorities to reduce the community's commercial tariffs by 50 percent. The appeal was successful.[31] In what reflects the social and political position that Hayyim reached in eastern Mediterranean diplomatic circles, his name appears in Venetian notarial records, the acts of the Senate and Council of Ten, and in Venetian judicial records. Hayyim's career reflects a larger pattern of Sephardic Jewish merchants being central to Ottoman political and commercial relations in the eastern Mediterranean in an era when the Ottomans sought dominance in the region.

What is unclear about Hayyim's story, beyond what it tells us generally about Sephardic Jews in Ottoman diplomacy, is indicative of how his career might be of the way imperial boundaries were increasingly contested and demarcated. On one level, his story highlights how Sephardic Jewish merchants, like Ottoman Christian subjects, navigated fluid political boundaries between polities like the Venetian republic and Ottoman sultanate, and how the Venetians' and Ottomans' mutually important commercial relations partly explain the two polities' longer history of peaceful relations than conflict. On another level, Hayyim's story also brings to mind the fact that Venetian and Ottoman administrators were continuously debating, especially through legal edicts, how to manage and police these boundaries. From the perspective of governance, administrators were aware of the political advantages of transimperial subjecthood given the government's need for political diplomacy and commercial negotiation. However, as in the case of the Venetians maintaining certain Ottoman Latin-rite Christians on the Venetian payroll in order to avoid their employment by other embassies, both Venetians and Ottomans were equally interested in managing and controlling the boundaries of their information networks. The Dutch, newcomers to the global trade scene in the sixteenth century, even sought to benefit from the overlap of diplomatic and merchant communities in Istanbul despite the possible transfer of Dutch information to other embassies. The Ottomans appear to have taken a similar approach, allowing centers like Thessaloníki to benefit politically and commercially from the commercial and diplomatic activities of high-level transimperial subjects like Hayyim with an apparent awareness that the Venetians might, in turn, learn about the activities of the Ottoman political elites. The outcome was that in his case, Ottoman subjecthood offered greater political security than any status the Venetians could offer.

Information Networks

In 1571, the Council of Ten in Venice sent Hayyim back to Ottoman territory, specifically to Istanbul, to gain information for Venice about Ottoman affairs. This event occurred five years after the Ottomans intervened on behalf of Hayyim in Venice's bankruptcy proceedings against him, an event that saw the Ottomans apply diplomatic pressure on Venice in order to claim as Ottoman royal property an amount of alum that Venice originally sought to confiscate. Three years prior to that event, the Ottomans intervened when Venetian authorities seized as contraband, and therefore state property, a shipment of textiles that Hayyim brought to Venice. The event turned into a diplomatic spat that saw the Ottomans claiming the material as their own, which prevented the *bailo* from leaving unless the cloth was delivered. From the perspective of Ottoman governance and its history, the question that arises is whether the high-level patronage of figures like Hayyim was part of a deliberate strategy on the part of Ottoman administrators to prioritize maximum commercial benefit over maximum demarcation of information networks.

Like the Venetians, the Ottomans were certainly aware that figures such as Hayyim, like the many Ottoman Catholic subjects working in the European embassies, could share information between the embassies.[32] The fact that misinformation was deliberately passed to other embassies, and the fact that dragomans were kept on the payroll to prevent their being hired by other embassies, is indicative of this reality. In the case of Hayyim, even in the years prior to 1571, it would certainly have been conceivable to the Ottomans that the Venetians might become privy to various Ottoman political affairs in the years when Hayyim and other Sephardic and Catholic transimperial subjects like him were in close contact with Venetian authorities. Therefore, the fact that Ottomans intervened time and again on behalf of Hayyim and others seems to reflect something that parallels the Dutch example of governance, which is that in the particular case of Ottoman–Venetian relations, Ottoman governance frequently showed a preference for maximizing the political and commercial benefits of transimperial subjecthood in spite of potential leaks across Ottoman and Venetian information networks. This aspect of Ottoman governance might be a specifically early modern outcome of a common Venetian–Ottoman political and commercial cause against growing Atlantic and Indian Ocean mercantile activity on the part of the Portuguese and Dutch.[33] The end result was that as long as Venetian and Ottoman political and commercial interests were in alignment, Catholic and Jewish subjects of the sultanate like Hayyim became the beneficiaries of cultural connections linking the Italian peninsula with the Ottoman world.

In sum, the history of the Venetian republic's and Ottoman sultanate's capture of eastern Roman (Byzantine) territories throughout the 1400s and 1500s saw naturalization become a key mechanism for expanding imperial boundaries and access to trade networks. One of the patterns that emerged out of this competition was the enduring pull of Ottoman subjecthood against its Venetian counterpart. Like the Genoese diplomats who became Ottoman subjects in service of the sultan even prior to the capture of Constantinople, Greek and Sephardic merchants became more closely intertwined with the Ottoman world than its Venetian counterpart in accordance with three specific legal advantages: residency privileges, movement along lucrative internal trade routes and frontiers, and lowered customs duties throughout commercial centers absorbed into Ottoman political dominion.

Still, the appeal of either remaining in Venetian territories or moving to the Venetian capital was strong for these Greek and Sephardic communities, just as it was for the Genoese who traded as Venetians in the Ottoman capital. In an Italian context, what the Venetian model of absorbing Mediterranean trade diasporas illustrated was how a maritime republic could grow both by expanding its domains centrifugally and absorbing, centripetally, the Mediterranean's increasingly global trade diasporas. It was a model of expansion that the Ottomans perfected, and that the Venetians likewise adopted in the aftermath of the eastern Roman collapse and start of the Age of Exploration. Where the Venetians found new competition was in Florence on the western Italian coast, where a resurgent Florentine government would begin transforming Tuscany and its port of Livorno into a modern global and multiethnic hub that would connect modern Florence with Fez, Algiers, Tunis, Alexandria, and the Ottoman Levant.

8

FLORENTINE COMMERCE AND THE RENAISSANCE

Figure 8.1 Pope Leo X (r. 1513–1521), born Giovanni di Lorenzo de' Medici, was a leading member of the Medici family that governed the Grand Duchy of Tuscany based in Florence. Leo's reign saw Ancona, a Papal-held Adriatic port used by Florentines for commerce with the Ottomans, become a central node in a growing Ancona–Ragusa–Istanbul trade route that competed with the Venetians' Venice–Spalato–Istanbul route. Like Venice, Ancona offered Muslim and Jewish merchants from the Ottoman Empire residency privileges in a pattern that foreshadowed Florence-held Livorno's absorption of the region's trade diasporas in the 1600s.

Source: https://en.wikipedia.org/wiki/Pope_Leo_X#/media/File:Portrait_of_Pope_Leo_X_and_his_cousins,_cardinals_Giulio_de'_Medici_and_Luigi_de'_Rossi_(by_Raphael).jpg, public domain.

HOUSE OF MEDICI

Lorenzo de' Medici's Diplomacy between the Mamluks of Cairo, the Ottomans of Istanbul, and the Papacy

The rise of modern Florence, a cultural crossroads of Italian trade with northern Europe and the Middle East, was closely intertwined with the House of Medici. In the earliest decades of Istanbul's Ottoman period (1453–1923), the Medicis were actively involved in banking and manufacturing activity throughout the empire. Francesco, Giovanni, and Raffaello de' Medici, for example, were active in Istanbul's Pera district and in the neighboring cities of Bursa and Edirne throughout the 1460s and 1470s.[1] Pera was the former Genoese-controlled district of Byzantine Constantinople. In 1470, Francesco was conducting business in Ottoman Pera, simultaneously making trips to neighboring Bursa and Edirne on behalf of Medici & Company. Other members of the family were involved in related manufacturing activities that included cloth, dyes, and other materials. Among them was Lorenzo, one-time diplomatic interlocutor with Cairo's Mamluks who became the de facto ruler of Florence in 1469.

Lorenzo was the grandson of Cosimo de' Medici, head of the Medici bank during the Ottoman conquest of Istanbul (1453) and the first of the Medicis to govern as de facto ruler of Florence (1434–1464). With the rise of the Ottomans in the eastern Levant, it was Lorenzo de' Medici who emerged as Florence's key political and cultural broker, mediating Florence's commercial position between the Levant's Mamluk past and its Ottoman future. What facilitated this process was the Ottoman administration's overtures to the Florentines at a time when the Genoese and Venetian republics dominated Italian connections with the Middle East.

When Mehmed the Conqueror (r. c. 1444–1481) came to power in Istanbul, one of the first policy shifts was his cultivation of relations with Florence over Venice. Despite Venice's successful cultivation of diplomatic and trade relations with the Ottomans on a scale evocative of earlier Genoese–Byzantine relations, the Venetians were engaged in conflict with the Ottomans around the Aegean from 1463 to 1479. In one of a variety of diplomatic moves, Lorenzo commissioned a medal for Mehmed in gratitude for Mehmed's extradition of the assassin of Giuliano de' Medici. Giuliano was Lorenzo's brother, who co-ruled Florence and who was assassinated at the age of twenty-five in the Duomo during the so-called Pazzi Conspiracy. Lorenzo was also involved in diplomatic exchanges with Mamluk Sultan Qaitbay, as it was only in the following century when Mamluk domains were taken over by the Ottomans.

Lorenzo's simultaneous diplomatic encounters with the Mamluks and Ottomans occurred during a crisis of succession following Mehmed's death. Sultan Djem was the third son of Mehmed the Conqueror and a pretender to the Ottoman throne during his half-brother Beyazid II's reign. Beyazid's defeat of Djem led to Djem's exile, which took him to the domains of the Knights Hospitaller of St. John in Rhodes in 1482. The Knights concluded a separate agreement with Beyazid to imprison Djem on the island in return for large payments. From there, he was transferred to the Duchy of Savoy along the Italian borders with France, and by 1483, he was moved to the Kingdom of France under Charles VIII, where he would remain for about five years. By 1489, the Papal States successfully managed to secure his transfer to Rome despite the Hungarian king trying to gain custody of him.

There were a variety of motivations to have Djem held in good condition, for as long as possible, under the equivalent of house arrest in European domains. For the Knights in Rhodes, the Papal States, and Hungary in particular, Djem's presence offered two things. First, it offered a source of massive funds sent by Bayezid, who remained concerned that Djem would use his continued connections with loyal and disgruntled officials to attempt to reconquer part of the empire. Secondly, it offered European powers significant leverage against Bayezid to deter Ottoman invasion through the Balkans, where the Ottoman dominion did eventually reach into Hungary. Lorenzo got involved in this whole process as a kind of go-between connecting the Mamluks with the papacy and France.

In Cairo, Mamluk Sultan Qaitbay had a strong interest in pulling Djem into Mamluk domains. Like the Hungarian king and the pope, the Mamluk sultan was interested in leveraging the potential arrival of an Ottoman pretender in Cairo to push back the Ottomans from their ongoing conquest of Mamluk-held Levantine and North African lands. War had already broken out between the Mamluks and Ottomans in 1485, and since several European powers were interested in mobilizing against the Ottomans, there was an opportunity for the Mamluks to collaborate in return for Djem's transfer from France to Cairo. The head of the diplomatic negotiations was none other than Lorenzo.

The Egyptian ambassador arrived to meet Lorenzo in 1487. Having cultivated commercial relations with both Cairo and Istanbul for twenty years, Lorenzo was aspirationally careful about balancing his relationship with the Mamluk and Ottomans. After initially attempting to focus negotiations in the realm of commerce and avoid the Djem affair, Lorenzo appears to have become more open to helping secure Djem's transfer to Egypt as the opportunities for commerce grew. Within months of the Mamluk ambassador's arrival, an agent in France named Lorenzo Spinelli secured a meeting with King Charles VIII. Acting on behalf of Lorenzo de' Medici, Spinelli presented Charles VIII with Mamluk Sultan Qaitbay's offer: 100,000 gold ducats for transfer of Djem to Cairo. In the end, the negotiations fell through. Pope Innocent VIII managed to edge out his Hungarian and Mamluk counterparts, and by 1489, Djem was in Rome. The Papal States began to receive vast sums from the Ottomans, whose financial transfers accounted for much of the sums used to maintain the Sistine Chapel.

Despite Lorenzo's inability to procure Djem for transfer from France to Cairo, the entire diplomatic encounter raised both the Medicis' and Florence's profile throughout Europe and the Middle East. When the Mamluk embassy arrived in 1487, the ambassadors entered the city as part of a vast procession that even included a giraffe. The Medicis maintained a menagerie, a kind of predecessor to modern zoo gardens, and the giraffe would make a welcome addition. Giraffes, which were native to Africa, had no recent history of being seen in person in the Italian peninsula until that moment, which meant that the diplomatic event was something of a spectacle that was enshrined in local memory for generations. A century later, when Cosimo I de' Medici adopted the Palazzo Vecchio as his new private residence and had its lions find a new home, he commissioned a certain Giorgio Vasari to decorate it.[2] The most remarkable work of art that Giorgio found in the vault was an art piece called *Lorenzo the Magnificent Receiving the Tribute of the Ambassadors*. The painting featured, among other things, the very giraffe that the Mamluks brought to Florence fifty years before Cosimo took power. Interestingly enough, by the time Cosimo was in power as the first Grand Duke of Tuscany (r. 1537–1569), Mamluk Cairo had already been subsumed into Ottoman authority, which made this painting a relic of a bygone era when Lorenzo de' Medici navigated Ottoman and Mamluk diplomacy and propelled Florence into the heart of global commercial and political affairs.

In the immediate decades that followed Lorenzo's diplomatic encounter, the Medicis were slow to compete with the Venetians for close commercial relations with the Ottomans. In fact, while the Genoese and Venetians had been entrenched in Ottoman politics and society for decades, Florentine rulers were still contemplating participation in a new and belated Crusade to capture Istanbul. In other words, in the lead-up to Ferdinando de' Medici's (r. 1587–1609) transformation of Livorno into a multinational commercial center on a par with Venice, military engagement with the Ottomans—like diplomacy—remained one of a variety of methods the Medicis experimented with in the process of growing Tuscany's stature in the eastern Mediterranean in the 1500s.

Lorenzo's Successors and the Limits of Medici Power

Giuliano di Lorenzo de' Medici was one Lorenzo's sons. In the lead-up to his reign as the leading political figure in Florence (r. 1513–1516), Giuliano was an exile in Venice, Florence's competitor. The reason for his exile, and the circumstances of his return, were indicative of some of the fundamental problems that the Florentine government faced in the early decades of Venetian–Ottoman exchange. Florence was not a centralized republic with the degree of political stability seen in Venice. This contrast meant that Florence's attempt to leverage or scale Tuscany's mercantile connections with markets further east ran into local obstacles in the early 1500s. Giuliano's exile was part of the ouster of the Medicis by the same Florentine republicans involved in the assassination of Lorenzo's brother, Giuliano's uncle.[3] As mentioned, Lorenzo's brother co-ruled Florence and was assassinated at the age of twenty-five in the Duomo during the so-called Pazzi Conspiracy. Lorenzo commissioned a medal for Mehmed in gratitude for Mehmed's extradition of the assassin. Giuliano's reign in the 1510s was part of a wider return and consolidation of Medici power in Florence, supported in part by the Medicis having risen to the papacy in Rome. Giuliano's elder brother Giovanni was named pope in Rome in 1513.

As Pope Leo X, Giovanni continued the work of his predecessor Pope Julius II in helping push western and northern European powers, including the Spanish and French, out of the Italian peninsula. The Spanish controlled the Duchy of Milan, while the French controlled the Kingdom of Naples and, indirectly, Florence. In practice, Julius attempted to play each European power against the other in order to consolidate papal control and influence over as much of the Italian peninsula as possible. This meant collaborating in one campaign with the French during a conflict against the Venetian republic in order to regain part of the Adriatic coast, and then partnering with the Spanish against the French in order to oust the French from Naples.

It was against this backdrop that when Giuliano returned to Florence from exile in 1513, he did so as Duke of Nemours under French authority. The French appeared to have been preparing Giuliano for rule in a French-aligned Naples, but their plans were cut short both by Giuliano's sudden death in 1516 and by the papacy's efforts to expel the French from Naples altogether with the help of the Spanish Habsburgs. It was, again, Giuliano's brother Giovanni—Pope Leo X—who participated in this process of reinstalling the Medicis in Florence through a complex set of diplomatic maneuvering. On the one hand, Giovanni helped to secure his younger brother's royal connection with the French through Giuliano's marriage into French royalty. On the other hand, Giovanni sought to consolidate both Florentine and papal influence over the Italian peninsula to the exclusion of the French. It was against this backdrop that Giovanni cultivated closer connections with Spain, even facilitating the process of Charles V—Habsburg on his father's side and both Castilian and Aragonese on his mother's side—being named Holy Roman Emperor. The fact that Charles V was able to claim titular rule over Naples upon the expulsion of the French, simultaneously playing the role of imperial protector of Medici-governed Florence, was indicative of how the Medicis navigated their relationships with these vast northern empires in order to exclude them.

It was in this context that Giovanni experimented with a more belligerent approach to the Ottomans and a more conciliatory approach towards local Greeks and Jews, both of whom were intertwined with trans-Mediterranean trade diasporas connected with Ottoman and Venetian domains.

The Medici Pope, the Ottomans, and the Competition over Greek, Jewish, and Protestant Loyalties

As in his father Lorenzo's case, Giovanni's political career (1513–1521) as pope and as an influential figure in Florentine politics occurred at a time of growing hostility between the empires of Europe and the Ottomans. The reigns of Selim I (1512–1520) and Suleiman the Magnificent (1520–1566) saw the Ottomans transform from an Anatolian power into both a European and Middle Eastern power. The final years of Leo's reign saw the Ottomans capture Mamluk Cairo (1517) and Belgrade (1521). Two years earlier, Hungary secured a three-year peace agreement with Selim I.[4]

In the lead-up to the Ottoman capture of Belgrade, Giovanni attempted to accomplish two initiatives that would consolidate his authority in the Italian peninsula. The first was to push back the Ottomans, whose ability to reach the Adriatic gates of the Italian peninsula had become a very real possibility. Giovanni attempted to declare a new Crusade against the Ottomans by attempting to bring about a truce across Europe, particularly between the French monarch and Habsburg Emperor Charles V. This initiative failed in part because peace with France remained elusive. The so-called Holy League, which included the Papal States and the Spanish Habsburgs, were still fighting campaigns against the French in 1521, which made the possibility of a truce and concomitant Crusade far-fetched.

Giovanni's second initiative was to leverage his authority as pope to penetrate circles of loyalty outside Catholic circles. The example of papal relations with Jews was discussed above in Chapter 7 on Venice. As much as Giovanni's personal interest in the arts and letters of the classical world helps to explain the establishment of a Hebrew printing press in Rome, Giovanni's patronage of Jewish communities fit neatly into the larger context of Italian states offering legal protection to trade diasporas active throughout the Mediterranean. Sephardic Jews escaping the Inquisition were welcome for decades in Ottoman and earlier Mamluk domains. Once in cities like Istanbul and Cairo, they maintained social and commercial connections with New Christians of Jewish heritage in Portugal, where many Spanish families of Jewish heritage fled in the 1500s. Those families who settled in New Spain (Mexico) were, thus, on the westernmost fringes of a truly global social and commercial network that had a solid eastern node in Istanbul. Across these networks, merchants traded in commodities like red cochineal, the high quality low-cost red pigment from Oaxaca that was used to produce red velvet.

It was against this backdrop that the thirty years of Medici governance in the Papal States—Giovanni as Leo X followed by his nephew Giulio as Clement VII—saw a variety of policies illustrative of papal tolerance towards Jewish communities that were in sync with wider Italian flexibility towards Jewish settlement. Ancona, which was subsumed into the Papal States in 1532, saw an increase in Sephardic Jewish settlement in the final years of Giovanni's nephew's reign as Pope Clement VII. Leo X himself employed

Jewish physicians and artists and offered tax-related privileges to Jews in Rome. The outcome was that by the end of Medici rule within the Papal States in the 1530s, papal-held Ancona was part of an Ancona–Ragusa–Istanbul trade route that competed with the Venice–Spalato–Istanbul trade route, and along both routes, Sephardic Jews were active conducting business. Another group active along these trade routes were the Greeks, over whom the Venetians and Ottomans competed for loyalty in the aftermath of the Byzantine Empire's collapse. Into this competition stepped Leo X.

As much as the Ottomans managed to subsume the Greek patriarchate into Ottoman political dominion, there remained the Greeks of the sprawling Venetian republic and the Italian peninsula who had a problematic relationship with the Roman Catholic clergy. The Greek Orthodox of the Aegean were subject to Venetian pressures to become Greek-rite Catholics, and then there were the Greek-rite Catholics of the Italian peninsula who faced heavy-handed Latin assimilationist pressures against their Greek liturgical and ecclesiastical traditions. Leo X's clerical authority over Catholic affairs within and outside the Papal States meant that he could institute policy changes even within the Venetian republic. Leo X issued two papal bulls in 1514 allowing the Greeks of Venice to have their own church, a cemetery, and to perform the liturgy according to their own rite. Leo also placed Venetian Greeks under the direct authority of the papacy rather than Venetian bishops. In 1521, the pope decreed that Greek monks and priests on the islands of Zante and Cephalonia were subject to the legal jurisdiction of their own bishops, which meant that Greeks could not be put on trial before Roman bishops.[5] Medici Pope Clement VII and his successor Pope Paul III renewed certain aspects of these decrees in what fit into a larger sixteenth-century attempt on the part of the Italian peninsula's political and clerical authorities to secure Greek loyalty.

The move to secure greater loyalty from the Greek-rite Catholics served at least two outcomes that were both related to Italian–Ottoman political competition. The first was to strengthen Latin–Greek ties against the backdrop of an enduring Latin–Greek schism that the Ottomans successfully exploited during their expansion into western Anatolia. The second was to offset the problem of Catholics founding a break-away movement, Protestantism, which the Ottomans likewise exploited.

It was during the reign of Leo X that Augustinian Catholic priest Martin Luther wrote the Ninety-Five Theses in 1517, while 1518 saw a series of negotiations between the Church and Martin Luther intended to force him to retract his theses. Rather than meet with Leo X directly in accordance with an originally scheduled papal summons, Luther met the Papal Legate Cardinal Cajetan in Augsburg in October 1518.[6] The cardinal's arguments in favor of indulgences did not manage to extract a retraction from Martin Luther, and the Papal Bull of November 9 required all Christians to believe in the pope's authority to grant indulgences. By January 1521, the pope had excommunicated Martin Luther altogether. Already in 1520, in what foreshadowed the rise of Lutheran Protestantism across Scandinavia, Lutheran theologians were invited to Copenhagen by King Christian II of Denmark and Norway (r. 1513–1523) as well as Sweden (1520–1521). King Christian promoted Lutheran theology against the backdrop of local Scandinavian clergy's dissatisfaction with papal authority. Among the key beneficiaries of this shift was the Ottoman administration, which keenly followed these developments.[7]

Protestant–Ottoman Connections during the Reign of Giuliano de Medici (r. 1519–1523)

The theory that the Protestant reformation and the Ottoman administration had a mutually beneficial effect on one another is an old one. When Martin Luther nailed his Ninety-Five Theses to the door of the Wittenberg church, his perspective on the Ottomans closely echoed that of the Syriac-speaking clergy at the time of the spread of Islam: the claim that the expansion politically of Islamic dominion was an outcome of divisions within the Church and the heavy-handedness of each faction against the other. In the Syriac case, this heavy-handedness could be seen in Byzantine Constantinople's intrusion into the affairs of the Oriental Orthodox churches, including the Syrian Orthodox of Antioch and Coptic Orthodox of Alexandria. In Martin Luther's case, he found the Roman Catholic Church's leadership partly to blame for the Ottoman capture of Constantinople. Contemporary observers, in turn, wondered whether Lutheranism (Protestantism) survived the Habsburgs' anti-Lutheran activities because of how preoccupied the Habsburgs became with pushing back Ottoman expansion in Europe, which saw the Habsburgs look for allies among rising Lutheran powers.

More specifically, one of the most interesting outcomes of this period was the trajectory of Charles V's recognition of Lutheranism (Protestantism) in Germany. In 1526, just three years after the end of Giuliano's reign, Charles V was forced to adopt an increasingly conciliatory policy towards the Lutherans in Germany in large part because of the need for military support against the Ottoman–French alliance. A series of meetings of the Holy Roman Empire's parliament-like Diet began in Speyer (Bavaria) in 1526, when the Diet resolved that each prince should "rule and act as he hopes to answer to God and his Imperial majesty."[8]

By 1529, however, the Lutheran movement was in crisis. Charles demanded the 1526 ruling be rescinded, and that German rulers implement anew the Edict of Worms of 1521. That edict, issued during the middle of Giuliano's reign as pope, indicated that no one should dare to "receive, defend, sustain, or favor" Martin Luther.[9] Surprisingly, most German rulers agreed with the exception of those who protested, that is, the "protesting" (Latin: *protestant*) signatories who came to be known by this *protestant* moniker in Latin. Already in 1532, Charles V signed a peace agreement with Protestant princes against the backdrop of growing military conflict. During the 1540s, however, Charles ran into difficulty with Ottoman and French forces, respectively, and in the third and fourth diets of 1542 and 1544 made concessions. By 1555, the Peace of Augsburg saw Charles officially recognize Protestantism, even as he later attempted to push it out by force.[10]

In a move that supports the historical theory that Protestantism survived as an outcome of Habsburg–Ottoman rivalries, Suleiman himself leveraged his connection with the Greek Orthodox Patriarchate of Istanbul by cultivating connections—via the Orthodox—with Protestant princes in his attempt to navigate the new European landscape. Philip Melanchthon (d. 1560), one of Martin Luther's associates and a key theologian of the Protestant Reformation, maintained a close connection with the Greek Orthodox patriarchate. In 1552, Suleyman sent a letter inviting select princes to form an alliance directed against Charles and later Ferdinand's forces.

By then, Florence was under the rule of Grand Duke Cosimo I de' Medici (1537–1569), for whom the threat of Ottoman expansion across the Mediterranean was serious enough to inspire discussion of a new crusade. Cosimo I was the founding head of the Knights of St. Stephen, which was authorized by the papacy on Cosimo's initiative in response to the reality that the Ottomans were making inroads into Tyrrhenian Sea along the western Italian coast. The Ottomans were already in control of parts of the Adriatic on the eastern Italian coast, and their inroads on the Tyrrhenian coast along the western coast meant a potential threat to the Tuscan duchy's key port: Livorno. Cosimo was simultaneously in contact with the Ottoman sultanate for Tuscan–Ottoman trade, which he had to represent to Habsburg Spain as an operation of security and information-gathering.[11] In the 1580s, a little over a decade after the end of Cosimo's reign, his third surviving son Ferdinando I (1587–1609) declared Livorno a free port.

In the long-durée of Tuscan commerce in the Middle East, the declaration of Livorno as a free port in the 1580s was the belated Tuscan response to the Venetian centripetal absorption of non-Catholic merchants from all around the Mediterranean. The Venetians' absorption, in turn, responded to the Papal States' reception of foreign merchants in the papal-held city of Ancona in the late 1400s and early 1500s in competition with the Ottoman Aegean. Those pope were the Medicis, completing a lesser known history of Medici encouragement of trans-Mediterranean trade.

Figure 8.2 The history of the Duchy of Tuscany and its predecessor, the Republic of Florence, saw the once-powerful city of Pisa become eclipsed by both Florence and the growing Tuscan port of Livorno. During the Medici era, including the reigns of the Medici governors in Florence and the Medici popes in Rome, Florentine commerce and culture rose to such prominence throughout the peninsula that the Tuscan dialect eventually eclipsed the prestige of the Venetian dialect as the peninsula's lingua franca. By the twentieth century, it had become the national Italian dialect and even eclipsed Rome's own dialect (Romanesco), which itself gradually became Tuscanized from the sixteenth century onward.

Source: https://pixabay.com/photos/florence-city-italy-il-duomo-duomo-2147625, public domain.

Florentines in Ottoman Territory

Across the entire history of Medici activity in Florentine and Ottoman affairs, from Lorenzo's navigation of the Ottoman–Mamluk rivalry in the 1480s to Ferdinando's declaration of Livorno as a free port attracting Ottoman subjects in the 1580s, Florentine merchants and diplomats were active throughout the Middle East and North Africa. That is, in parallel with Venetian history, the push and pull of Florentine political friction with the upstart Ottomans developed simultaneously with Florentine–Ottoman commercial exchange. Florence's exchange with the Ottomans was built, in part, on Florence's relationship with the Mamluks, and its trajectory varied partly in accordance with the history of the rival Venetian republic's relationship with the Ottomans.

In the decades before the Ottomans conquered Mamluk Levantine and North African lands, Florentine merchants flourished in the region in the shadow of Venetian and Genoese merchants. Like merchants coming from the Most Serene and Most Superb republics, the Florentines had consular privileges in cities like Alexandria and Damascus. These privileges were successively renewed in 1489, 1496, and 1497. The appointment of a Florentine consul in Ottoman Istanbul itself, meanwhile, dated back to 1461, which marked the start of a decade of Venetian–Ottoman tensions. This appointment was in many ways the culmination of a long history of Florentine–Ottoman commercial relations that dated back even before the Ottoman conquest of Istanbul, when the Florentines managed to compete successfully with the Venetians and Genoese even in the Byzantine Aegean.

By the 1430s, some twenty years before the Ottoman conquest of the Byzantine capital, Constantinople saw a general revival of Italian–Byzantine exchange decades after problems in security plagued the city's trade. Tensions between the Byzantines and Genoese in Pera, which even drew in the Ottomans on occasion, likewise began to ease in the 1430s. Giacomo Badoer, a French-born Venetian diplomat and scientist, was one of these merchants who reported on Byzantine Constantinople's commercial culture in the late 1430s. Badoer was in a unique position to comment on the affairs of the day given the long-standing connections of the Venetians throughout the eastern Mediterranean. The accounts in his *Il Libro dei Conti* (1436–1440) reference a variety of Genoese businesspeople who were active in Constantinople between the years between 1436 and 1440.[12] Bertrandon de la Broquiere likewise noted the presence of Genoese among Catalans and Venetians during his visit around 1423.

By 1439, the Florentines were granted a set of commercial and residency privileges that would carry into the Ottoman period. These privileges, which included the establishment of a residential quarter, were an outcome of the Council of Florence. The council, which had its origins in an earlier council in Basel related to papal authority, was a contested initiative that imagined—among other things—a unionist resolution to the Latin–Greek split of the 1000s. In theory, from a Byzantine perspective, the union would have secured a united Latin–Greek front against a continuing Ottoman conquest of Byzantine-held territories. In practice, the Latin Crusader conquest of Byzantine Constantinople in the 1200s still loomed large in local memory, from the general populace to civil authorities and in clerical circles. These circles, including both monks and nuns, were well aware of how either Latin political rule over Byzantine lands or Latin–Greek unionism would involve a loss in autonomy over clerical affairs. They were in favor of negotiating with the Ottomans in accordance with the terms that other newly Ottoman Byzantine cities like Adrianopolis had accepted, which included the preservation of clerical autonomy. What likely made this position more appealing was the growing financial contrast between Constantinople's upper socioeconomic echelons and the increasingly impoverished wider populace of the 1430s and 1440s.[13] Individual high-level Byzantine cardinals, however, were actively working towards unionist goals, including Isidore of Thessalonica, who had been sent by Emperor John VIII Palaiologos to articulate a pro-unionist position at the Council of Basel in 1434. The ruling dynasty, in other words, was exceptionally interested in cultivating close connections with Latin Europe until the last days of the empire. While the political reasons for the dynasty's self-preservation are obvious, the commercial dimension adds interesting context to how Florentine and other Italian merchant groups became so closely connected with the city's ruling circles both before and after the transition to Ottoman rule.

In what adds a commercial context to the dynasty's exceptionally pro-unionist position, the ruling Palaiologos dynasty was personally invested in Italian trade in ways that were in contrast to the wider economic problems faced by the general populace amidst the final collapse of the empire. Contemporary Latin and Greek authors claim that the wealthiest in Constantinople feigned poverty in the final years of the empire, and both archeological evidence and Ottoman literary sources support the claim. In what potentially reflects the financially lucrative dimensions of unionism for the ruling dynasty personally, Giacomo Badoer's acountbook references the leading Byzantine families: Palaiologoi, Kantakouzenoi, Doukai, Doukai Rhadenoi, Notarades, Sophianoi, Goudelai, Iagareis, Argyroi, Laskareis, Synadenoi among others.[14]

With the final Ottoman conquest of the capital, the Florentines simultaneously participated in the defense of Byzantine Constantinople while navigating a certain continuity in their commercial activity across the empire's new centers. From the start in 1454 in the first full year of the Ottoman period, Florentine ships arrived in the city and grew to a convoy of three ships annually.[15] The Florentines paid an annual payment of 5,000 gold pieces in order to keep their agents in Galata. By 1461, they had managed to become the beneficiaries of Venetian–Ottoman political problems. That year, the Ottomans expelled the Venetians from government-owned houses and allowed the Florentines to settle in them. What followed two years later was a sixteen-year period of rocky Venetian–Ottoman relations resulting in the rapid growth of the Ottoman navy, the navy's dominance over the Venetians and Knights Hospitaller throughout the Aegean, and the Ottoman conquest of previously Venetian-held domains throughout present-day Albania and Greece, including the sprawling Greek island of Evia (Negroponte) across from Istanbul.

The Florentines were keen to demonstrate their support of the Ottomans' expansion in the region. Three Florentine ships that were anchored in the Golden Horn even participated in celebrations following the capture of Mytilene on the island of Lesvos.[16] With the capture of part of Bosnia in 1463, the Florentines decorated their houses and streets in celebration of the empire's victories, with some in attendance together with the sultan at a banquet in Florentine banker Carlo Martelli's mansion in Pera.[17] The year also marked the start of Venetian–Ottoman hostilities, with Florentine consul Mainardo Ubaldini and his associates in Pera having even actively participated in the process of the Ottomans declaring war on Venice.

Benedetto Dei and the Road to the Indian Ocean

Benedetto Dei (1418–1492) was one of these merchants active in Galata, and his activities in Istanbul illustrate how Florentine–Ottoman relations grew in proportion to Venetian–Ottoman tensions. Dei worked closely with both the Medici and the Portinari merchant houses. His *La cronica dall'anno 1400 all'anno 1500* reads like a kind of biographical dictionary of the city's notables, illustrating his own connection to Florentine elites. Dei's extensive traveling career helped to cultivate trading connections on behalf of Florentine merchant houses, taking him from Germany and France to Timbuktu, Sfax, Oran, Jerusalem, and, most significantly for Florentine–Ottoman relations, Istanbul. Dei rose to prominence in Istanbul in the 1460s, when he developed close relations with Mehmed II against the backdrop of increasingly contentious Venetian–Ottoman relations.

The period of Dei's activities in Istanbul—1460–1472—saw the Ottoman sultanate invest in Florentine espionage and insights. In one episode, Dei intercepted a series of Venetian letters in the harbor around Chios, bringing them from there to the Florentine consul in Pera and, in turn, to the sultan. Dei tells us that the sultan then summoned four Florentines, Mainardo Ubaldini, Iacopo Tedaldo, Niccolo Ardinghelli, and Carlo Martelli, who in return recommended various defense mechanisms.[18] Dei himself, he claims, was dispatched to Mamluk Cairo on the sultan's behalf to warn the Mamluks about the Venetians. Dei's accounts are frequently unable to be substantiated by Ottoman and Venetian accounts, and in this case, the Ottomans' own plans on Mamluk Cairo are worth noting.

Dei's accounts, which frequently border on the grandiose, point to Florence's rivalry with Venice in Italian–Ottoman commerce. Dei was himself a member of a Florentine silk merchants' guild as well as a wool dealer's guild in the early 1440s.[19] By the 1460s, he was traveling around Istanbul wearing multiple hats as merchant, ambassador, and informer along the intertwined information networks of the eastern Mediterranean. In those days, when Pisa remained Tuscany's key port city, Livorno was more than a century away from being adopted by the Medicis as a new center of commerce. Dei's activities around the eastern Mediterranean were part of a larger phenomenon of enterprising merchant-business people traveling around the region on behalf of families like the Medicis to conduct business.

The Florentines' activity in Bursa even put them in direct contact with Indian Ocean trade networks that predated the Age of Exploration. The Bahmanid sultans (1347–1527), the progenitors of the five so-called Deccan sultanates in present-day India, were involved in Ottoman trade via Bursa and as far west as the Balkans. Mahmud Gawan (d. 1481) was a minister at the court of Humayun Shah and Muhammad Shah III, and his center of learning still stands in Bidar Karnattaka. Gawan was among the Indian Ocean politicians who sent merchants to Bursa, from where they continued to the Balkans. Bursa in the fourteenth and fifteenth centuries, in other words, was a crossroads of European and Middle Eastern trade with what later Dutch and British merchants came to call the Far East. The ports of Antalya and Bursa linked trade in Egypt and Syria with Anatolia, which meant that Bursa became an alternative to Alexandria and Cairo for European access to the Indian Ocean. From a Florentine perspective, what distinguished Bursa from other Mediterranean ports was its access to the overland routes to Adana, Konya, and the world of Iranian silks. Bursa was the international center of high-quality raw silk in the fifteenth century, specifically the fine silks of Asterabad and Gilan. In the decades before the Iberian-led Age of Exploration bypassed Middle Eastern trade with the Far East, Bursa offered the Medicis and other Florentine banking families direct access to Central, South, and East Asian commodities.

In what points to why the Medicis eventually promoted Livorno as a local Tuscan access point to global trade in the late 1500s, the complexity of Florentine trade with Istanbul and Bursa in the early 1500s meant certain risks. Specifically, because Italian cloths were cheaper than rare Iranian silks, Florentine merchants experimented with incorporating Ottoman Bursa and Istanbul into Florence's export market. The market, however, was unpredictable. While the Ottoman archives offer a picture of the bustling import of Italian cloth in Bursa, they also point to cases of Florentine cloths being sent back from Bursa unsold.[20] Shipping to and from Ottoman ports across the Adriatic was a costly affair. Still, there were other ways to make up losses. A certain Christofal Bonifazio, a brother of the Giacomo Badoer based in Venice, bought a piece of camlet in Bursa that he sent to a certain Jeronimo. In other words, Bursa was not only a transit point for East–West trade, but was also the center of intra-Italian commerce.

The growth of Florentine–Ottoman trade meant that in the lead-up to the rise of Livorno in Tuscany, particular transit points in the Italian–Ottoman trade routes began to expand. Specifically, while the Venice–Spalato–Istanbul route continued to grow in accordance with the rise of Venetian–Ottoman trade throughout the 1500s, the growth in Florentine trade meant the expansion of Ragusa as a transit point, which in turn benefited papal-held Ancona along the Ancona–Ragusa–Istanbul route. That is to say, the rise of Florentine–Ottoman exchange meant the expansion of commerce in the Papal States in competition with the Venetian Republic, which still meant that the Florentine republic remained both removed from and dependent on centers closest to the Ottoman Empire. It was in this context that the Medicis became increasingly aware that the port of Livorno on the Tuscan coast was worth developing to bring all of these trade networks to Tuscany itself. In the meantime, the rise of Florence saw a growth of intermediary centers that became central to early modern European exchange with the Ottoman Empire: Foca, Novi Pazar, Saraybosna (Sarajevo), Skopje, and Mostar.

Broadly speaking, in sum, despite the intermittent friction between the Medicis and the Ottoman ruling families, there was a continuous history of commercial exchange between Tuscany and the Ottoman world that predated the dominance of either family in eastern Mediterranean commerce.

Figure 8.3 Florentine paintings representing biblical scenes, like earlier Norman mosaics in Palermo depicting St. Mark in Alexandria, incorporate visual cues that accurately depict select aspects of the contemporary Middle East and North Africa in imaginative contexts. In the Norman case, mosaics depicted ancient scenes of St. Mark adjacent Alexandria's lighthouse in its specifically Islamic-era medieval iteration, complete with a crescent on top. In the case of *The Gathering of Manna* (1540) by Francesco Bacchiacca, the painting offers an accurate representation of a giraffe as likely seen by the painter himself during a Mamluk procession that passed through the city decades earlier. The procession included the gift of a giraffe for the Medicis' menagerie. The giraffe itself was depicted in a variety of paintings in distinct contexts throughout the 1500s, which makes Bacchiacca's representation likely based on either his own visual encounter, his access to earlier paintings of the giraffe, eyewitness testimonies, or a combination. More than an attempt to capture life and society across the Mediterranean, these paintings—and the mosaics before them—offer a window into the way Florentine and wider European painters variously imagined, remembered, or heard about the Middle East and North Africa.

Source: https://upload.wikimedia.org/wikipedia/commons/4/4a/The_Gathering_of_Manna-1540_1555-Bacchiacca. jpg, public domain.

Imagining the Orient

Florentine Philo-Hellenism from Acciaioli to the Medicis

Like the Genoese and Venetians, the Florentine political establishment was hardly removed from the depths of local cultures in the eastern Mediterranean. While the Genoese ruling circles became linguistically Hellenized in semi-independent Genoese island regions around Constantinople, the Venetians cultivated a certain philhellenism in terms of a parallel interest in Greek antiquities and contemporary Byzantine Greek learning. In both cases, there was a kind of fusion of interest in the Aegean's ancient Hellenistic past and an attempt to cultivate the loyalty of local Greek-speaking circles. As seen in the early Ottoman court, the Ottomans likewise incorporated aspects of the region's ancient and contemporary Greco-Roman heritage into Ottoman political culture, bolstering the Ottomans' self-representation as both inheritors of the ancient Greek heritage and patrons of the Byzantine Greek Orthodox Church. The Florentines were very much part of this fifteenth-century phenomenon, which amounted to both a multifocal renaissance and a kind of cultural turn eastward.

In the decades before the Medicis welcomed Greeks and other non-Catholics to Livorno, Florentine ruling circles in Tuscany and the Aegean were likewise involved in this philhellenism specifically in terms of cultivating classical Greek learning and collecting Greek antiquities. For Nerio II Acciaioli, the Florentine ruler of the Duchy of Athens, ownership of the most important monuments of the Hellenistic world was a central part of its ruling culture in the Aegean. Athens during the Florentine period also saw the central propylaea of the Acropolis become repurposed as the palace, while the Parthenon served as the Duchy's Catholic church. The Acciaioli dynasty remained in power in Athens, perched between the Venetian and Ottoman Republics, until the city was subsumed into Ottoman rule. In Florence, the Medicis were likewise intertwined with this renaissance interest.

Lorenzo il Magnifico de' Medici, seen previously negotiating with both the Mamluks and the Ottomans during the Djem affair, was born a decade before the Ottomans captured Florentine Athens. While Lorenzo spent most of his life in the Italian peninsula itself, he nonetheless cultivated an eclectic taste for Hellenistic learning as part of a larger interest in the worlds of Europe's *levante* (east). Part of this interest correlated with the circle of intellectuals with which he surrounded himself. Pico della Mirandola, a philosopher and nobleman, enjoyed the patronage of Lorenzo and was connected with the so-called Latin Averroists, that is, the circles of Italian philosophers studying the Arabic works of Averroes and Maimonides in translation. Della Mirandola supplemented his knowledge of Greek and Latin with Semitic languages Arabic and Hebrew in what rounded out an eclectic understanding of philosophy, science, and history.[21] One of the outcomes was Lorenzo's creation of the Italian peninsula's first chair for the study of Greek, which in turn bolstered the study of Greek throughout the Italian peninsula and all of Renaissance Europe.[22]

Gifts for the Medicis

The objects that traveled to and from the worlds of the Italian peninsula were as varied in form as they were in provenance. Some fifteen years after sending the Venetian doge Nicolo Tron Chinese porcelain together with a variety of rare luxury items, Sultan Qaitbay sent Lorenzo de' Medici a variety of diplomatic gifts in 1487: Chinese porcelain, Valencian vases, sweets spices, textiles, medicinal herbs, essential oils, and exotic animals.[23] The animals would fit nicely in Lorenzo's menagerie.

The porcelains Lorenzo received pointed to the Mamluks' growing access to the Great Ming's Chinese exports via the Indian Ocean and Red Sea. This Mamluk–Ming exchange echoed earlier centuries of Abbasid–Song exchange, when Fatimid Cairo along the Red Sea competed with Abbasid Basra along the Persian Gulf. Both in the ninth century and the fifteenth century, the Red Sea and Persian Gulf on either side of the Arabian Peninsula constituted the Indian Ocean's gateway to the Mediterranean and Europe. The presence in the Italian peninsula of objects from the silk and spice routes grew increasingly common in the late sixteenth century, and given Lorenzo's predilection for collecting rare objects, it comes as no surprise that even Timurid objects passed into Florentine hands. In 1471, Lorenzo acquired the so-called Tazza Farnese, which was a Ptolemaic sardonyx cameo once part of the Timurid treasury.

The Medici family ended up with one of the largest collections of porcelain in the Italian peninsula owing both to Lorenzo's tastes and the growth of Florentine exchange with the Middle East. The collection was kept in Lorenzo's bedchamber and included mostly blue-and-white porcelains and a celadon piece. One Ming-era celadon piece, currently in Florence's Museo degli Argenti (Palazzo Pitti), bears an unsurprising inscription: it was a gift from Mamluk Sultan Qaitbay for Lorenzo. By the sixteenth century, the Ottomans and Safavids became the largest collectors of Ming porcelain

Inventory of the Medici Household

Upon his death, Lorenzo's family members undertook an inventory of his estate, which included the largest private palace in Florence. The anonymous clerk who went through the palace, recording each and every piece of porcelain and art piece, left a detailed account of what he saw in the palace. While the original was lost, a copy made in 1512 survives. The clerk noted furniture, clothing, and artwork in all of their varieties: Chinese porcelain, tapestries, Middle Eastern silk fabrics, necklaces, rings, and other miscellanea like wine barrels.

Some of the terms used by the clerk point to the eastern dimensions of the items. In reference to the various flowing men's gowns that patricians wore on formal occasions, the clerk used terms like *saio*, *vesta*, *lucco*, *robetta*, and *turca*. The last term points to a resemblance with some kind of caftan found further east, where elaborate gowns were similarly intertwined with the display of wealth and taste. One of these items is described as a *turca* of Moroccan cloth lined with ermine.[24] There were also hooded capes that included *gabbanna* and *gabbannella*, that is, cloaks that were hooded. The term's origin is Arabic, *jubba* (colloquial variants: *gubba*, *gibba*), and points to the incorporation of eastern garments into the repertoire of Italian clothing.

These *gabbannella*s were, of course, not the only items coming from the Middle East. There were Turkish bowls, some sixteen Turkish bows, three pieces of red Moroccan leather,[25] a Turkish crossbow target, a shield and horsehead armor in Turkish fashion, five bolts of Egyptian linen from Cairo,[26] two pieces of Syrian jasper,[27] three "caskets inlaid and decorated with ivory in the Damascene style."[28]

One of the interesting outcomes of this transfer to Tuscany of objects and forms from the North African and Levantine *levante* was the transformation of Italian ceramics. The Medicis were one among various mercantile families who collected Chinese blue and whites together with pseudo-porcelains from the most western parts of Asia, that is, the Ottoman world, as well as Iberia. Slipware from Iznik and Kutahya, for example, was also brought into the Italian peninsula. Giovanni Bellini's (c. 1430–1516) *Feast of the Gods* depicts three blue-and-white bowls that foreshadow Dutch painter Vermeer's taste for Chinese ceramics two centuries later. One of the hypotheses surrounding Bellini's *Feast of the Gods* is that one of the three pieces is not an original Chinese blue-and-white, but rather Ottoman slipware potentially brought to the Italian peninsula by Giovanni's brother Gentile during the latter's time in Istanbul.[29]

This mix of Ottoman and Chinese porcelain in late fifteenth-century Italian commerce had an impact on local Italian ceramics. In neighboring Liguria to the north of Tuscany, where the Genoese republic was situated, Ligurian calligraphic patterns began to use the same spirals and comma-shaped leaves found on Ottoman blue-and-white slipware. In cities around Venice, including Padua, local potters began integrating Iznik polychrome patterns that included tulips and carnations.[30] In Tuscany itself, Tuscan potters in cities like Montelupo also drew on Spanish ceramics, especially Valencian potters, in the employment of vine and leaf patterns. Spanish ceramics, in turn, drew on the world of Andalusi art of the *Maghrib*. All of these influences, in turn, shaped so-called "Medici porcelain."

Medici porcelain, most of which was produced at the Casino Mediceo di San Marco during the lifetime of Francesco, survives in the form of some seventy pieces. During the reigns of Ferdinando I de' Medici (r. 1587–1609) and Cosimo II (r. 1609–1620), production continued at factories in Cafaggiolo and Pisa.[31] One of the most striking aspects of Medici porcelain is the evidence it shows of Ottoman influence, specifically Iznikware's blue-and-white and polychrome palette with floral and foliate ornamentation: carnations, feathery leaves, roses, and palmettes.[32] Medici porcelain's connection with Iznikware could also be seen even in its production technique. Both Iznikware and Medici pseudo-porcelain used a frit-paste technique common in Persian pseudo-porcelain ceramics, which mixed clay with quartz or sand. In what points more explicitly to the transfer westward of Ottoman decorative forms, Medici inventories likewise make reference to "earthenware from Saloniki resembling porcelain."[33] That is, the inventories use resemblance to porcelain to identify and compare individual pieces transferred from the Ottoman world.

Medici pseudo-porcelain, in sum, was part of an era of Italian visual culture that was in dialogue with both Chinese and Middle Eastern design.

Middle Eastern design was itself partly shaped by a synthesis of medieval Greco-Roman, Persian, and Chinese design—especially in floral and faunal motifs—that ultimately impacted how Italian designers cultivated their own floral Chinoiserie in the production of pseudo-porcelain. In the case of Medici pseudo-porcelain, decorations integrated Chinese and Iznikware decorative motifs with Renaissance motifs and a variety of other floral and scroll elements. The outcome was the shared language of peony blossoms, palmettes, lotus palmettes, and wheatsheaf designs.

The trajectory of Florentine pseudo-porcelain developing in the context of a budding European variety of Chinoiserie and Turquerie fit neatly into the wider trends of Renaissance-era bookbinding, glasswork, and metalwork. Venetian glass, for example, developed in close dialogue with Syrian glass, which led global glass production for 200 years prior to the Timurid conquest of Damascus in 1401 and the transfer of the industry to Samarqand.[34] The impact of Byzantine and Syrian glass on Venice's glass industry, which was confined to Murano, continued well into 1550s until the invention of crystal.

The Medicis' collection of Middle Eastern and North African art and objects, in other words, was part of a larger history of medieval and early modern Renaissance Italian absorption of objects and artifacts from the Midde East. The impact of this absorption stretched from private collections and taste like that of the Medicis in Florence to the art and architecture of the Venetians and Genoese. The case of representations of St. Mark in Venice's central cathedral, depicted in contemporary Egyptian settings rather than ancient ones, points to how this cultural transfer stretched into the sacred. The more familiar examples of Mary represented with a veil embroidered in pseudo-Arabic script, or royal Mamluk textiles preserved as saintly relics after being gifted to clerical figures in the church, illustrate more broadly the premium placed throughout the Italian peninsula on the Middle East's material and visual cultures.[35]

9

LIVORNANS IN NORTH AFRICA DURING ITALIAN UNIFICATION

Figure 9.1 Ferdinando de' Medici (r. 1587–1609) was the primary figure associated with the rise of Livorno as an international port that attracted merchants from a variety of backgrounds and imperial associations: Protestants from northern Europe, Muslim exiles from Iberia and North Africa, Greeks from the Venetian and Ottoman territories, Jewish merchant networks, and the like. His career began as a cardinal in Rome, where he simultaneously served as an administrator of the Villa Medici. In an illustration of the continuing political and cultural relevance of Rome since the establishment of the Papal State almost a millennium earlier, ruling circles throughout the Italian peninsula owned properties throughout early modern Rome. Estates like the Villa Medici allowed them to maintain diplomatic relations and conduct business with a wide variety of patricians. The Medicis' decision to develop Livorno as a kind of new Pisa, coupled with the policy of inviting a variety of merchant circles to conduct business with tax exemptions, reflected the enduring aspirations of ruling circles to center the peninsula around their own capitals and ports. The rise of the Tuscan dialect as the peninsula's prestige lingua franca illustrated the Medicis' success in this process.

Source: https://simple.wikipedia.org/wiki/Ferdinando_I_de%27_Medici,_Grand_Duke_of_Tuscany#/media/File:Ferdinando_i_de'_medici_12.JPG, public domain.

A NEW GATEWAY TO THE MIDDLE EAST

In the ancient world, Cicero wrote of a port called Labrone on the western coast of the Italian peninsula. For the Genoese, the port was known as Ligorna. The Florentines called it Livorno. Throughout Crusader history, Livorno remained an inconsequential port and coastal village in the shadow of Pisa and Florence. All three cities are situated in Tuscany, giving its residents the characteristic Tuscan dialect that came to be the Italian kingdom's national language in the late 1800s. The confessional variety of the language's speakers following the *Risorgimento*—Roman Catholics, Jews, Greeks, Protestants— was a reflection of Florentine governance under the Medicis in the 1500s, when the port of Livorno became one of the Mediterranean's most politically and economically powerful cities in the early modern world. The Medicis even invited Iberian Muslims to take up residence in the city at a time when the Spanish Inquisition was at its peak. The goal was not only to make Livorno a commercial microcosm of the global Mediterranean on a par with Venice and Istanbul's Pera district, but also more simply to build a viable inheritor of Pisa's long lost legacy.

Matilda of Tuscany appears in the early history of Livorno because of the tower she built in the port in 1077. By 1103, Livorno had been subsumed into the Republic of Pisa, when the Pisans built the *Quadratura dei Pisani* fort that incorporated Matilda's tower. The fort was built in order defend Livorno, which as early as the 1100s was becoming increasingly important to Tuscan commerce. By 1399, the city had been purchased by the Visconti of Milan, who in turn sold it six years later to the Genoese republic based further north. Just two decades later on August 28, 1421, the port was back in Tuscan hands when the Republic of Florence (r. 1115–1532) purchased it. It was under Florentine rule that Livorno's modern history began.

The House of Medici's legacy saw Livorno rise to political, commercial, and intellectual prominence in the sixteenth and seventeenth centuries. Cosimo de' Medici (r. 1537–1569), the second duke of the Duchy of Tuscany and the first Grand Duke of Tuscany, laid out plans for the city's surviving *Fortezza Vecchia* in 1519. The castle, completed in 1534, was part of a Florentine government push to encourage settlement in the port and incorporated the older tower of Matilda and the *Quadratura dei Pisani* fort surrounding it. Still, there were less than 1,000 permanent residents in the port by the middle of the century, just decades before Livorno would begin its rapid planned expansion that would take the population to over 10,000 by the mid-1600s.[1]

In tandem with that growth was the rise in prestige of Tuscany in the European political world. While Tuscany was technically part of the Holy Roman Empire in the early 1500s, it was in practice independently governed in accordance with the decentralized nature of the Holy Roman Empire's power. The empire recognized the title grand duke in 1575 during the reign of Francesco de' Medici (r. 1574–1587), the son and successor of Cosimo who was the first to be named grand duke by Pope Pius V.[2] Cosimo's aspiration to be crowned grand duke by the pope was part of his broader consolidation of independent political and naval power in the shadow of the Habsburg Holy Roman emperors Maximilian II (r. 1564–1576) and predecessor Ferdinand (1556–1564), the successor of Charles V. Charles was the influential inheritor of the Habsburg throne who was simultaneously Castilian and Aragonese on his mother's side, making the Habsburgs a powerful political force not only in northern and western Europe, but also across all the domains of the Spanish empire as far east as Manila. For Cosimo, elevating the royal prestige of Tuscany to a grand duchy meant increasing the political rank and prestige of both the Medici dynasty and the Tuscan polity at a time when the political powers further north were simultaneously consolidating their domains and going global. The pope's willingness to accommodate Cosimo's aspirations was part of Rome's strategy to find local supporters for the Counter-Reformation, which included having dissenters sent to Rome.

The figure most closely associated with Livorno's rise to prominence was Francesco's successor Ferdinando I de' Medici (1587–1609), Grand Duke of Tuscany at the end of the sixteenth century and start of the seventeenth. Ferdinando was the fifth son of Cosimo I de' Medici and Eleanor of Toledo. Despite never having being ordained as a priest, he was made a cardinal in 1562 in Rome, where he established the illustrious Villa Medici. His brief career in Rome at the Villa Medici illustrated his abilities as an administrator and cultural critic. Ferdinando acquired the property in 1576 and ensured that just as other royal houses had an institutional presence in Rome, so the villa would be able to offer Rome a window into the splendid intellectual and political life of the Florentine court. Villa Medici's place in Rome among the properties of other Italian royal houses illustrated the extent that in the centuries following the start of the Italian Renaissance, Rome was emerging as a key node of cultural transfer and convergence connecting the Italian peninsula's variety of political and intellectual cultures.

On one side of this Italian cultural convergence was the value that royal houses assigned to Rome's ancient past. When an ancient Roman marble sculpture of wrestlers (*The Two Wrestlers*) was discovered and excavated in 1583, Ferdinando moved quickly to purchase it to include in the Villa Medici's gallery of antiquities. The Medicis purchased the sculpture together with the *Niobids*, sculptures depicting the children of Amphion of Thebes and Niobe in Greek mythology.[3] Far from dilettantes in the world of patronizing and collecting classics, the Medicis were patrons of Leonardo da Vinci (d. 1519), rival of fellow Florentine Michaelangelo (d. 1564).

On the other side of this Italian cultural convergence was the increasing settlement of various mercantile communities of the Mediterranean in the Italian port cities, making cities like Venice and Ancona centers of the commodities, tastes, and peoples whom the Italian peninsula's itinerant merchants previously encountered abroad. For Ferdinando de' Medici, the previously sleepy village of Livorno represented a perfect opportunity for Florence to cultivate its own Venice-like center of international commerce, taste, and people. Upon the death of his brother Francesco I in 1587, the young thirty-eight-year-old cardinal and administrator took power as the next grand duke. In a move evocative of Venice's decision to allow long-term Jewish settlement in the city, Ferdinando issued an edict that allowed Jews and Muslims to reside in the city.

One of the key outcomes of Ferdinando's edict was the rise of a prominent Sephardic Jewish mercantile community in Livorno, which became simultaneously one of the youngest and most prominent throughout the region. Muslims from the Ottoman Empire likewise took up residence in the city. A second outcome was the governing patronage of the intellectual cultures associated with these communities, whose cultural heritages were closely intertwined with Andalusi, North African, and Ottoman history. Accordingly, Ferdinando established the Medici Oriental Press (*Typographia Medicea*), which was among the first publishing houses to publish books in the Arabic script. Robert Granjon (d. 1590), a French printer and type designer, developed a variety of types for Middle Eastern characters for use among Catholic missionaries while he was working in Rome. These included printing types for Armenian (1579), the Syriac variety of Aramaic (1580), Cyrillic (1582), and various Arabic types (1586). It was with Granjon's scripts that the *Typographia Medicea* published the Gospels in Arabic. The novelty was not the publication of Christian Arabic writing. Indeed, various Orthodox churches of the Middle East had already adopted Arabic as an ecclesiastical and liturgical language in the early Abbasid era, from the Greek Orthodox (Melkite) to the Assyrian (Nestorian) and Syrian Orthodox Churches.[4] The use of the printing press to print Arabic was new, predating by several centuries the displacement by printing press of handwritten Arabic-script copyist and pedagogical dictation traditions in the Middle East.[5]

Livorno's Global Diplomacy

This dual connection that Ferdinando cultivated with the Italian's peninsula's ancient Roman past and its similarly international present extended beyond residency laws, material culture, and intellectual culture to include new trends in diplomatic relations. On the one hand, like the republics of Pisa and Venice since the Crusades, Ferdinando supported aggressive military campaigns that might help Florence to gain a foothold on the administratively Arabic and Turkish side of the Mediterranean opposite Latin Europe. He developed Tuscan naval power and fought against both Barbary pirates in 1607 and an Ottoman fleet in 1608. On the other hand, Ferdinando was equally aggressive in identifying and cultivating relations with powerful princely sovereigns of the eastern Mediterranean who could help facilitate the growth of Livorno as a hub of West–East commerce.

Among these eastern Mediterranean sovereigns was Fakhr al-Din ibn Qurqumaz al-Ma'ani (1572–1635), who ruled as governor of Mount Lebanon (r. 1590–1633) inside the Ottoman Empire. Fakhr al-Din appears in a letter written during the reign of Ferdinando's grandson Ferdinando II (r. 1621–1670). Sheikh Abu Nawfal al-Khazel, a Maronite Christian "overlord" residing in Tuscany (1635–1637), wrote a letter to Ferdinando II on behalf of Fakhr al-Din's grandnephews Amir Qurqmaz and Amir Ahmad. The letter asked Ferdinando II to lend them a portrait of Fakhr al-Din housed in Tuscany. Against the backdrop of the death of their father Amir Milhim ibn Yunus al-Ma'ani, the letter asks specifically that, "Your Highness kindly allow the Jesuit Fathers, delegated by their Superior, to bring to the amirs the painted portrait of their uncle Amir Fakhr al-Din in the palace of Your Highness, or allow them to copy it, and send it here [to Beirut] from Livorno in the first vessel to sail to

Saida or Beirut."[6] The letter points to the reality that early seventeenth-century Livorno had risen to become one of key nodes of present-day Lebanon's commercial access to European markets.

This Livornan connection with Mt. Lebanon and the ports of Beirut and Tyre was a product of Ferdinando I's policy moves. The Medicis' connection with Fakhr al-Din's family dates back to the late 1500s, when Tuscany competed with France, Spain, and England for access to the eastern Mediterranean. Fakhr al-Din controlled not only Beirut but also Sidon and Tyre. Ferdinando I offered Fakhr al-Din safe passage to Tuscany in 1608 in an illustration of increasingly direct bilateral relations between the Medicis and the Ma'anid dynasty. From the perspective of Ottoman governance, these talks were alarming because they constituted illicit political and commercial negotiations outside the purview of regional Ottoman powerbrokers. During the reign of Ferdinando's son Cosmio II de' Medici (r. 1609–1621), Ottoman governor Ahmad Hafiz of Damascus raided Fakhr al-Din's domains in 1613. Fakhr al-Din fled together with his family and an entourage of some seventy-five people to Livorno, where he was received by a delegation sent by the Medici family.

The Ma'anids and their Maronite representatives did not represent a rare phenomenon of the Christian and Muslim subjects among the Ottomans residing in Tuscany. Livorno under Ferdinand became a crossroads of Ottoman Jews, European Jews, Muslims, Greeks, and a variety of merchants, refugees, and exiles. There were two elements to this shift in the fortunes of Livorno. The first predated Ferdinando I, dating back to his predecessor Cosimo. The earlier duke promoted Livornan commerce by commissioning a new building to replace the earlier customs shed in 1546 and simultaneously issuing a variety of customs privileges to attract mariners. The newer customs house would include several warehouses and would be joined by a variety of other structures that would simultaneously promote commerce and facilitate defense of the city: a stockpile for the Tuscan galleys, underground grain silos, and an arsenal for both shipbuilding and repairs.[7] There were also infrastructural updates: the new *Canale dei navicelli* was built to connect Livorno with the Arno River, allowing the transport of imports to Pisa and cities further island. A pier was built adjacent to the port's lighthouse, allowing an increased number of ships to dock.

Ferdinando I's declaration of Livorno as a free port (*porto franco*), in sum, had the long-term effect of transforming the city both culturally and infrastructurally. In continuity with Venice before it, Livorno simultaneously

Figure 9.2 The Chiesa della Santissima Annunziata is one of several Greek Catholic (Byzantine-rite Catholic) churches in Livorno illustrative of the Florentines' ability to pull eastern Mediterranean trade diasporas towards Tuscany and away from Venetian and Ottoman territories. Echoing the career of Cardinal Bessarion in Venice in the early years of the Ottoman period, Greeks who settled in Livorno faced pressure from the papacy and local ecclesiastical authorities to adhere to Roman Catholicism in order to avoid spreading Greek Orthodoxy through local intermarriage. The Medicis themselves were less concerned about Catholic–Greek boundaries.

Source: https://commons.wikimedia.org/wiki/File:Livorno_Chiesa_Santissima_Annunziata_04_@chesi.JPG, public domain.

became a new crossroads between Europe, on the one hand, and the Middle East and North Africa, on the other. In parallel with the case of Venetian–Ottoman exchange throughout the fifteenth and sixteenth centuries, Livorno became one of the key sites of Italian–Ottoman exchange.

Muslims, Christians, and Jews across Cultures

Muslims and Jews from Iberia

In 1555, the city of Pisaro issued a charter that would be echoed in an edict issued by Ferdinando de' Medici in Florence in the 1590s. Pisaro's charter offered commercial privileges to five groups: Turchi, Armeni, Greci, Mori, and Ebrei. The names of the groups indicate the extent that confessional identity was only one of the many ways merchant networks were formed. Two of these groups referred to Muslims: Turks and Moors, references in broad brushstrokes to Muslims of Turkish-speaking lands to the east and Muslims of Iberia and North Africa to the west. Two other groups referred to Christians: Armenians and Greeks. The Greeks straddled Venetian and Ottoman subjecthood, while the Armenians additionally included Iranian Armenians under Safavid rule.

The edict inviting all of these groups was issued against the backdrop of restrictions against the settlement of these communities in other Italian port cities. In an effort to compete with the Venice–Spalato–Istanbul trade route, the Florentines originally relied on Ancona as an international trade hub connected with the Ancona–Ragusa–Istanbul route. Ancona was more accessible than Levantine ports, and Florentines in any case were unable to negotiate the same flexible trade arrangements in Ottoman Istanbul that the Venetians and Genoese secured. Ancona, however, became an increasingly unreliable point of access to the Ottoman market via the Ancona–Ragusa–Istanbul trade route. In Ancona, which was absorbed into the Papal States in 1532, Pope Clement VII found it problematic that there were so many "Turkish merchants in the city" and took steps to restrict commercial privileges. Pope Clement VII was Giulio di Giuliano de' Medici, the second of the two Medici popes who embraced the movement in and out of Ancona of Sephardic Jewish merchants active along the Ancona–Ragusa–Istanbul trade route. Restrictions on Muslim settlement in the city illustrated the extent that the Medicis—whether those based in Florence or the Medici popes of Rome—did not have one view on foreign settlement in lands that they governed. As Pope Clement VII, Giulio's intermittent restrictions on certain foreigners from settling echoed the haphazard restrictions seen in Venice, where Iranian Muslims complained of being asked to remain overnight in the Ottoman *fondaco* rather than with their Iranian Armenian business associates. Cities like Pisaro and Livorno, in this way, were in a position to become the beneficiaries of nearby Ancona and Venice's commercial shortcomings in the mid-sixteenth century.

Iberian Muslim Families between the Medici and Ottoman Domains

In the case of the Muslims who came to Livorno, the story of the Iberians is particularly interesting. Interestingly, Florentine ruling circles imagined that the often privately Muslim "New Christian" Moriscos might find a place in Livorno. Moriscos traveling throughout Europe came from linguistically

Hispanized families throughout Castile and Aragon and were not typically distinguishable—both in Iberia and beyond—from Old Christians. Ferdinand I's successor Cosimo II, in particular, worked through his agents to have wealthy Moriscos settle in Florentine domains in the interest of growing the region's capital and skills in accordance with trends already established by *conversos* who had settled there. As many as 3,000 Moriscos may have settled in and around Livorno during this period, but the enduring settlement of a large and wealthy community somehow never materialized.[8] The case of Lopez Stalavella is particularly illustrative of the tension between the contrasting pulls of the Medicis and Ottomans at a time when both ruling circles were making explicit overtures to Iberia's Morisco and *converso* exiles.

Lopez Stalavella was a wealthy Morisco who was courted by a Medici agent named Pesciolini during Cosimo II's reign. Cosimo II was the successor of Ferdinand I (1587–1609), and his reign saw the Medicis turn specifically to the Moriscos as a potentially lucrative community for business. There were a variety of Moriscos who had scattered throughout Europe, North Africa, and the Levant in the aftermath of the Alhambra Decree restricting Muslim observance and confessional identity in Iberia. Some were wealthy entrepreneurs, while others worked in infrastructural projects as day laborers.[9] For many, the Italian peninsula was not a final destination but a transit point along the way to centers in the Islamic world. A certain Morisco named Molina, for example, left for Marseille and Livorno together with Moriscos from the Trujillo community around 1610.[10]

Others including Diego Bejarano, also known as Ahmed b. Qasim al-Hajari, went to North Africa via Morocco. Al-Hajari (Bejarano) left in 1598 for Marrakesh, where his career as an interpreter eventually took him back to Europe to centers like the Netherlands. There, he met the Orientalist Jacob Golius, known for his meeting with famous China-based Jesuit Martino Martini during the latter's sojourns through Amsterdam. Golius was a specialist of Arabic and Persian manuscripts, and his meeting with Maritini confirmed that the "Cathay" of ancient and medieval Persian writings was the same China that the Jesuits visited themselves and that was known in Southeast Asia as "China," not "Cathay."[11] After al-Hajari returned to Morocco, he kept in touch with Golius by letter to an extent indicative of how Moriscos—Spaniards of Muslim heritage—remained an enduring element in Europe's many political, social, and commercial landscapes during the rise of Dutch shipping in Asia. For both the Medicis and the Ottomans, these mercantile polyglots and polymaths of Muslim heritage were potentially as much an asset to Livorno and Istanbul as Spaniard networks of Jewish heritage.

Still, many Moriscos were not entrepreneurs and merchants. Many others worked as skilled laborers in public works and infrastructural projects more generally. Interestingly, the Medicis appear to have been interested in both. For Stalvella and many wealthier Moriscos, Livorno was not an attractive enough destination to justify remaining given greater opportunities in Istanbul, Alexandria, Cairo, and the Levant. For a smaller group, there were business opportunities to be had specifically in connection with fellow Iberian exiles, especially Sephardic Jews.

Surviving notarial documents in the city of Tunis indicate that Morisco merchants sent shipments of leather to Jews in Livorno. Mostafa Barragan, for example, shipped a load of white animal skins in 1619 to Livorno, while Cristobal de Beldar shipped red and black leather. Dominico Fernandez procured a loan in 1615 that he guaranteed using a shipment of leather goods.[12] The international connections of Morisco merchants, likewise, were not limited to those who shared their Iberian heritage. A certain Juan Perez, also known as Mahamet Khayyar, partnered with a certain Mahamet Cimeniz and opened a soap-making factory in 1621 together with two Frenchmen and a German. The Frenchmen provided additional finances while the German added technical expertise.[13] The surviving Andalusi district of Tunis points to the history of specific Morisco families building a fortune from industries like leather tanning and textile or soap manufacturing, specifically in cases where they were able to expand the scale of the business and export. Al-Surdu Street, in particular, is a vestige of Ali al-Surdu (Spanish: El Sordo), who like Mustafa de Cardenas, Luis Zapata, and Juan Perez, was able to expand the scale of his business.

Given the parallel Iberian heritage of Sephardic Jewish exiles as well as the similarly trans-Mediterranean activities of both Iberian Muslims and Jews from Europe to North Africa and the Levant, Medici interest in the Moriscos comes as no surprise. In the long run, however, Morisco and *converso* communities diverged in terms of the longevity of their networks across time. In terms of language and identity, Moriscos did not hold onto their Iberian heritage and use of Romance languages to the extent that *converso* families did, and the dimensions of assimilation with co-religionists contrasted sharply. In the former case, Iberian Muslim family and business networks became absorbed into the Arabic- and Turkish-speaking milieu of Muslim commerce in North Africa and the Middle East, with enduring Hispano-Arab identities manifesting less in terms of commerce and more in terms of select cultural practices, clothing, and oral heritage connected with family genealogies. In the latter case, Spanish-speaking Iberian Jewish family and business networks remained an enduring phenomenon from Europe to the Middle East well into the twentieth century. The cultural and commercial prestige of the community caused other Jewish communities, especially Arabic-speaking North African Jews, to be absorbed into a Iberian (Sephardic) genealogical and linguistic cultural heritage—especially through marriage—that was celebrated well into the twentieth century through fluency in the community's archaic variety of Spanish and preservation of Spanish last names. Livorno's Jewish community, in particular, offers a multifaceted window into how the Italian peninsula was connected with Ottoman domains—from the Balkans and Istanbul to the Levant and North Africa—through a clear fluidity that characterized the region's cultural and legal borders.

Sephardic Jewish Networks in Livorno between Europe and North Africa

While Moriscos increasingly lost the Iberian languages that once connected their short-lived networks from France to Istanbul, Spanish and Portuguese became the long-term community languages of Sephardic networks. The situation in Livorno paralleled Venice in certain ways, but there were key differences. In Venice, Sephardic Jews' fluency in both a community language—Spanish—and the local Venetian language facilitated the ability to conduct business across cultural, geographical, and political boundaries. The population of Jews in Venice generally, including Sephardic and non-Sephardic Jews, grew from almost 2,000 individuals in the 1580s to almost 3,000 in the 1640s, and to about 4,000 in the 1660s.[14] Sephardic Jews were just one component of the larger Jewish community of Livorno that included Ashkenazi and Levantine Jews. Together with the growth of the Jewish population in Venice was an expansion in the variety of their commercial activities and access to Venice's economy. Following an edict in 1516, Jews in Venice were required to remain in the *Ghetto Nuovo* and were limited to trade in fields like money lending and the textile trade, the latter having been one of the lucrative taxable enterprises motivating the Venetian Senate to allow long-term settlement of Sephardic Jewish communities.[15]

While Livorno paralleled Venice in terms of an official policy of cultivating Iberian Jewish interest in conducting trade in the city, the circumstances of Jewish residence could hardly be more different. Livorno was a port city separated from Tuscany's capital city of Florence, while Venice was both the capital of the Duchy of Tuscany and its central port city. Among the outcomes of this contrast was that even if the Florentines and Venetians shared questions about the ethics of allowing Catholic citizens unfettered opportunities to intermingle with non-Catholic subjects and foreign subjects in public and private spaces, the realities of geography called for different answers.

In Livorno, there was no Venetian debate about establishing hotels for Muslims who numbered among the Ottoman Empire's subjects (*fondaco dei turchi*), and there was no question of whether the Safavid domains' Muslim subjects had to stay in Venice's Turkish *fondaco* or rather at the residencies of Safavid Armenian subjects in the heart of the lagoon. There likewise was no debate about where to house German merchants, whether throughout the city or the German residence (*fondaco dei alemani*). The entire port city of Livorno was a center for foreign subjects and was intended to be one. For Jewish communities, this meant Livorno became a major crossroads of European, Middle Eastern, and North African mercantile networks in a way that was unprecedented in Europe. As in the case of Venice, Livorno's Jewish community was, in fact, multiple communities that grew from a meager population of 114 long-term residents in 1601 to 3,000 by 1689.[16] There were two demographics of Jewish merchants that were of particular significance in the city. The first were the previously mentioned *conversos*, that is, Jewish subjects of the Spanish and Portuguese crowns who had converted to Catholicism around the time of the Alhambra Decree. While Catholic in Iberia, many secretly observed Jewish practices. Once abroad, many converted back to Judaism, especially in Livorno. The second group overlapped with the first. These were Jewish subjects of the Ottoman Empire living throughout the Aegean and the Levant. They included Greek- and Arabic-speaking Jews of the earlier Byzantine, Fatimid, and Abbasid lands as well as generations of Iberian emigrants in the fifteenth century.

For Ferdinando I, the ambiguously Catholic and Jewish identities of many Sephardic Jews posed no obstacles in his initiative to build a bustling merchant community in Livorno. In his charter issued in 1593, known as the *Livornina*, he wrote that, "None shall be able to make any inquisition, inquiry, examination, or accusal against you or your families although living in the past outside our Dominion in the guise of Christians."[17] In other words, while New Christians from Jewish families were fending off accusations of Judaizing in the Spanish Americas, those who made it to Livorno in the same century were free to revert to Judaism. In the short run, the policy was inconsistent in its treatment of new arrivals. Within twenty years of its issuance, the implementation of the *Livornina* began to regard Iberian Catholics of Muslim heritage (Moriscos) and Jewish heritage (*conversos*) with greater scrutiny.

More specifically, in accommodation of the local offices of the Inquisition as well as pushback from Rome, Tuscan officials attempted to delineate Catholic from non-Catholic arrivals more sharply in order to prevent Livorno's general populace of Catholics from becoming interspersed with Iberians who might still observe Jewish and Muslim practices.[18] For Spanish *conversos*, whose networks included Portuguese *conversos* and reverted Jews in Amsterdam, this scrutiny commonly meant being pressured to revert to Judaism and living with Jews who arrived at the start of the *Livornina*. For Moriscos, who did not have a local Muslim community in Livorno, this greater scrutiny meant identifying as a Muslim from an Islamic kingdom or identifying as a run of the mill Spanish Catholic. In both cases, the result was a pattern of hiding all evidence of Morisco heritage.

The long-duration outcome was that Livorno became intertwined with Venice and a variety of eastern Mediterranean ports as one of multiple nodes of Sephardic Jewish commercial and social exchange. Sons were sent abroad for apprenticeships under other Jewish businesspeople, while daughters were married into families that became increasingly intertwined together through new kinship relations. These networks were far from limited to trans-Mediterranean contexts and extended to include northern European cities like London, Amsterdam, and Hamburg. Even further east and south, these networks extended to the Portuguese *Estado do India*'s capital city of Goa. In the northern case, Sephardi and Ashkenazi Jews occupied a similarly liminal space between local and foreign commercial networks, with each community's networks abroad stretching across vastly different geographies. The trajectories of their business and financial transactions were as broad as their origins. The Cardoso brothers, for example, were among a variety of merchants who straddled the many worlds of the Mediterranean. The Cardoso brothers were originally from Venice. Michael Cardoso was born in Venice in 1630 and practiced medicine both in Venice and Livorno. His skills eventually took him to Ottoman Tripoli, where he worked as the personal physician of the city's governor.

In the realm of charity, likewise, Livorno closely followed and eclipsed trends in Venice. Throughout the sixteenth and seventeenth centuries, Venice was a key center in Jewish charity networks whose services included freeing captives and responding to requests for support from communities both distant and near. By the eighteenth century, it was increasingly Livorno rather than Venice that was the central node in these global networks. In 1745, for example, a major fire caused Ottoman Izmir's Sephardic community to request funds from Jews in Livorno. Rather than donate the sum or hold a fundraising (*nedavah*) campaign in Livorno's central synagogue, as proposed by Livorno's *parnasim*, the governor had Izmir's community take a loan that would be paid back over four years and was guaranteed by Livorno-based merchants.[19]

In 1747, similarly, the Jewish community of Urbino dispatched two emissaries to raise funds not only in Livorno but also Venice, Ancona, Pesaro, Mantua, and Ferrara. The event illustrates the extent that Livorno, like Venice before it, became the central node of a growing regional network of Jewish commercial and civic life inside the Italian peninsula.[20] The city's reputation among Jews further north in England and further south in North Africa meant that individual Livornese Jews were involved in some of the most global Jewish events. In 1782, the Sephardic communities of Tetouan, Mogador, and Sale sent an emissary named Isaac Nahon to several Italian cities, Amsterdam, and London to help resolve problems related to debt and poverty. The Livornese community decided to step in and provide financial assistance, including the expenses for Isaac Nahon's travel.[21]

Fundraising to provide donations for Jewish communities in need abroad, the ransoming of captives (*pidyon shvuyim*) captured by pirates, and the provision of loans was as much an expression of Livornese Jewish solidarity with Jews abroad as it was a reflection of their own internal cohesion in the port city itself. That is, despite the variety of their activities, origins, and the multiconfessional nature of their own individual business networks, Livornese Jews were connected together by the variety of civic activities that were specific to their community in Livorno.[22] What also exerted a kind of centripetal force on Livornese Jews, keeping the community together despite the centrifugal dimensions of their sprawling business partnerships and even marriage networks, were the financial dimensions of the community's semi-autonomous legal existence.

In what echoed Ottoman law, Livorno saw a certain legal pluralism that was instituted in the city. Livorno's Jewish community was afforded a certain semi-autonomous legal jurisdiction with dual authority due both to the republic and to various sociopolitical institutions internal to the community. In the former case was the grand duke himself, who appointed five members from the Iberian Jewish community's leading families to a council with legislative and judicial authority. It was this latter council that represented an authoritative structure internal to the community. The council, known as the *massari della sinagoga*, was established in 1593 and administered the community's affairs. The members were typically wealthy merchants and were elected for one year. For civil cases and minor offenses, the directors of the community were assigned a certain legal authority held in check by the duke's own authority. The doge assigned a judge to confirm more severe criminal cases.

Taxation, likewise, served as a kind of centripetal force that connected the many Jewish merchants of Livorno both to the community's institutions and to the state. The *diritto nazionale* was a duty at the rate of ⅛ percent for resident Jews and ¼ percent for non-resident Jews on all goods imported and exported through Livorno. The *zorke zibbur* was an income tax of ½ percent for merchants with an income of more than 1,500 lira. There was also a tax on meat prepared according to the rules of *kashrut*. The affairs of the *massari*, preserved in part by archival evidence, illustrate that while Livorno was just a point of transit for the previously discussed Iberian Muslims heading across the Mediterranean to Istanbul and elsewhere, it was an enduring center of cultural production for Iberians Jews all around the world. This was particularly the case in the realm of printing.

Like Venice, Livorno became a center of a multiconfessional printing culture that included Greek, Armenian, and Hebrew printing presses. In the case of Hebrew printing in the seventeenth and eighteenth centuries, Livorno's print culture attracted rabbis from Ottoman lands and North Africa. Yedidiah Gabbai established the city's first printing press in 1649, called *La Stamperia del Kaf Nachat*. The *Yalkut Shimoni*, its first book, was published in 1650. The press was named after a treatise written by Gabbai's father published forty years earlier in Venice. By 1657, however, the press had closed, but it was not the last. Another press was established in 1740, while a full growth in Hebrew printing culture began to flourish in the 1800s. The connection of the name of Gabbai's original press to his father's early seventeenth-century work in Venice points to the continued relevance of Venice as a model for the printing culture in formation throughout seventeenth- and eighteenth-century Livorno. That earlier print culture in Venice saw the proliferation of writings in Hebrew, Armenian, and Greek scripts among languages printed on both sides of the Adriatic. As in the case of Venice, this mix of languages in Livornese print culture paralleled Livorno's mixed social culture. For Livorno, what it meant to be Christian went beyond Latin Christendom's Roman Catholics and included, respectively, Greeks connected with the Ottoman Empire and Armenians connected with both the Ottoman and Safavid empires.

Livorno's non-Catholic Christians: Greeks, Armenian, and English Networks

While the early Greeks of Livorno were Venetian subjects, the Greeks increasingly arrived as Ottoman subjects. Cosimo I invited Greeks to Livorno in 1564 in the context of the city's need for maritime labor. Dionisio Paleologo, a Basilian monk, facilitated the initial invitation of Greeks, leading to the arrival of a variety of sailors and individuals who worked in maritime industries. Part of the challenge was to incentivize Greek arrival through the promise of both financial and social benefits. At the heart of the Medicis' strategy to recruit Greek maritime expertise to the city was the construction of a Greek church, which would function as a shared communal space for sacred and social activities.

The Florentine government's promise of a Greek church to recruit Greek maritime experience ran into one obstacle, however. The Ecumenical Council of Florence (1438–1439) called for Greek churches to be in communion with the Catholic Church. The Greek Patriarchate in Byzantine Constantinople never ratified the Council's conclusions, but the Roman Catholic

Church restricted the independence of Greek churches in the Italian peninsula anyway. The Medicis attempted to navigate Latin–Greek tensions by simply forgoing the tradition of securing papal approval for a new church for the Greeks. In 1562, on the site of a former Augustinian hermitage, the Greek church of San Jacopo was established just a mile from Livorno's city center.[23] Despite the Medicis' not having secured papal approval for the church, San Jacopo was still officially expected to be in communion with the Catholic Church in accordance with customs seen previously throughout the Venetian republic. In other words, the Greek church in Florence was expected to be Catholic even if it followed the Byzantine liturgical rite. By 1601, Ferdinando also allowed the community to build Livorno's Santissima Annunziata on Via della Madonna, known also as the Chiesa dei Greci Uniti.[24] Despite similarly not securing papal approval for the church, the Medicis still supported the guidelines of the Ecumenical Council of Florence.

While the Medicis' construction of Greek churches certainly facilitated the movement of Greeks from the Venetian republic and Ottoman sultanate, Greeks were under intermittent scrutiny by the offices of the Inquisition that suspected Greeks—whether Byzantine-rite or Latin-rite—of adhering to Orthodox rather than Catholic practices. Part of what propelled the activities of the Inquisition was the social proximity of these Greeks, who were officially Catholic, with the wider Catholic population with whom they intermarried. Indeed, on the one hand, Greeks represented a kind of residential national unit similar to what the growing Sephardic Jewish community became.

This conception of a Greek *nazione* in Tuscany is what allowed Manoli Volterra, a Greek immigrant from Venetian-held Zakynthos, to be named governor of Livorno and "protector of the Greek nation" (Florentine: *protettore della nazione greca*) simultaneously in 1589. On the other hand, Livorno's Greeks were unlike Livorno's Jews in terms of the close confessional proximity between the Greeks and the wider Catholic population. At least nominally, Livorno's Byzantine-rite and Latin-rite Greeks were Catholics insofar as their association with local unionist Greek churches was concerned. Rather than promote a kind of solidarity between the two groups, however, the proximity undergirded the Catholic Church's suspicion of enduring Orthodox practices among the Greeks generally and the activities of the Santissima Annunziata church specifically.

In some sense, in other words, the Inquisition attempted to work against the reality that Venetian and Ottoman Greeks who came to Tuscany had begun to straddle the worlds of their own Greek *nazione* within Livorno and the wider Latin population. It was a kind of cultural porousness and cultural convergence within a wider Catholic sociocultural context that caused church officials in the early 1600s to push Livornese officials to have Iberian *conversos* revert to Judaism. That is, from the Inquisition's perspective, Catholics of Jewish heritage should revert to Judaism for the same reason that Catholics of Greek heritage should be held under greater suspicion: in order to more clearly delineate Catholic and non-Catholic boundaries. What reveals something about the disunity of the Catholic Church's policies was the very fact that it was Ferdinando de' Medici himself who invited to Livorno all of these groups, that is, the Iberian Catholics of Muslim heritage (Moriscos), the Iberian Catholics of Jewish heritage (*conversos*), and the Greeks. His inclination to have these groups come to Livorno echoed the earlier Medici popes' flexibility with Jewish settlement in papal-held Ancona along the Ancona–Ragusa–Istanbul route.

In a surprising escalation of tensions, the 1620s saw the Catholic Church launch formal accusations against "Greeks who reside in Livorno, who are not only schismatics but heretics as well. They live as such and thus cause great scandal and damage to the Catholic Italians."[25] The escalation coincided with the push to have newly arriving *conversos* declare themselves Jewish and live with other Jews. This distinction between Greeks being pushed to adhere to Catholicism and *conversos* having to revert to Judaism became intertwined with a broader shift in Christian and Jewish access to Tuscan citizenship. While Livorno's Jewish community was able to acquire Tuscan citizenship without converting to Catholicism, non-Catholic Christians were required to conform to Catholicism at least outwardly. Protestant captains, for example, could be granted grand ducal corsairing licenses upon becoming Roman Catholic.

The outcome was that Tuscan citizens in Livorno, while technically just Catholic and Jewish, were actually a cultural variety in accordance with the variety of people petitioning to naturalize as Tuscan citizens. The *cento cittadini*, Livorno's governing body, included a mix of figures eligible for citizenship in 1604: Thomas Hunt of England, former German–Dutch consul Matteo

Bonade, an applicant from Ireland, and two Greeks.[26] In 1665, a prominent Armenian merchant named Antonio Bogos was on the list. The presence of Armenian Catholics in Livorno comes as no surprise given their influence in Venice. Armenian Orthodox families that became Catholic in Venice included the famous Scerimani (Shahriman) family, who played a prominent role in Venetian–Safavid relations a century earlier. All of these examples of naturalization and its outcomes—Venetian and Ottoman Greeks intermarrying with local Catholics, Armenians making Livorno a new node in their Venetian–Ottoman–Safavid networks, a former German consul becoming Tuscan—points to the unique possibilities of social and political mobility that Livorno offered non-Catholics in the Mediterranean world. The appeal of this mobility, however, was mixed. This was particularly true of the English, for whom Livorno's Catholicism was less appealing than its commercial importance as a potentially key Mediterranean node for the rising British Empire.

Englishmen and the Rise of the British Empire

The arrival of British merchants in late sixteenth-century Livorno coincided with the Tudor policy of expanding into the Mediterranean. In 1592, the last of the five Tudor monarchs, the renowned Queen Elizabeth I, granted a charter to four Englishmen to establish the Levant Company. The company's purpose was to cultivate British trade with the Ottoman Empire, especially the Ottoman Levant. It was one of a variety of companies that predated the East India Company and was tasked with fostering British trade in a particular part of the so-called Orient, in this case the Middle East as opposed to the Far East. The names of the Levant Company's predecessors, namely, the Venice Company and the Turkey Company, fit the realities of early sixteenth-century European trade. Going into the sixteenth century, the Venetian republic was the premier player in European competition for access to Asia's silk, silver, and spice commodities. By the mid-sixteenth century, advances in Iberian shipping and navigation technology allowed the Portuguese to secure trade privileges in Macau adjacent to Hong Kong. It would be another century before the British and Dutch almost entirely eclipsed the Portuguese in seventeenth-century East Asia through the activities of the British and Dutch East India companies. By the end of the eighteenth century, on the heels of the French revolutionary wars and Napoleon's invasion of the Italian peninsula, Livorno had become one of the central Mediterranean nodes of a global British trade network.

In comparison with the Greeks, what was unique about the arrival of Englishmen in Livorno was the extent that they were connected with an increasingly powerful and industrial British Empire. The outcome was that the English of Livorno increasingly eluded the expectation of fitting into the Catholic mold and, simultaneously, increased British cultural capital in Tuscany in the lead-up to the French invasion. In other words, moving into the eighteenth century, the English increasingly represented a local connection to one of Europe's rapidly industrializing superpowers that, through the English of Livorno, played a role in some of the political and industrial reforms of the Italian peninsula's northern regions.

This connection of the English with the British Empire in the eighteenth century was in contrast to their earlier presence as merchants who, like the Greeks, frequently naturalized as Tuscan Catholics in accordance with the political and cultural capital that the Florentines cultivated in competition with the Venetians. In those earlier decades of English presence, there was even some resistance to newer English arrivals more closely connected with the rising empire. Thomas Hunt, recorded as being eligible for citizenship, was simultaneously consul of the English nation (*nazione*) and a vocal critic of the English captains who came to Livorno in the 1600s. Hunt thought they might pose a problem for English political and social life in Livorno.[27] In 1610, Hunt warned Livorno's regional administrator (*provveditore*) about the arrival of three English ship captains whom he described as "men of nefarious business," "not Catholic," and "rebels of the King" who would likely "do something to lose the grace of their Highness and of the entire [English] *nazione*."

By the mid-1600s, the tide had turned. The English nation was increasingly Protestant and formed the basis of the British Factory. Archival evidence preserved in *Lloyd's List* illustrates that by the 1770s, Livorno had grown to become the most frequent port of call for British vessels.[28] In the decades before the British were able to negotiate a one-sided trade deal with the Ottomans to allow English cotton to flood the Ottoman market, English products were shipped to the eastern Mediterranean from Livorno. According to a merchant from Bristol, the impact was massive:

At least one half of Italian people wore English cloth and almost two thirds of them ate about three days in a week the salted fish which 800 to 900 English ships yearly carried here [Livorno] from the far English fisheries. Moreover, the most elegant houses were fitted up with English furniture and the rich families bought produce of East and West Indies.[29]

British presence, in other words, saw a certain cultural convergence between English cultural production and Tuscan social customs, particularly among Florentine elite circles with perpetually increasingly tastes for the British Empire's global fashions. Livorno's future, however, would not be British but rather French. In the lead-up to the French occupation of both Italy and North Africa, the French became the beneficiaries of certain patterns of cultural convergence that linked North Africa with Italy.

Figure 9.3 In an illustration of the global connections of Livornese Jewish networks, travelers to Fez who met local Livornese Jewish communities were struck by how individual members were multilingual—frequently able to speak Arabic and Tuscan (Italian)—and dressed variously according to both local and European fashions.
Source: https://en.yabiladi.com/articles/details/81428/jewish-pilgrimage-morocco-shlomo-aben.htm, public domain.

Transnational Tuscans in Fez and Tunis

Livorno's centripetal attraction of Mediterranean trade diasporas to Tuscany had an interesting centrifugal counterpart: the expansion of Tuscan culture, including language, back into the global communities connected with these trade diasporas. One of the most unique and complex examples of this pattern was the case of Livornese Jews. Largely Iberian in heritage, Livornese Jews in the sixteenth and seventeenth centuries frequently spent extended periods of time in North Africa among other Iberian Jews who settled in the Arabic-speaking worlds of North Africa. The result was an interesting pattern of cultural convergence. Some Livornese Jewish communities became gateways for local Jews to become Italianized, while others became acculturated to the local Arabic-speaking Jewish milieu. With the rise of the Napoleonic Empire and the subsequent growth of an Italian national movement, Livornese Jews became one of the earliest communities to cultivate Italian cultural transfer outward throughout the cities of North Africa.

By the nineteenth century, in the lead-up to the rise of an Italian kingdom and the competition between France and Italy over control of North Africa, Livornese Jews with access to French citizenship found themselves in the middle of competing European cultural policies oriented around expanding French and Italian cultural influence in the so-called orient. It was a precarious position fraught with the complexities, as both France and Italy were in the process of deciding what it meant not only to be French or Italian, but also European. That conversation about European identity, discussed in the next chapter, was in formation within the Livornese Jewish community itself as it began to straddle the worlds of Italian-speaking Tuscany and Arabic-speaking North Africa in the decades leading up to the Napoleonic conquests of Venice, Genoa, and Florence.

From Between Morocco, Tuscany, and the Netherlands

According to the *ballottati*, between 1753 and 1807, some 29 percent of immigrants in Livorno were Jews from North Africa. By the end of the nineteenth century, 13 percent of Livorno's total Jewish community was North African. Families in Livorno of North African origin included the Abudarham, Ben Attar, De La Mar, Akrish, and Delevante.[30] Names like De La Mar and

Delevante tell us something about origins. Among the Arabic-speaking Jews of North Africa were families of Iberian origin, just as the Livornese Jews were largely Iberian in their heritage. What is more, both in North Africa and in their travels to Livorno, North African Jews defied trends of custom and culture. Linguistically, at least a sizeable portion adhered to the use of Arabic once in Livorno. Still, the use of Arabic did not preclude fluency in Italian, and specifically the prestige Florentine dialect used in Livorno that became the national language in the twentieth century. North African Jews were multilingual and were able to straddle the worlds of North Africa and Europe in a way that observers found remarkable. The example of Samuel Romanelli's observations during a visit to Morocco offers one example of this.

In the writings of Samuel Aaron Romanelli (1715), a Lombardy-born Jewish writer, the image of cultural convergence emerges with some clarity. Romanelli observed how North African Jews were able to bridge the semiotics and customs of multiple geographies in what reflected the reality that multiple waves of European Jews from Iberia and the Italian peninsula settled in North Africa throughout the 1500s and 1600s. In his travels to Mogador, he describes the following:

> It was the day prior to Rosh ha-Shana even, and there was a circumcision celebration being held in the home Abraham de Lara. He was from Amsterdam and had come to Morocco, where he became successful and settled down. He married the daughter of R. Gedalya, the richest man in all Morocco. I was among those invited, so I went. I must confess that I was indeed astounded when I saw a group of men there actually seated on chairs and dressed in our fashion. They included the master of the house and his brother, the four sons of Gedalya, a member of the Abudarham family from Gibraltar with his two sons, three members of the Akrish family from Livorno, and a man named Pinto, who though a Moroccan, was also splendidly dressed in our style. The rest of the people were local inhabitants.[31]

The mix of Jews from Morocco, Amsterdam, and Livorno in the Mediterranean port, together with the description of their clothing, is illustrative of the various ties of kinship, commerce, and culture that connected Jewish communities across the Mediterranean. "Abudarham," Rossellini explains, "was proficient in many languages, examined my words, tested my ability in languages, and cited many proverbs to test my knowledge."[32] The names appear in a variety of contexts in Livorno. Hayyim ben Attar was a seventeenth-century Moroccan rabbi who spent more than a year in Livorno, where he raised money to publish his major torah commentary known as *ha-hayyim*.[33]

Gorni (Livornese) Jews and Tunsi (Tunisian) Jew in North Africa

While the activities of Livornese Jews around the Middle East and North Africa would suggest that they were a cohesive cultural group around the Mediterranean and an agent of Livornese cultural transfer in Arabic-speaking and Turkish-speaking regions, the situation was naturally more complex. Tunis was just one many cities where Livornese Jews conducted business. They were also in Tetouan, Safi, Essaouira, Gibraltar, Algiers, Alexandria, Cairo, Sidon (Sayda), Aleppo, Salonica, and Smyrna. Across these cities, there were varying patterns of cultural convergence between the Livornese Jewish merchants, who were subjects of the Tuscan duke, and local North African Jews, who were often under Ottoman authority. Many of these Arabic-speaking Jews shared the Sephardic heritage of the Livornese, even if their respective customs had diverged sharply throughout the sixteenth century.

In Arabic, the Jews of North Africa came to be identified as either Tunisians (*tunsi, twansa*) or those from Leghorn (*gorni, grana*), that is, the Livornese. The reference to local North African Jews as the *tunsi* Jews, or the *twansa* in the plural, dates back to the Hafsid period (1229–1574) of Tunisia, which followed the Almohad period and preceded the Ottoman period. The term *gorni*, technically *il-gorni*, is connected to the Arabic word for Leghorn (Livorno). The *grana*, as the Livornese Jews were called in the plural, were not a static European group in seventeenth- and eighteenth-century North Africa. In fact, the distinction between them and local Arabic-speaking North African Jews was a blurry one because of an interesting outcome of their frequent travel to and from North Africa: some Livornese Jews became acculturated to the local Arabic-speaking Jewish milieu, and in some cases never returned to Tuscany.

In the case of Livornese Jews who came to Tunisia in particular, there were successive waves of immigration that saw arrivals become acculturated to the local Arabic-speaking Jewish milieu. After the initial Inquisition-era wave of earlier Iberian Jews who went directly to Tunis, there was the early wave that came some one hundred years in the late 1500s. Many of these new Livornese arrivals, like their fellow Iberian-heritage predecessors, lived in Jewish neighborhoods, became subjects of the Tunisian *bey*, and experienced the same kind of cultural convergence seen among earlier Iberian Jews who were Arabized by the pull of the markets and North African Jewish social life.

Other Livornese Jews arriving in the late 1500s as part of a second wave appear to have held more strongly onto their identities, including the use of Spanish or Italian in speech, the use of Portuguese in account books, and the use of Spanish and Portuguese names rather than Hebrew names and naming patterns. One of the enduring pulls towards Tuscany for these emigrants was the arrival in the 1600s and early 1700s of even more waves of Livornese Jews, who worked as bankers, physicians, business representatives, and advisors to the bey. Echoing the exchange between Tunisian ruling circles and Norman Sicily in the twelfth century, Livornese Jews facilitated the export of local agricultural commodities like olives, almonds, cereals, and dates in exchange for a variety of European goods.[34]

By 1710, Livornese Jews formally distinguished themselves from the Arabic-speaking Jews by forming a distinct synagogue.[35] The two communities, which were supplemented by new arrivals from Christian and Muslim regions, had demarcated their social institutions with distinct synagogues, schools, butchers, cemeteries, and governing structures.[36] By 1741, they had their own burial grounds. From a governing perspective, the fundamental distinction of the two groups was one in status. The former were subjects of the bey, and the latter subjects of the Tuscan doge. Given the existence of wealthy groups on both sides, what tied down the contrasting pull were socioeconomic distinctions oriented less around class and more about markets and geography. While the *grana* were oriented around Tuscany's markets, the *twansa* were oriented around the local Arab markets.

What was new about the eighteenth and nineteenth centuries of this history was the Napoleonic Empire and its impact on citizenship. Napoleon's conquest of the northern Italian peninsula subsumed those Livornese Jews who were still under Tuscan subjecthood into French citizenship, which meant that vast swaths of Jews on both sides of the Mediterranean were suddenly French in the 1800s. What was interesting about this shift was how it fit into a much longer process of North African Jewish circles that predated and followed the Napoleonic conquest being pulled into the Tuscan side of this two-way cultural transfer. That is, while the sixteenth and seventeenth centuries saw waves of the *grana* assimilate into the local Arabic-speaking Jewish communities, the eighteenth and nineteenth centuries frequently saw Arabic-speaking North African Jews become Livornese. What points to the growing pull of the Livornese market in this eighteenth- and nineteenth-century process is the experience of North African Jews further west, specifically in Morocco. In places like Fez, a larger percentage of the local Arabic-speaking Jews shared the Iberian heritage of Livornese Jews who traveled southward for business. While the early centuries of this history saw strong trends of cultural convergence that pulled Livornese Jews into Fez's Arabic-speaking Jewish worlds, the immediate lead-up to the Napoleonic invasion saw numerous Morocco-based Jewish families head to Livorno and settle throughout Europe.

With the rise of the Napoleonic Empire in the late eighteenth century, large swathes of Livornese and North African Jews on both sides of the Mediterranean became French subjects. The shift in status of Jewish communities from the subjecthood of Florentine and North African rulers to that of the French foreshadowed the start of what would become, by the late nineteenth century, a contested relationship between the Italian and French kingdoms over political and cultural influence in North Africa.

10

ITALIAN CITIZENS BETWEEN ROME AND THE EAST (*LEVANTE*)

Figure 10.1 By 1812, the Napoleonic armies—unprecedented in their scale and organization—brought the first French Empire to its greatest territorial extent. In the Italian peninsula, the empire took control of the Grand Duchy of Tuscany (est. 1569) and set the stage for the transformation of Ottoman Algeria and Tunisia into French protectorates in 1830 and 1881, respectively. The French empire's conquests, occurring in the aftermath of the antimonarchist French Revolution, helped to set in motion a variety of local debates throughout the eastern Mediterranean about the value of French antimonarchist ideals and the potential benefits of a move towards a more elective constitutional republic. In cities like Livorno and Ottoman Istanbul, these debates would see a political turn away from the varieties of communitarian subjecthood seen for centuries under the governance of the Medici doges and Ottoman sultans.
Source: https://www.avvo.com/legal-guides/ugc/history-immigration-in-us https://www.dante.global/en/la-dante/history, public domain public domain over than fifty years.

The Italian Unification Movement in the Aftermath of Napoleon

Napoleon and the French Conquest of Tuscany and North Africa

By the late 1700s, France was on the brink of a revolution that would have a massive impact on Italy's later unification as a single Italian kingdom. The

French Revolution (1789–1799) transformed the French state from a monarchy into a republic that brought about massive shifts in the institutional structure of the French military. The French Revolutionary Army, which was a mix of the old aristocratic army and new recruits, was the force that led the notorious French revolutionary wars across Europe and gave rise to the enduring Napoleonic empire.

What came to be known as the War of the First Coalition saw the First French Republic engage in armed conflict against various European powers that included, by 1792, the Habsburg-controlled regions of the Low Countries (Netherlands) and the kingdoms of northern Italy. The Netherlands was also the heart of the global Dutch empire, which seceded from the Habsburgs in 1581 and oversaw the mighty Dutch East India Company (VOC). In the Dutch empire's place, the French established the Batavian Republic in 1795. The Treaty of Campo Formio, signed in 1797 by Napoleon Bonaparte and Austrian monarch Count Philipp von Cobenzl, saw much of the Netherlands pass into French hands. Northern Italy was turned into a variety of French republics. By 1797, the First Coalition had collapsed, leaving only Britain on the battlefield against the French Republic.[1]

It was during this War of the First Coalition that the so-called Italian campaigns were fought, witnessing the rise of Napoleon Bonaparte. In 1796, Napoleon was appointed Commander in Chief of the French *Armée d'Italie* and set out for the Italian peninsula. The last prominent member of the Medicis, Gian Gastone de' Medici, had already been succeeded by Francis Stephen of Lorraine and his wife Maria Theresa in 1737, initiating the Habsburg–Lorraine line of rule during the last decades of the Grand Duchy of Tuscany's existence. By 1801, the Duchy of Tuscany was dissolved altogether and replaced by the Kingdom of Etruria under the rule of the Bourbon–Parma dynasty.

By 1807, the kingdom was annexed to France, with Napoleon reviving the grand duchy under the rule of his sister Elisa. The following decades would see a new French-controlled Duchy of Tuscany begin a process of breaking with the political legacy of Medici governance. While the Medicis built Livorno as multicultural trade zone on Tuscany's periphery, the new French government's politically liberalizing policies brought Livorno closer to the center of Tuscan political and civic life.[2] Both the Genoese and Venetian republics had succumbed to Napoleonic rule just ten years earlier in 1797 in what laid the groundwork for a unification of the former empires under a single political entity.

Outcomes of the Napoleonic Period

From the perspective of a rising unified Italian kingdom (est. 1861), there were three outcomes of the Napoleonic period and the tumultuous political and social shifts of the 1800s. The first outcome was the eruption of an Italian national movement oriented around democratic liberal citizenship, which contrasted both to communitarian conceptions of citizenship and monarchical notions of ruler–subject relations. This process pulled Roman Catholics, many Jews, and many families of religiously or linguistically Greek parentage into a shared conception of being "Italian." What offset this centipedal pull were a variety of connected centrifugal forces that included the following: rising debates about whether the fourteenth-century Tuscan dialect of Dante and Petrarch ought to be so strictly fashioned into the prestige national language; how "Italian" exactly were Roman Catholics of frontier ports like the heavily Slovenian-speaking Adriatic city of Trieste; the multidimensional linguistic orientation and sprawling kinship networks of groups like Sephardic Jews; and the adherence of many Livornese and Venetians of Greek parentage to Greek Orthodoxy and the Greek language amidst the simultaneous emergence of Greek nationalism.[3]

The second outcome of the Napoleonic period, which builds on these centrifugal forces offsetting the centripetal pull of Italian nationalism, was the rise of a French–Italian political rivalry in the Mediterranean. This rivalry impacted the sprawling Tuscan-speaking worlds outside the peninsula. More specifically, large swaths of the Italian-speaking diasporic communities—especially Tuscan Jews resident in North Africa—became linguistically and politically French.

That is, in summary of these first two outcomes, the political developments of the 1800s saw contrasting forces that simultaneously pulled a linguistically and religiously diverse variety of peninsular residents into a rising modern "Italian" subjecthood while pushing others out. The middle position of Tuscan Jews, rising to the position of Italian prime ministers in the 1860s while simultaneously losing their Italian political status over in Algeria and Tunisia, illustrated the way the political and cultural boundaries of Italy were still taking shape. The same can be said of the many Italo-Greeks of Tuscany who became central players in the rise of Greek nationalism, even as the contemporary history of the Venetian Greek colony illustrates the extent that much of the peninsula's Greek-speaking Greek Orthodox world had largely become Catholic and lost the Greek language.

A third outcome was the rise of a new diaspora of Roman Catholic Italians, distinct from the older Genoese families of the Spanish Americas and the Venetian families of the Ottoman domains, who headed for the industrializing late nineteenth-century worlds of cities like Alexandria (Egypt) and Ottoman Istanbul in search of opportunities that eluded them in the early Italian kingdom. By the start of the twentieth century, these so-called Levantine Italians represented one of the last chapters of a millennium-long history of connections between Italy and the worlds of the Middle East and North Africa. Changes in the legal privileges of foreign passport holders in the rising Republic of Turkey and Arab Republic of Egypt saw a variety of these Cairo- and Istanbul-born *Italiani Levantini* head to their "homeland" from the 1920s through the 1960s, marking an almost total end to the millennium-long history of Italy's involvement in the worlds of the Middle East and North Africa. For some of the famous Levantine Italians, such as Cairo-born singer and actress Dalida (Iolanda Gigliotti), countries like France would be their final home. For a select few, an enduring life in a modern Turkish subaltern was worth living. What follows is a closer look at the beginning of this post-Napoleonic redefinition of Italian-ness starting in Tuscany.

The Short-Lived Rise of a Multiconfessional Tuscan Republic 1848–1849

In 1848, Grand Duke Leopold II agreed to popular demands for a constitution that would establish a more democratic form of shared governance. In what moved Tuscany further away from the history of communitarian subjecthood seen in Livorno, the new constitution (*statuto*) declared all subjects equal before the law, though Roman Catholicism was declared the state religion.[4] This statement constituted the culmination of growing republican conceptions of liberal citizenship, which was in contrast to earlier communitarian notions of subjecthood encouraged by the Medicis in Livorno and the ruler–subject relationship dictated by traditions of royal governance. Leopold's statement represented the culmination of a decades-long process that saw politically liberal reformers push antimonarchist ideals. These antimonarchist ideals were solidified during the 1822 Congress of Vienna, which saw the so-called four Great Powers—Austria, Britain, Russia, Prussia—redraw the boundaries of European powers during the aftermath of the French revolutionary and Napoleonic wars. The three decades following the Congress of

Vienna saw antimonarchist nationalist revolutionary ideals continue to pick up pace throughout the Italian peninsula, which remained divided under partial Austrian rule following the Congress of Vienna.

Like the Duchy of Tuscany, a variety of northern regions that originally fell to Napoleonic rule were also subsumed into Austrian rule. Aside from Modena and Parma, the most significant was the Republic of Venice. Its historical competitor, the Genoese Republic, was subsumed into a restored Kingdom of Piedmont-Sardinia. The Papal States, meanwhile, were restored to papal authority. It was against this backdrop that Livornese Jews, like Tuscans more broadly, participated in the growing discourse of republican liberal citizenship and the rise of the *Risorgimento* (unification) movement.

The three decades from the 1820s through the 1840s were a particularly formative period when both Tuscan subjects and Tuscan ruling circles became intertwined with the wider language of liberalism pushed elsewhere in the Italian peninsula by figures like Giuseppe Mazzini. Mazzini's "Young Italy," a secret society, promoted Italian unification under the guise of a single independent nation. By 1840, following failed uprisings, Mazzini was in exile in London. In spite of the apparent failure of the "Young Italy" movement, liberal reform movements remained active in provinces like Tuscany, where they called for changes in governance and the establishment of constitutions. And despite Grand Duke Leopold's (r. 1824–1859) nods to liberal modes of thought, including his implementation of a Tuscan constitution in 1848 and his allowance of a degree of free press, Tuscan reformers Francesco Domenico Guerrazzi and Giuseppe Montanelli still managed to rise to power at the head of a series of newly established parliaments and assemblies that eventually declared a short-lived republic lasting from 1848 to 1849. The grand duke went into exile, but only temporarily.

Upon Leopold's departure from Tuscany, Livorno and Lucca along the Tuscan coast fell under direct Austrian rule. Upon the invitation of a municipal council, the duke returned in order to maintain independence from the Austrians. In practice, the duke served only semi-independently of the Austrians. Following the near simultaneous arrival of the Austrians and Leopold himself in the city just days apart, Leopold—under the influence of the Austrians—cut short Tuscany's liberal reforms and had Guerrazzi and others imprisoned. By 1859, however, with France and Piedmont engaging

Austria in war, Leopold turned on the Austrians and joined the war under pressure from the wider Tuscan populace. Leopold formed a ministry under the leadership of Don Neri Corsini, who in turn presented Leopold with a popular demand for a Tuscan alliance with Piedmont and the reorganization of Tuscan governance as part of an eventual union with the rest of Italy. By June 1860, Leopold abdicated the throne, and Tuscany became part of the growing kingdom of Italy. Guerrazzi returned to prominence as a deputy in the Italian parliament from 1862 to 1870.[5]

Interestingly, as much as these decades saw the formation of a single Italian kingdom built on liberal citizenship, they also saw the beginnings of a still indefinite disappearance of Italian Jewishness and the burgeoning of a Roman Catholic Italian diaspora population in the Middle East, that is, the so-called Levantine Italians. In the former case, despite the fact that the office of the prime minister saw the appointment of two Jewish politicians (Alessandro Fortis 1905–1906, and Venetian-born Luigi Luzzatti 1910–1911), many Jews with ties to the Italian peninsula had long since become permanently disconnected culturally and linguistically. In particular, as discussed in the next section on the Italian diaspora, many Livornese Jews resident in North African cities like Tunis were permanently separated from Tuscany by unprecedented laws enacted after the Napoleonic period that required Livornese Jews resident in North Africa for more than a year to naturalize as subjects of the Tunisian beys. Across these same decades, new generations of Roman Catholic Italians similarly headed abroad to centers like Tunis, Alexandria, and Istanbul in search of new opportunities afforded by the Ottoman and Ottoman-affiliated domains' expansive industrialization reforms.

The long-term outcome was that precisely as the discourse on liberalization and unification was in formation from the 1820s to the 1860s, a multiconfessional Jewish and Roman Catholic Italian national diaspora came into existence across the Middle East and North Africa. It was a diaspora that had inconsistent claims to Italian citizenship and that was unevenly connected with the older diasporic populations, whether earlier generations of Livornese Jews or earlier generations of Venetians resident in Istanbul. What was most notable about this diaspora was how its trajectory diverged internally amidst the expansion of French political and cultural influence across North Africa and, in the long run, the Mussolini-era redefinition of Italian-ness: in the first

Figure 10.2 Yaqub Rafael Sanu (1839–1912) was of Livornese Jewish parentage on his father's side and Arabic-speaking Jewish heritage on his mother's side. Fluent in Italian (Tuscan), French, vernacular Egyptian Arabic, and a variety of other languages, Sanu was a Francophile and deep admirer of the vernacular Egyptian dialect of Arabic. His primary legacy was in his role as a foundational figure in cultivating Egyptian Arabic—as opposed to standard Arabic—as a written medium for new literary genres like political satire and modern Egyptian theater. Sanu received part of his education in Livorno under the patronage of the Turco-Egyptian khedives, who encouraged his early work as a playwright in the formation of Egypt's national theater. By the late 1800s, the rise of an Italian kingdom saw the rise of debates about what constituted "Italian-ness." Though Livornese Jews were native speakers of what became the national dialect (Tuscan), debates about Italian-ness eventually began to regard Roman Catholicism as a central part of Italian identity to the exclusion of Greek and Jewish identities. Greek-heritage Livornese in Tuscany even participated in the formation of Greek nationalism in the late 1800s, just as some Alexandrian Italians in Egypt like Tommaso Marinnetti participated in the evolution of Italian nationalism in the early 1900s. Sanu, in other words, lived in a time when debates about nationalism and citizenship throughout Europe, the Middle East, and North Africa saw transnational communities like Livornese Jews, Venetian Greeks, and the later "Levantines" (*Levantini*)—immigrants from the new Italian kingdom to the Middle East and North Africa in search of work (c. 1860s)—begin to debate which of the rising kingdoms-turned-republics was their rightful home.

Sources: https://hsje.org/Galleries/abu_naddara/image001.jpg, public domain; https://en.wikipedia.org/wiki/Isma%27il_Pasha#/media/File:Isma'il_Pasha.jpg, public domain; https://www.newyorker.com/books/page-turner/the-egyptian-satirist-who-inspired-a-revolution, public domain.

case, the French government both encouraged and coerced generations of Tuscan Jewish families in North Africa to become linguistically and politically French throughout the entire nineteenth century, leaving later generations to head to France together with the so-called *pieds-noir* upon the withdrawal of France from North Africa. In the second case, the so-called Levantine

Italians—Roman Catholic immigrants in search of opportunities in North Africa and the Levant—developed a permanent path to Italian citizenship in accordance with a Second World War-era re-identification of Italian-ness in terms of a vaguely defined mix of geographical, racial, and confessional criteria. For these Levantine Italians, memories of exile were not memories of an Italian homeland while living in the Middle East. On the contrary, having been born in cities like Cairo and frequently having become acculturated to the cosmopolitan worlds of centers like Alexandria and Istanbul, memories in exile were memories of their birthplaces "in the orient." Their stories were similar to those of the Alexandrian Greeks, who included offspring of refugees from the 1923 Greek–Turkish conflicts in Izmir. Like the Alexandrian Italians, they eventually looked for new opportunities in Europe following Egypt's turn to socialist Arab nationalism in the 1960s and 1970s. What follows is a closer look at the formation of this multiconfessional Italian national diaspora, and how both abroad and in Italy itself, the boundaries of Italian-ness by the end of the Second World War separated modern Italy from its millennium-long connections with its "orient."

A Multiconfessional Italian National Diaspora in Formation

The Separation of Livornese Jews from Italy

In the long run, the century and a half between the Napoleonic conquests and the Second World War-era career of Mussolini saw "Italian-ness" both within the Italian peninsula and abroad pegged to a combination of language, geography, Roman Catholicism, and, in the Mussolini era, race. Older Jewish families in Livorno were native speakers of the prestige Tuscan dialect that pushed out Venetian as the peninsula's prestige literary language and eventually national language. Still, in the aftermath of the Napoleonic era (*c*. 1801–1814), Livornese Jews occupied an increasingly ambiguous position in Italian political and social life. What caused these shifts were major changes in the legal and commercial dimensions of both Livorno and the entire peninsula.

Upon the restoration of the Duchy of Tuscany, Livornese Jews originally negotiated to reestablish the Jewish *nazione*, but they did so with limited results. Specifically, the communitarian political and social identity of Livornese Jews ran into legal challenges during the Napoleonic era. While three of the five *masarri* seats were restored, judges were not reinstated, which meant that all Livornese Jews were subsumed under the municipal and civil laws of the rest of the Livornese population. In a related development, in accordance with the growth in revolutionary fervor across the Italian peninsula, the early decades of the Napoleonic era saw Livornese Jews adopt an attitude towards the government more in line with liberal citizenship. At the same time, there was a contrasting political process that pulled Tuscan Jews away from Italy. Long before this process of Jews "becoming Italian" was both contested and undone in the lead-up to the Second World War, there already were examples in early nineteenth-century Tuscany of boundary delineation that curtailed the longstanding ability of Livornese Jews to straddle the many worlds of the Sephardic Mediterranean.

More specifically, as early as 1822, Tunis and Tuscany came to an agreement on bilateral trade stipulating that Livornese Jews resident in Tunis would have to become subjects of the Tunisian bey after just one to two years of residence. That is, in contrast to the way successive generations of Livornese Jews in seventeenth- and eighteenth-century Tunis maintained a linguistic and cultural connection with Tuscany, and in contrast to the way many late eighteenth-century North African Jews headed to Livorno in accordance with patterns of frequently shared Sephardic cultural convergence, this new legal arrangement in the early nineteenth century would facilitate a political severance of North Africa's many generations of Livornese Jews from the Tuscan duchy. This change was in sharp contrast to the way Roman Catholic Italians of the early twentieth century, the so-called Levantine Italians (*gli italiani levantini*), were welcomed back to Italy despite their reputation for having become deeply acculturated by marriage and language in the worlds of North Africa and the Levant.

In the 1820s, the policy of having Livornese Jews naturalize as subjects of the Tunisian bey had its detractors. Felice Padova, the Jewish community's chancellor, offered a clear criticism that amounted to wishful thinking: "I believe that our government in its policies and justice will not agree to such a condition so prejudiced against some of its subjects and so injurious to commerce."[6] The stipulation was clear, however, and it was implemented in the end. After one to two years, Jews in Tuscany "can no longer be regarded as Tuscan subjects under the protection of our consul but instead must be regarded as Tunisian subjects and therefore pay taxes and other duties as Jews."[7] Against the backdrop of a rising Italian–French political rivalry over cultural influence in the region, large swathes of these Tuscan Jews—together with North African Jews more broadly—became French. The origins of that process lay simultaneously in the French government's legal policies, which oversaw Jews in French Algeria register in French schools, as well as the activity of French Catholic clerics, whose hospitals and schools represented the first introduction of local Muslims and Jews to French culture.

From the Soeurs de St. Joseph to the Alliance Schools: French Hospitals and Schools from Algiers to Tunis

The late nineteenth-century rivalry between France and Italy over political and cultural influence in North Africa had its roots in the early decades of French expansion. France's power over Tuscany eventually challenged long-established Tuscan civic institutions—hospitals, schools, cultural organizations—in cities like Algiers, Tunis, and Alexandria. Algiers was annexed to French rule very early on in this rivalry in 1830. Tunis was subsumed into French rule in 1865 at the end of a much larger process of expanding French-Tunisian relations. A closer look at growing French-Tunisian connections will help to contextualize the story of how even Livornese Jews—that is, Jewish families with the closest connections with the Italian peninsula—became intertwined with the expanding Francophone Mediterranean world.

In the lead up to Tunisia's transformation into a French mandate, and in parallel with developments in Egypt under Muhammad Ali, Tunisia's officially Ottoman-appointed ruling Husaynid dynasty attempted to reform or "modernize" Tunisian governing institutions along French models. Between 1830 and 1860, the number of southern European immigrants in North Africa swelled from 2,000 or 3,000 to 10,000, including Sicilians, Sardinians, Maltese, Greeks, French, and less so, English, Spaniards, and Austrians.[8] This growth is partly explained by the increasingly direct and close relations the Tunisian Husaynid dynasty had with European ruling circles. Ruling beys Ahmed I ibn Mustafa (r. 1837–1855) and his successor Muhammad II ibn al-Husayn, officially Ottoman vassals, oversaw a series of modernizing reforms modeled after an industrializing Europe. Ahmed Bey's reign was notably contemporary with Muhammad Ali (r. 1805–1848), the famous modernizing reformer of Egypt.

Like Muhammad Ali in Egypt, Ahmed Bey had pretensions to conduct diplomatic and local affairs in at least partial independence of Ottoman ruling circles. Two of King Louis Philippe's (r. 1830–1848) sons, the duc de Montpesier and the prince of Joinville, visited Tunisia in 1845 and 1846, respectively. Part of the diplomatic missions' goal was to build French–Tunisian relations to the exclusion of British and Ottoman influence in the region.[9] The British were themselves wary of damaging their relationship with the Ottomans through direct diplomacy with the Tunisians, even eschewing the possibility of Ahmed Bey visiting London without an Ottoman envoy. In the long run, in the aftermath of French intrusion in Algerian and Tunisian affairs, the British were following closely behind in their own pursuit of Egypt.

Among the outcomes of French–Tunisian connections was the rise of French institutions of education and public health. In the 1840s, the most prominent among these institutions were run by clerical figures connected with the French Catholic clergy, specifically the nuns of the Soeurs de St. Joseph. The congregation was founded by Emilie de Vialar (1797–1856), a nun whose work in Tunisia built on her earlier work in French-held Algeria.[10] The French consul in Tunis and his wife had a positive view of charitable institutions run by French nuns, whose work in education and public health raised the French national profile in the eyes of competing powers simultaneously present in North Africa—especially the British.

Vialar established a hospital in Tunis, a pharmacy-like dispensary, and two schools with five nuns staffing each institution.[11] Ahmed Bey gave Vialar permission to rent a house in the non-European Muslim section of the city where Muslims and local Jews lived. There, she established a pharmacy, an outpatient clinic, and later an attached hospital called St. Louis. The congregation went on to establish a variety of establishments in Algeria and Tunisia with healthcare facilities, which were part of the early global use of anesthetic agents like chloroform for more complex procedures.

In parallel with these healthcare institutions were a variety of educational institutions. As in the case of the hospitals, the congregation's schools came to serve not only Catholics but also Jews and Muslims. Interestingly, Livornese Jews became intertwined with this world of French education and public health, and the story of a certain Abbe François Bourgade illustrates the extent that Livornese Jews were at a crossroads between enduring Italian influence and growing French influence in the affairs of both Europeans and North Africans in Tunisia.

Figure 10.3 Danielle Frida Hélène Boccara (1940–1996) was a French singer of Italian Jewish heritage. Though her career spanned several decades of the late twentieth century, her biography echoed the stories of Jewish lives of the late 1800s and early 1900s that had origins in the Italian peninsula, lived in Francophone North Africa, and eventually moved not to Italy but to France. Frida's family, like many families before hers, was of Italian origin and originally lived in Tunisia before moving in the early 1900s to Morocco, where Frida was born. As an adult, Frida moved to France where she embarked on a storied singing career with hits in both French and Italian. Her biography likewise paralleled the lives of Roman Catholic descendants of the Levantine Italians who moved to Alexandria in the late 1800s. Iolanda Gigliotti (Dalida), the Cairo-born daughter of Lombard immigrants, moved to France in the 1950s after starting her career in Arabic-language cinema in Cairo and reinventing herself in Paris as a singer of French, Italian, and Arabic songs.

Source: https://en.wikipedia.org/wiki/Frida_Boccara#/media/File:Grand_Gala_du_Disque_in_RAI_Amsterdam._Frida_Boccara,_Bestanddeelnr_923-3017.jpg, public domain.

Livornese Jews in Tunis between the Italian and French Worlds

The story of how the Soeurs de St. Joseph coexisted with the Francophone Alliance Israelite schools and the Colegio Italiano in mid-nineteenth-century Tunisia offers a window into how the multiconfessional Arabic-speaking worlds of North Africa became intertwined with a rising French–Italian cultural rivalry in the region. The example of French Catholic cleric Abbe François Bourgade and his connection with a Tunis-based Livornese Jewish family offers a particularly interesting window into how North African Jews broadly—long before they moved to France together with the French *pieds-noir*—came to straddle the Italian and French worlds even before the French claimed Tunisia as a protectorate.

When Abbe François Bourgade was active in Tunis opening a kindergarten in 1846, one of his closest associates was a Catholic woman from a Livornese Jewish family. Her name was Giulia Maria Giovanna. Giulia, in fact, had been known as Esther Sulema just three years earlier prior to her conversion from Judaism to Roman Catholicism. Esther's sister was Pompeo Sulema. In 1831, the sisters Esther and Pompeo Sulema were the Livornese Jewish co-founders of a primary school for local students.[12] By 1843, during her friendship with Bourgade, Esther had converted to Catholicism and married a French Catholic trader named David Menard. By 1845, the Sulemas' primary school merged with Bourgade's school. In the same decade, Bourgade's associates among the Soeurs of St. Joseph opened two girl schools in 1840. The congregation followed this with the establishment of another school where Europeans and Livornese Jews lived, and following that, more schools in three other Tunisian towns. Other French Catholic congregations likewise began to open schools, clinics, and orphanages in accordance with the example of the sisters of St. Joseph. Unsurprisingly, in the lead-up to Italian unification, Italian political authorities were working in parallel to build Italian schools throughout North Africa that rivaled French educational institutions. Interestingly, the same Livornese Jewish Sulema family involved with French Catholic schools participated in the Italian side of this development.

In 1863, the Italians of Tunis could be seen building schools under the patronage of the Italian government. That year, three years after the Huseynid bey granted the newly united Italian government land for a new educational institution, the Colegio Italiano was established.[13] Pompeo Sulema, sister of Giulia Maria Giovanna (Esther Sulema), was active in the school's administration. By the 1870s, the Italian government expanded its support for Italian educational institutions in Tunis. By that point, in the lead-up to Tunis' transformation into a French protectorate in 1881, the European population was far more linguistically Italian than it was French

Interestingly, precisely as Italian schools were starting to proliferate in Tunis, the famous Alliance Israelite French school system came into existence. The

Alliance Israelite Universelle (AIU) was known for having made North African Jews French speakers en masse. What distinguished the AIU's newer schools from Vialar and Abourgade's older schools was the explicitly multiconfessional dimensions of the older French educational project. While Bourgade and the Soeurs de St. Joseph came from a French Catholic tradition of bringing both public services and exposure to Catholicism to a variety of non-Catholics, the AIU was specifically oriented around the French education of Jews and not the wider Muslim population. What helped the AIU schools overtake the French Catholics' mission, and what ultimately facilitated the linguistic gallicization of North African Jews even beyond the borders of French colonial regions, was the support of the French government.

The French government supported the Alliance schools in what had the effect of linguistically gallicizing en masse both Italian- and Arabic-speaking Jews in North Africa and bringing them into closer cultural alignment with French Catholics. In neighboring Algeria, which became a French protectorate (1830–1962) some fifty years before Tunisia saw the same fate, Algerian Jews were legally required by the French government to register in French schools. The law, enacted in 1845, required Jews in Algeria to attend French schools and simultaneously prohibited rabbis from accepting students in rabbinical schools who were already registered in a French school.[14] The chief rabbi himself became an employee in the French civil service, and by 1920, French observers like historian Gautier could document what appeared to be a new and uncanny blending of North African Jewish and French Catholic cultural worlds:

> Apart from some important and imponderable exceptions, one cannot distinguish the Jews from the Christian anymore in Algeria. One needs to make an effort to remember that he is also a Maghrebi, as deeply rooted to the place as the others ... For fifteen centuries, it was clear that the Jews had lived in the Maghreb. And it was impossible to show that they came from anywhere else. They were not foreigners; they simply represented the mentality which had been formed and chosen among the mentalities of the Maghreb.[15]

This law contested the Italian- and Arabic-language dimensions of North African Jewish life. By the end of Algeria's French period, what had become an entirely Francophone Jewish population came to be viewed by local Muslims as being just as French as the French settlers known as the so-called *pieds-noir*. In a sense, North African Jews "returned to France" with the *pieds-noir*, even though it was only the latter who actually came from France while the latter only did so in the wider imperial sense of "France." What blurred the lines most between these French-speaking North African Jews—some of whom were of Livornese parentage—and French-speaking French Catholics was that technically, in terms of political status, North African Jews had been officially "French" ever since the French government granted French citizenship to Algerian Jews en masse in 1870. This change occurred three decades after Algerian Jews were required to register in French schools.

In neighboring Tunisia, which avoided French rule (est. 1881) as late as the 1870s, Jewish communities had a longer history of contesting the growing influence of French language and culture in Tunis. Jewish religious authorities criticized specifically the AIU schools' secularization of Jewish cultural institutions and social norms. This criticism amounted to a losing battle. In the long run, with respect to North African Jews across the spectrum of Livornese parentage and local Arabic-speaking parentage, the AIU schools contributed both to the cultural alignment of North African Jews with France and to their separation from the Maghribi Jewish legal customs that had a long history in North Africa's majority-Muslim lands. Notably, this Francophone Jewish separation from Maghribi Jewish legal customs also included the erosion of Italian Jewish customs.

In one of the most interesting windows into the degree that North African Jewish life was in the process of being Italianized before it was gallicized, AIU founders themselves remarked on the Italianization of local Jewish communities. Paul Mellon, one of the founders and a critic of the French clergy's decidedly multicultural and multiconfessional schools, noted in 1885 that, "The truth is that the Brothers and the Sisters employ both Italian and French as language of instruction, even giving Italian more emphasis in order to retain in our schools Sicilians and Italians who are the object of anti-French campaigns."[16] In other words, given the previously discussed cultural currency of Tuscan-speaking Livornese Jews among Arabic-speaking Tunisian Jews for several centuries, this new nineteenth-century French orientation of North African Jews represented a major rupture in what was originally becoming a very Jewish demographic within a rising Italian national diaspora in North Africa.

Interestingly, this process was already being offset both in North Africa and in Tuscany by two dimensions of the Tuscan government's mid-nineteenth-century laws: the first was the previously discussed law on naturalization, which pushed Livornese Jews resident in North Africa to give up pre-*Risorgimento* Tuscan subjecthood in favor of Tunisian subjecthood. The second was the complex choice created by the Italian unification movement: eschew Jewish transimperial communitarian identity as a multilingual Livornese *nazione* and become "Italians" within the growing discourse of liberal citizenship, on the one hand, or travel abroad throughout the communitarian networks of Sephardic commerce and culture and enjoy the benefits of a sprawling world of business and family, on the other. What made the latter option appealing at least for some Livornese Jews was the same attraction that pulled Roman Catholic Italians to cities like Alexandria and Istanbul: business opportunities in the modernizing kingdoms of North Africa and the Levant. For Italian Catholics, this process meant the rise of the so-called Italian Levantine community.

11

THE LAST LEVANTINES (*GLI LEVANTINI*)

Figure 11.1 While Italian "Levantine" (*Levantini*) families still live in Turkey and maintain connections with Italy through institutions like Italian private schools, the heyday of Istanbul's Levantine community was in the final decades of the Ottoman Empire. One of the principal events that saw the departure of the community from the Ottoman heartlands was the Italian–Ottoman War of 1911, which saw Ottoman administrators, in anticipation of the Italian invasion of Ottoman Libya, warn that any invasion would lead to the expulsion to Italy of the Levantine Italians.
Source: https://www.opiniojuris.it/levantini, public domain.

Italians in Late Ottoman Istanbul

In the lead-up to the First and Second World Wars, the Italian citizens who came to be known as the Levantines (*Levantini*) formed a robust group active throughout the heartlands of Ottoman and former Ottoman domains, from Istanbul and Izmir to the Ottoman-affiliated khedivate-turned-kingdom of Egypt. A mix of older Tuscan communities in exile and newer *Risorgimento*-era immigrants looking for opportunities in the industrializing cities of the Middle East and North Africa, the Levantines participated in a variety of trades across cities like Istanbul, Alexandria, and Cairo: insurance, banking, publishing, healthcare, food and beverage production, sales in the food and beverage industry, military manufacture, architecture and design, and various forms of design and aesthetic taste-making from apparel to architecture. The enduring legacy they left in the urban landscape, visual and material culture, black-and-white film culture, and the linguistic vocabulary of present-day Arabic-speaking Alexandria as well as Turkish- and Greek-speaking Istanbul offers a window into how much the modern social fabric of these regions was a product of Italians from all walks of life.

The Venetian Palace (*Palazzo di Venezia*), the current Italian consulate, presents one of the most interesting examples of how the Pera district continued to be a meeting place for Italians some 500 years after the Venetians established their extraterritorial agreements in the Ottoman capital. The reconstruction of the palace in 1853, in particular, offers an illustrative window into the variety of workers living in Istanbul who were part of construction contracts. In the decades leading up to the reconstruction, the palace had fallen into the hands of the Austro-Hungarian Empire, whose monarch Franz Joseph I sought to "raise the declining prestige of Austria in the Orient in every respect."[1] Architects Gaspare and Giuseppe Fossati received a lump sum as remuneration for the twenty-two week project, which employed a variety of Italian trades people.

According to the surviving inventory of restoration tasks and subcontractors hired, Italian artisans worked on every part of the building. Among them was Luigi Leoni, who was hired to renovate the fresco paintings throughout the palace.[2] Achille Bottazzi was hired to paint the entire palace, including ceilings and ornaments as well as its vestibules. A variety of local suppliers were likewise hired to work on more specialized parts, from metalwork and door handles to bronze and iron screws and locks. Among these suppliers was a certain Bianchi, who provided some of the metalwork, as well as a locksmith named Ravetti, a plumber named Rozario, and a bronze metalworker named Dapei. The family name Dapei appears throughout the Ottoman metropolis after 1835 in the world of metal-casting and metalwork. These suppliers typically operated factories and warehouses around Istanbul for industrial work. This was the case of the Camondo family that operated a brick factory after 1874.

In many cases, these companies operated up to the very end of the empire in the 1920s. The Ansaldo Company, active from 1882 to 1921, is just one example of a long history of late nineteenth- to early twentieth-century Italian private industry operating in service of Ottoman industrialization.[3] The company was involved among other things in the modernization of the Ottoman naval fleet. What was unique about the Ansaldo Company was the way it appears to have weathered the storm of Ottoman–Italian geopolitical conflicts, which erupted in the late nineteenth century and left an enduring impact on Levantine Italian communities that never regained their mercantile and social foothold in their adoptive "oriental" (*oriente*) homelands. What conditioned this late nineteenth-century political conflict was the transition of Italy from a unified kingdom to an expansionist imperial power, one with aspirations for conquest in the eastern Mediterranean in accordance with the contemporary models of colonial France and Britain.

For the *Levantini*, who stretched across the Ottoman Aegean and Levant to Egypt and North Africa, the rise of an expansionist Italian empire proved to be problematic. The Italian–Ottoman War of 1911–1912, which was sparked by an Italian invasion of Ottoman Libya, resulted in the Ottoman administration expelling to Italy anyone who had acquired Italian citizenship and who was working in the Ottoman Levant (Aleppo, Beirut, Jerusalem). Following on the heels of the Italian–Ottoman conflict were the Balkan Wars of 1912–1913, which saw the bulk of Adriatic Ottoman territories west of Istanbul secede in the lead-up to the First World War. The aftermath of the First World War, in turn, saw the British and French acquire the empire's Middle Eastern territories. Italy and Greece's postwar aspirations of claiming western Anatolia, secured by the Treaty of Sevres (1919), were cut short by the war that led to the establishment of the Turkish Republic and the updated Treaty of Lausanne (1923).

War and Flight 1911–1923

It was these years, from the Italian invasion of Ottoman Libya (1911) to the establishment of an independent Turkish Republic (1923), when Italian passport-holding residents of the Ottoman Levant witnessed the biggest upheavals in their own demographic. A certain Sir Robert Graves, a financial adviser to the Ottoman authorities in 1911, was able to comment on the situation first-hand. Graves wrote that a "large Italian colony" lived in Ottoman territory with "little interference" from the government.[4] What put their position in jeopardy was the Italian threat of invasion of Ottoman territories, especially Libya. By 1911, the year of the Italian invasion of Libya, the Ottomans found themselves in a militarily defensive position vis-à-vis the two major blocs that were in formation: the so-called Triple Entente consisting of France, Britain, and Russia, and the Triple Alliance made up of Germany, Italy, and the Austro-Hungarian Empire.

In the lead-up to the 1911 Italian invasion of Ottoman Libya, the Italian press back in the peninsula pushed for public support of the invasion. This anti-Ottoman media blitz took place against the backdrop of an enduring Austrian (Austro-Hungarian), British, and French presence throughout formerly Ottoman-held eastern Mediterranean regions dating back to the late 1800s. Ottoman losses occurred on all sides of the empire in the late 1800s, including the northwest frontiers with Russia. The Russian–Ottoman War of 1877 saw Russia annex the Ottoman-held Caucasus, including southwestern Georgia. The war also coincided with the formal emergence of independent political powers in the Balkans, including the Principality of Bulgaria.

The Congress of Berlin in 1878, one year after the Russian–Ottoman War, allowed other powers to annex various Ottoman territories: the Austro-Hungarian Empire claimed Bosnia-Herzegovina, Britain claimed Cyprus, while the French were allowed to occupy Ottoman Tunisia some fifty years after their annexation of Algeria. The French occupation of Tunisia, which took the Francophile Bey of Tunis Muhammad III al-Sadiq by surprise, occurred despite Italy's protests. By 1902, France and Italy agreed that Italy would have priority over any future intervention in Ottoman Libya and the Moroccan sultanate. By 1911, the Italian press joined the fervor for invasion, calling for the conquest of Libya. The Italians sent an ultimatum to the Ottomans to transfer the territory, to which the Ottomans partly conceded on the condition that Libya remain under official Ottoman rule at least in name. Italy refused and invaded, and despite promises by the Italian press of a quick and easy war, the process lasted for a year and saw various episodes of prolonged violence.

The Italian invasion of Libya proved to be a much darker and more drawn out affair than the image originally sold by the Italian press, and it was during this invasion that Ottoman diplomats in Europe began to predict an Italian invasion of the Ottoman Aegean. Anticipating the very real threat of Italian hostilities extending as far east as Anatolia's Mediterranean coast, Ottoman diplomats in early twentieth-century Berlin and Vienna—Nizami Pasa and Fuat Bey, respectively—were told to communicate to the major powers of Europe the following message: the Porte would not shy away from a general expulsion of all Italian citizens from Ottoman territories if Italy invaded the Anatolian coast and the Aegean islands where the British were active in Cyprus. Despite multiple threats across several months in 1911, Italy invaded the Ottoman Aegean anyway, and the Ottomans went ahead with the expulsion. Like the Ottoman Greeks during the 1923 Greek–Turkish population exchange, some of these Italians poured into the Egyptian khedivate's port city of Alexandria.

Alexandria, where an Italian and Greek population continued to thrive well into the 1950s, was shielded from the kind of Italian invasion and Italian Levantine population transfer seen in the region for at least two reasons. Firstly, it was already within the political sphere of a European power, namely, the British. Secondly, the longer survival of the originally Ottoman affiliated dynasty until 1953—with its Ottoman-like demographic mix and its enduring legal pluralism complete with broad extraterritorial agreements for foreign passport-holders—meant that Egypt became a refuge for a variety of Ottoman exiles, from Italians and Greeks to Armenians and even Ottoman royals. Greeks from Izmir frequently moved to Alexandria and Cairo, where they joined older Greek communities. Royals of the Ottoman dynasty, including the last sultan's daughter, likewise moved to Egypt where they intermarried with the khedival dynasty. And then there were the Alexandrian Italians, who earned the reputation of being among the most culturally intertwined of these groups with Arabic-speaking Muslim and Coptic Christian circles in accordance with the history of Italian emigrants taking on a variety of jobs across classes.

Figure 11.2 While Livornese-heritage Cairene Jewish writer Yaqub "James" Rafael Sanu (left) connected the literary worlds of Arabic with French and Italian in the late 1800s and was a foundational figure in vernacular Egyptian Arabic literature and performing arts, Alexandrian writer Tommaso Marinetti (middle) in the early 1900s left a legacy not in Egypt but in Italy as a formative player in the Italian literary and artistic movement known as Futurism. Marinetti became a supporter of Mussolini's Fascist Party at a time when other Italian Alexandrians, including Fausta Cialente (right), were vociferous critics.

Sources: https://arabcomixproject.weebly.com/uploads/9/0/7/4/90744849/published/abou-naddar1_2.jpg?1575418712, public domain; https://en.wikipedia.org/wiki/Filippo_Tommaso_Marinetti#/media/File:Filippo TommasoMarinetti.jpg, public domain; http://www.voxmilitiae.it/2016/12/fausta-cialente-il-destino-di-una-scrittrice-straniera-dappertutto, public domain.

What was unique about Italian Alexandrians—that is, residents in early twentieth-century Alexandria with Italian legal status or familial roots in the Italian peninsula—was the extent that their nationalistic inclinations contrasted so sharply. On the one hand, there were figures like Tommaso Marinetti, who would be seen retrospectively as ultranationalist Italians with roots in Alexandria. On the other hand, there were figures like Yaqub Rafael Sanu, who was of Livornese parentage on his father's side, and who had the same Italian and French fluency shared by Marinetti. But unlike Marinetti, he also spoke Egyptian Arabic fluently and pioneered the use of colloquial Egyptian Arabic in writing.

Tommaso Marinetti (1876–1944) was born in Alexandria, and became a supporter of Mussolini later in life. His father was from Piedmont, and his mother was the daughter of a Milanese professor. They came to together to Alexandria in 1865, just years after the unification, on the invitation of khedive Isma'il Pasha, who invited them to work as legal advisors for the many new companies involved in Egyptian industrialization. Marinetti's educational career was typical of many well-educated Italians in Alexandria in terms of its multicultural dimensions: while originally educated in Egypt, he received a baccalaureate degree not in Italy but in Paris in 1894, receiving a law degree from Italy five years later. This mix of French and Italian education was illustrative of the cultural phenomenon at play in Alexandria that existed in Tunis decades earlier: the competing cultural presence of France and Italy. In Egypt's case, the British managed to edge out both powers in terms of political clout, making any French–Italian rivalry in Alexandria less a question of military power and more of cultural currency.

More specifically, with the reconstitution of Tunisia as a French protectorate in 1881 and the growing hold of the British over Egyptian governance and commerce by the 1890s, any potential Italian national aspirations for imperial expansion in Egypt were militarily limited. Still, there were possibilities for Italian cultural dominance in the eastern Mediterranean in competition with the global cultural clout of the British and French. The idea was hardly unrealistic. In accordance with the long history of Pisans, Genoese, Venetians, Florentines, and Livornans conducting business throughout the eastern Mediterranean, Italian was the European *lingua franca* in Tunis and Alexandria in the mid-1800s before being edged out by French. Italian cultural revival, then, meant the revival of education in Italian language and literature.

For Marinetti, this revival of Italian in eastern Mediterranean lands would not be his project. It would be that of institutions like the Dante Alighieri Society, which had begun to promote language and literature even among local Arabic-speaking Muslims and Christians in what evoked the enlightening or civilizing mission of the French Catholic and AIU schools in Algeria and Tunisia. While institutions like the Italian Dante Alighieri Society in Egypt could have been the center of Marinetti's activities and interests as a supporter of the Italian nationalist cause, his professional life as a literary and artistic figure—and later military figure—took him to the circles of Mussolini and Italians who straddled the worlds of Italian militarism and the Italian avant-garde.

Within a year of the Italian racial laws (1938–1943) directed against Italian Jews and various avant-garde artistic movements, Marinetti defended these movements—modern art and futurism specifically—by distancing them from anything foreign and from anything Jewish. That the Italian political leadership generally and Marinetti specifically placed special emphasis on Jews seems shocking giving the degree that Italian Jews had so recently permeated the highest echelons of Italian political life and, as will be seen below, Italian social life in Marinetti's own birthplace of Alexandria. Marinetti went on to volunteer for service in the Italo-Ethiopian war, which began when he was fifty-eight. At the time of his death, Marinetti was completing a collection of poetry in praise of the Decima Flottiglia MAS.

Marinetti's overall profile represented a rather significant contrast to the world of Italian culture in Alexandria, where Livornese Jews played a very prominent role in Italian educational, cultural, and political movements. It was in these circles where an interesting array of positions on Italian nationalism developed. The case of Yaqub Rafael Sanu, of Tuscan parentage and similarly adept in Italian and French, offers an example of the complete opposite of Marinetti. Decades before the Arab Republic of Egypt co-founder Gamal Abdel Nasser popularized the use of colloquial Egyptian Arabic rather than formal Arabic as the language of aural public political engagement, Sanu pioneered the written use of colloquial Egyptian Arabic in political cartoons critiquing the reigning Egyptian–Turkish khedives.

Like Marinetti, Yaqub Rafael Sanu was the son of an immigrant from Italy to Egypt who worked as an advisor to the ruling dynasty. His mother was Egyptian-born, which means that she may have been of earlier Livornese descent, more broadly Sephardic descent, still earlier Egyptian and North African Jewish descent, or a mix of these and other backgrounds connected to the Levant and beyond. In his youth, Sanu spent three years in Livorno, Italy, where any Italian he learned from his father became polished enough for him to publish a variety of successful Italian translations of Arabic literature. Sanu also earned fame in France for his French-language political cartoons depicting British–Egyptian relations in critique of British influence and in praise of Egyptian independence.

Where Sanu was most pioneering was in his publication of works in the Egyptian dialect of Arabic. In stark contrast to the many Livornese Jewish families of the mid-nineteenth century that straddled France and Italy's expatriate political and cultural worlds in Alexandria, Yaqub Sanu pioneered the use of the local Egyptian dialect of Arabic in modern literary and theatrical cultural production, most famously in the realm of political satire. In Sanu's day, the reigning khedive was Isma'il Pasha. Isma'il was the grandson of former Ottoman governor Muhammad Ali, who famously established a semi-independent dynasty of viceroys intertwined with Ottoman Turkish-speaking ruling circles.

The reigning Isma'il Pasha knew Yaqub personally. He funded Yaqub's vision of creating an Egyptian theater tradition, which included original Arabic and adapted French screenplays. Following Isma'il Pasha's bankruptcy, however, the khedival dynasty and, more so, the British government became the object of Sanu's political satirical cartoons written in both Egyptian Arabic and French. Yaqub accomplished this almost one hundred years before the leading figure of Egypt's Arab nationalist socialist revolutionary regime—Gamal Abdel Nasser—broke from the tradition of using classical Arabic in his use of Egyptian dialect Arabic for oratorical effect.

Marinetti and Sanu were on opposite sides of a world of Alexandrians of Italian parentage who participated in a semi-distinctly Italian expatriate social and political life. What made this Italian presence semi-distinct was the fact that the distinctiveness of Italian life in Alexandria was somewhat aspirational on the part of Italian government officials in the Italian peninsula and in Italian consular circles, who supported the Dante Alighieri Society and its Italian language and education activities. In practice, Alexandrians with distant and recent connections with Italy—from Livornese Jewish families active in North African commerce to recent migrants seeking opportunities in Egypt's growing variety of industries—worked across a variety of professions illustrative of their socioeconomic or class diversity. Apart from the variety of experts attracted by opportunities connected with industries like cotton production and the various European companies connected with them, there were smaller scale merchants, shopkeepers, domestic servants, clerks, laborers, artisans. Livornese Jews were part of the earlier wave of long-term Italian immigration from Tuscany, and as mentioned, the borders separating short- and long-term Livornese Jewish residents in North Africa from one another and from older Sephardic and non-Sephardic Jews in North Africa were frequently murky. Far from the picture of a mercantile elite, and in parallel with the situation of Catholic migrants, Jews were represented across professions: bankers, merchants, store owners, commercial agents, brokers, clerks working in firms and retail stores, bank administrators, and workers in the tobacco industry.[5] This was of concern to the Dante Alighieri Society.

Dante Alighieri Society

The Dante Alighieri Society worked in collaboration with the Italian government to promote Italian language and cultural relevance abroad. In parallel with the British Council and Alliance Française, the society had an office in the khedivate-turned-kingdom of Egypt and cultivated a large audience of both Alexandrian Italians as well as Arabic speakers who had no connection with Italy.[6] The outcome of its work in the late 1800s and early 1900s was intertwined with the equivalent of modern soft power. In other words, despite the clear limits of Italy's political power in what was quickly becoming a largely Francophone Algerian and Tunisian world and an increasingly British-influenced Egyptian kingdom, the Italian government continued competing with the British and French for cultural influence across the industrializing cities of what were once Ottoman tributary states.

Interestingly, in the decades before Mussolini's racial laws targeting Italian Jews, the Italian government and the Dante Alighieri Society placed special emphasis on pushing back against French-language instruction within Alexandria's Jewish community. The Society sought to slow the turn to French in the first years of the twentieth century as the primary language of instruction amongst Alexandrian and Cairene Jews.

The Dante Alighieri Society's overture to Jews in Egypt, which included a large number of old and new Livornese Jewish families, was intertwined with a parallel Italian governmental concern over the potential decline of Italian cultural influence in Egypt. Salvatore Tugini was the Italian consul in Cairo in 1901, when he lamented in a report the enduring relevance of French in administrative offices as well as the rising influence of English.[7] The centrality of Italian to eastern Mediterranean political and social life was still a recent phenomenon, having only been replaced by French in Egyptian post offices, consular offices, and business firms in 1876.[8]

It was against this backdrop that the question of an Italian diaspora (*italiani all'estero*) rose to a certain political urgency from the perspective of Italian nationalists. On the one hand, the existence of colonies of Italians dating back centuries offered Italy a ready-made template for political and cultural dominance over the British and French in the Mediterranean. On the other hand, the profiles of Marinetti and Sanu, coupled with the activities of the Dante Alighieri Society, illustrated the extent to which the boundaries of

Italian and non-Italian identity remained as blurred in the Italian peninsula as they were abroad. Long before Italian unification, Livornese Jews spoke natively the variety of Italian (Tuscan) that was only a second language across much of what would become the Italian kingdom in the 1860s. In the decades leading up to unification, Livornese Jews participated in the spirit of liberalism that brought all Tuscans under a single legal system. By the start of the twentieth century, however, the Italian-ness of Italian Jews was in question in a political movement that would erupt with the racial laws. The early twentieth century simultaneously saw the Slovenes of Trieste on the boundaries with Austro-Hungarian Empire subjected to a forced Italianization process in what had the effect of assuming anyone on the Italian side of the kingdom was Italian. Abroad, with long-standing emigrant communities from the Italian peninsula being joined by newer communities that left Italy in the decades after unification, those who either spoke a variety of Italian or who were of recent Italian parentage stretched from South America to North Africa and the Ottoman Aegean.

It comes as no surprise, therefore, that the activities of the Dante Alighieri Society stretched from Argentina and Brazil to Tunisia, Libya, Egypt, and Greece. To some extent, this was a losing process given the extent that the Italian peninsula's diaspora had a long history of being willing to remain abroad and, in some cases, even become linguistically acculturated to their new geographies. Genoese nobility and mercantile circles had a long history of naturalizing as foreigners, especially in the Greek-speaking worlds of the Byzantine and Ottoman empires and in the Castilian-speaking worlds of the Habsburg Spanish empire. In these cases, languages like Castilian, Greek, and Turkish were the prestige languages of diplomacy and commerce, not the communal Ligurian language of Genoese. Likewise, segments of the Livornese Jewish population were seen as becoming intertwined with the Arabization process of earlier generations of Sephardic Jews, just as the same Livornese Jewish communities sometimes served as conduits of North African Europeanization.

This same process of Italian acculturation and cultural convergence could be seen in nineteenth-century Alexandria, where French as a prestige language and Arabic as a useful local language competed with Italian. With the British came another prestige language: English. These realities contextualized the Dante Alighieri Society's ambitious project of reviving Italian among Alexandrians

Figure 11.3 Dalida, born Iolanda Gigliotti, remains Egypt's most famous "Levantine" Italian. Born in Cairo to Lombard parents, Dalida began her career in Arabic-language cinema and was awarded Miss Egypt at the start of the Arab Republic of Egypt in 1953. By the late 1950s, years after her childhood saw her father and swathes of Italians in Egypt detained by the British during a time of British–Italian tensions, she left for France for a career as a singer. While most of her songs were recorded in French and Italian, her few Arabic-language songs like "My Beautiful Homeland (Egypt)" remain in wide circulation. An interview in Arabic during the later part of her career demonstrated her continued proficiency in vernacular Egyptian Arabic, which together with English slowly replaced French and Italian as prestige languages among Egypt's aristocracy.
Public domain after fifty years.

with both strong and weak connections with Italy in Egypt. In what offers a window into the complexity of this project, an Egyptian census in 1917 contrasted British and Italian settlement practices in Egypt in terms of degrees of acculturation. According to the 1917 Egyptian census, "The large Greek and Italian populations are colonies of settlers, who, for long periods of years look upon Egypt as their home."[9] The British, in contrast, "regard Egypt as a foreign country in which, by force of circumstances, they are destined to spend a part of their lives, but do not, as a rule, look forward to the prospect of their children establishing themselves in the country." That Alexandria resembled an Italian city in the eyes of Italian visitors, and that Italian remained a widely spoken prestige language of commerce and social life alongside French, likely made the prospects of long-term residence more palatable for Italians than British. What would eventually prompt the final exodus from Egypt to Europe of these mixed Italian-speaking communities was a series of unexpected events that began most obviously with the rise of Mussolini in Italy and that culminated with the start of the Egyptian revolution.

The Last Alexandrian Italians in the Era of Mussolini

The final exodus of the Levantine Italians from Alexandria was connected with a series of events coinciding with the Mussolini era. While the rise of Mussolini and Italian ultranationalism pulled Alexandrians like Marinetti into the heart of Italian nationalist politics and culture, it also made Alexandria a center of anti-Fascist Italian activity. While Italians throughout the 1920s, 1930s, and 1940s continued to play a central role across Egypt's many worlds of French- and Arabic-language commerce and entertainment, they were also caught between the growing forces of Egypt's rising multiconfessional Arabophone Arab nationalism, the Egyptian dynasty's tension with the British, British tensions with Italy, and the rise of Italian ultranationalist fascism. A key event in this history was Mussolini's invasion of Egypt's (the Kingdom of Egypt and Sudan) southern neighbors in East Africa.

Mussolini's invasion of East Africa came at the heart of his career at the helm of the National Fascist Party (Partito Nazionale Fascista), which was active from the 1920s through the 1940s. The Levantine Italians navigated his career and impact, including the invasion, in complex ways. On the one hand, there were Alexandrian figures like Tommaso Marinetti, who had already left Egypt by 1935 and participated in the Fascist Party upon moving to Italy. On the other hand, there were a variety of Italians still in Alexandria who were opposed to the movement. One of these critics was Fausta Cialente, who made Alexandria a center of anti-Fascist thought.

Fausta Cialente was a vocal critic of the Fascist movement. Cialente spent twenty-six years in Alexandria from 1921 to 1947, when she was active enough in the expatriate life of the city to make Egypt the setting of many of her novels. Cialente founded the anti-Fascist journal *Fronte Unito* (United Front) during the Second World War and participated in broadcasts for Radio Cairo on behalf of the Allied Powers.[10] Still, despite the activity of Italian anti-Fascists in Alexandria like Cialente, British conflict with Mussolini-era Italy put Italians in Egypt at the center of political suspicion. The British commanded significant political authority over the Muhammad Ali dynasty, which meant that Italian–British tensions played out locally in Alexandria. On top of the effect of Italian–British tensions on Alexandrian Italian life, the other unpredictable force was the rising tide of Egyptian and Arab nationalism.

In the years leading up to the 1953 overthrow of the Egyptian monarchy, Egypt saw a rise in popular and political debates about the distinction between locals and foreigners. This debate became intertwined initially with reforms in the system of legal pluralism and extraterritoriality, and it eventually escalated into a debate about the place of foreign-owned large and small businesses in the country. One of the key turning points in this history was the Montreux Convention of 1937, which had a major impact on Alexandrian Italian citizenship as it formally abolished the European capitulation system. Previously, Alexandrians associated with the Greek, Italian, French, and British consulates occupied a legally ambiguous place between the European legal systems and local Egyptian law jurisdictions. By 1938, Alexandrian Italians had a choice, which would have been familiar to their Genoese forebears in newly Ottoman Istanbul in 1453: remain Italian citizens and give up a variety of legal privileges associated with extraterritorial legal status, or naturalize as Egyptians.

In 1938, to the surprise of the Italian consulate, a variety of Alexandrians opted to take Egyptian citizenship.[11] What coincided with this shift was an ongoing diminishing of Italian cultural currency in the city despite Italy's imperial pretensions and land acquisitions. In the lead-up to Alexandria's encounter with Mussolini-era Italian fascism, Italian was no longer one of the main languages of Alexandria's mixed legal tribunals. Government administration was heavily oriented around the use of French and its newcomer counterpart: English. In education, even Alexandrians with Italian citizenship preferred to have their children attend French schools, which is a phenomenon visible in Cairo-born Iolanda Gigliotti's largely Francophone and later France-based singing career.

The culmination of these shifts was a sharper Second World War-era delineation of political and economic boundaries that eventually saw the rise of the Arab Republic of Egypt. What distinguished both Arab and Egyptian varieties of nationalism from many of its nationalistic counterparts—Turkish, Greek,

Italian nationalism—was the extent to which it was not limited to the majority confessional identity. In the legally multi-ethnic state of the Turkish Republic, for example, the Turkish ethnic community was defined in terms of being Muslim, which made various Christian and Jewish citizens of the republic official minority groups. By the Second World War, Greek and Italian nationalism were likewise exclusively Greek Orthodox and Roman Catholic affairs, making the Muslims of present-day Thrace on the Greek–Turkish border an officially designated minority group.

Egyptian and Arab nationalisms, in contrast, had an old history dating back to their origins in the 1800s of being led by both Muslims and Arabic-speaking Christians. In the days of Egyptian bureaucrat Saad Zaghloul, leader of an Egyptian revolution in 1919 that saw the khedivate-turned-sultanate become a constitutional monarchy, Egyptian nationalists like Zaghloul were suspicious of pan-Arab nationalism and its association with contemporary late Ottoman-era Muslims and Christians of the Syrian Levant. The goals of these Arab nationalists, who were active both in the Levant and in exile throughout Egypt, were in Zaghloul's eyes distinct from a more specifically Egyptian variety of nationalism. Part of what shaped these differences between Egyptian nationalists and Arab nationalists since the 1910s was the reality that Alexandria and Cairo were the centers of large and culturally diverse populations of Arabic-speaking Christians associated with a variety of origins, Christian denominations, and even socioeconomic circumstances: bilingual French- and Arabic-speaking political administrators and large business owners from Coptic Christian and Syrian Christian families; exclusively Arabophone Coptic Christian farmers; countless Ottoman Armenian refugees, whose children were in the process of being raised among the older Arabic-speaking Egyptian Armenian and Syrian Armenian communities; Ottoman Greek refugees from Izmir with children likewise raised among the earlier generations of variously Arabized Aegean Greeks resident since the early 1800s; and the large swathes of mixed interdenominational Arabic-speaking Christian families of Alexandria and Cairo.

It was within these circles of Arabic-speaking Christians in Alexandria and Cairo that the 1940s saw a brief window of a variety of Italian and Greek families who were legally associated with the Italian and Greek kingdoms in the 1930s simultaneously naturalize as Egyptians and, if they were not themselves already Arabic speakers as products of mixed Arabic-speaking

Christian families (Syrian–Italian, Egyptian–Greek, and so on), begin raising their children as Arabic speakers in the increasingly widespread bilingual Arabic–French and Arabic–English national schools.

The memory of the most famous products of this era can be seen still in black-and-white cinema dating back to the so-called golden age of Arabic-language Egyptian film in the 1950s: polyglot actors Stefan Rosti, Iolanda Gigliotti ("Dalida"), Maria Cariades ("Nadia Gamal"), and others. In the first years of the 1953 revolution, Alexandria's Greeks even played a prominent role in the rise of the Egyptian national army, where Alexandrian Greek men and women participated on the Egyptian side of the Egyptian–British military conflict following revolution-era President Gamal Abdel Nasser's nationalization of the Suez Canal. What followed that incident, however, were larger legal reforms nationalizing both large and small private industries that still had foreign ownership, whether British and French or Italian and Greek. While the Greeks in particular—a community of mixed foreign nationals and naturalized Egyptians similar to the Italians—were originally promised an exception, Nasser included them in the new policy. The outcome was a slow and final episode in the drawn out two-century-long separation of the eastern Mediterranean's previously connected worlds. By the 1970s, the vast majority of Alexandria and Istanbul's Greek and Italian communities had taken up residence in Europe, the United States, and South America.

EPILOGUE
MEMORIES OF THE LEVANT IN EXILE

What kept the memory of Italians in the Middle East alive were both surviving institutions and shops—Groppi's chocolatier in the heart of present-day Cairo—as well as a smattering of Levantine Italian families living either locally or in exile. In Egypt, Dalida's legacy in Arabic-language film and music remains a prominent part of the Egyptian national heritage, particularly as her most famous Arabic-language song—"My Beautiful Homeland" (Egyptian Arabic: *hilwa ya baladi*)—remains a widely known tribute to her country of birth. It was recorded relatively recently in 1979. She even gave an interview in Italian-accented Arabic for Egyptian television around the same period, frequently mixing in French words for Arabic.

Since the 1980s and 1990s, the Egyptian media has more broadly celebrated the memory of Alexandria's mid-century past. The omnipresence of black-and-white Arabic-language "golden era" Egyptian cinema, for example, has preserved the legacy of those Arabophone Alexandrian actors (*c.* 1920s–1970s) who were fully or maternally Italian. Stefan Rosti was the son of an Austrian ambassador to Egypt and an Alexandrian Italian mother, who insisted on staying in Egypt upon the departure of her husband and who enrolled her son Rosti in local Arabophone schools. Nadia Gamal was the stage name of Alexandrian actor and dancer Maria Cariadis, who was born to an Italian mother and Greek father and who popularized various "eastern" dances (*raqs sharqi*) in Egyptian and Lebanese cinema. Rushdy Abaza, ubiquitous in black-and-white and color films of the 1950s–1970s, was the son of an Alexandrian Italian mother who married a member of the prominent Circassian–Egyptian Abaza family. Egyptian documentaries since the 1980s with an overlay of mid-century nostalgia frequently recount the stories of these actors and their lives in cosmopolitan 1940s-era Alexandria and Cairo. That Alexandrian exiles born in the 1930s were only in their fifties in the 1980s meant that their stories, as told in these widely circulating documentaries, remain as vivid as depictions of Italians and Greeks in mid-century Egyptian films. There is also the handful of Greek families still resident in Egypt with their bilingual millennial offspring as well as the millennial grandchildren of Italian mixed marriages. Together with Egypt's Armenian population, much of which counts late Ottoman eastern Anatolian refugees in its ancestry, Egypt's visual culture and lived experiences offer a vibrant memory of the country's mid-century past and its once large Italian demographic

Further north in Istanbul today, one of the last Levantine Italian families can be seen pondering its legacy and identity in an interview with an Italian news agency. One of its youngest Generation-Z members, bilingual in Italian and Turkish, wonders what the right answer is when asked: "Where are you from?" Is the answer, "I am Italian" in accordance with heritage, or is it "I am Turkish" because of birthplace. "I just explain my background and people find it . . . interesting!" The fact that an explanation is even warranted in Turkish public life suggests the obvious: that the picture of Italians and Greeks perfectly straddling multiple sociocultural worlds in the port cities of Tunisia, Egypt, Syria, and Turkey has become, today, a kind of charming oddity. In the two millennia spanning the history of the Roman Empire and the Italian republics, however, it was far closer to the norm.

NOTES

Chapter 1

1. Leonardo di Niccoló Frescobaldi (fl.1384–1405), "Pilgrimage of Lionardo di Niccoló Frescobaldi to the Holy Land," in *Visit to the Holy Places of Egypt, Sinai, Palestine and Syria in 1384*, trans. Theophilus Bellorini, Eugene Hoade, and Bellarmino Bagatti (Jerusalem: Franciscan Press, 1948), 29–90; Giorgio Gucci (fl.1379–1383), "Pilgrimage of Giorgio Gucci to the Holy Places," in *Visit to the Holy Places of Egypt, Sinai, Palestine and Syria in 1384*, 91–156; Simone Sigoli (fl.1384–1390), "Pilgrimage of Simone Sigoli to the Holy Land," in *Visit to the Holy Places of Egypt, Sinai, Palestine and Syria in 1384*, 157–201.
2. Frescobaldi, "Pilgrimage of Lionardo di Niccoló Frescobaldi to the Holy Land," 29–90, 45–46.
3. *Itinerarium Symonis Semoneis ab Hybernia ad Terram Sanctam*, ed. Mario Esposito (Princeton, NJ: Institute for Advanced Study, 1960), 97–103.
4. Antonio de Sosa, *Topografía e historia general de Argel*, eds. Ignacio Lauer and Landauer, 3 vols. (Madrid: Sociedad de Bibliófilos Españoles, 1927–1929), 1:52–53.
5. William Rosen, *The Most Powerful Idea in the World: A Story of Steam, Industry, and Invention* (Chicago: University of Chicago Press, 2012), 90–114.
6. Matteo Gommellini and Gianni Toniolo, "The Industrialization of Italy, 1861–1971," in Jeffrey G. Williamson and Kevin O'Rourke (eds.), *The Spread of Modern Industry to the Periphery since 1871* (Oxford: Oxford University Press, 2017), 115–141.

7. William T. Rowe, *China's Last Empire: The Great Qing* (Cambridge, MA: Harvard University Press, 2010), 175–200.
8. George L. Van Driem, *The Tale of Tea: A Comprehensive History of Tea from Prehistoric Times to the Present Day* (Leiden: Brill, 2019), 631–649.
9. Dimitri Gutas, *Greek Thought, Arab Culture: The Graeco-Arabic Translation Movement in Baghdad and Early 'Abbasid Society (2nd–4th/8th–10th centuries) (Arabic Thought and Culture)* (London: Routledge, 1998), 2–27.
10. Fernand Braudel, *The Mediterranean and the Mediterranean World in the Age of Philip II: Volume I* (Berkeley: University of California Press, 1995), 103–137.
11. Olivia Remie Constable, *Housing the Stranger in the Mediterranean World: Lodging, Trade, and Travel in Late Antiquity and the Middle Ages* (Cambridge: Cambridge University Press, 2004), 306–354.
12. Janet L. Abu-Lughod, *Before European Hegemony: The World System AD 1250–1350* (Oxford: Oxford University Press, 1991), 3–32.
13. Peter Borschberg, *Hugo Grotius, the Portuguese, and Free Trade in the East Indies* (Singapore: University of Hawaii Press, 2011), 20–39; Andre Gunder Frank, *Reorient: Global Economy in the Asian Age* (Berkeley: University of California Press, 1998), 52–62.

Chapter 2

1. Penny MacGeorge, *Late Roman Warlords* (Oxford: Oxford University Press, 2002), 269–293.
2. Janett Morgan, *Greek Perspectives on the Achaemenid Empire: Persia Through the Looking Glass* (Edinburgh: Edinburgh University Press, 2016), 2–19.
3. T. Corey Brennan, *The Praetorship in the Roman Republic: Vol. 2: 122 to 49 BC* (Oxford: Oxford University Press, 2000), 414–416.
4. Tom Stevenson, *Julius Caesar and the Transformation of the Roman Republic* (London: Routledge, 2014), 154–166.
5. H. Galsterer, "A Man, a Book, and a Method: Sir Ronald Syme's Roman Revolution after Fifty Years," in Kurt A. Raaflaub and Mark Toher (eds.), *Between Republic and Empire: Interpretations of Augustus and His Principate* (Berkeley: University of California Press, 1990), 1–20, 14–18.
6. Nathanael J. Andrade, *Syrian Identity in the Greco-Roman World* (Cambridge: Cambridge University Press, 2013), 315–321.
7. Hans A. Pohlsander, "Philip the Arab and Christianity," *Historia* 29 (1980): 463–473; Glen W. Bowersock, "Review of Irfan Shahîd's Rome and the Arabs and Byzantium and the Arabs in the Fourth Century," *Classical Review* 36 (1986): 111–117.

8. Guy de la Bédoyère, *Domina: The Women Who Made Imperial Rome* (New Haven, CT: Yale University Press, 2018), 280–283.
9. Warwick Ball, *Rome in the East: The Transformation of an Empire* (London: Taylor & Francis, 2002), 101–106.

Chapter 3

1. Jeffrey Richards, *The Popes and the Papacy in the Early Middle Ages 476–762* (London: Routledge, 2014), 33–45.
2. Judith Herrin, *Ravenna: Capital of Empire, Crucible of Europe* (Princeton, NJ: Princeton University Press, 2020), 214–220.
3. Eamon Duffy, *Saints and Sinners: A History of the Popes* (New Haven, CT: Yale University Press 2006), 97–98.
4. Donald M. Nicol, *Byzantium and Venice: A Study in Diplomatic and Cultural Relations* (Cambridge: Cambridge University Press, 1992), 20–49.
5. Maya Maskarinec, *City of Saints: Rebuilding Rome in the Early Middle Ages* (Philadelphia: University of Pennsylvania Press, 2018), 88–89.
6. Caroline Goodson, *The Rome of Pope Paschal I: Papal Power, Urban Renovation, Church Rebuilding and Relic Translation, 817–824* (Cambridge: Cambridge University Press, 2010), 34–40.
7. Robert K. Sherk (ed. and trans.), *The Roman Empire: Augustus to Hadrian (Translated Documents of Greece and Rome 6)* (Cambridge: Cambridge University Press, 1988), 258–264.
8. Thomas F. X. Noble, *The Republic of St. Peter: The Birth of the Papal State, 680–825* (Philadelphia: University of Pennsylvania Press, 1984), 181–182.
9. Irfan Shahid, *Byzantium and the Arabs in the Sixth Century* (Washington, DC: Dumbarton Oaks Research Library and Collection, 1995), 143–148; James G. Clark, *The Benedictines in the Middle Ages* (Woodbridge: Boydell, 2014), 17–26.
10. Rutger Kramer, "Monasticism, Reform, and Authority in the Carolingian Era," in *The Cambridge History of Medieval Monasticism in the Latin West* (Cambridge: Cambridge University Press, 2020), 432–449.
11. James G. Clark, *A Monastic Renaissance at St Albans: Thomas Walsingham and His Circle c.1350–1440* (Oxford: Oxford University Press, 2004), 31–41.
12. John J. Contreni, "Carolingian Monastic Schools and Reform," in *The Cambridge History of Medieval Monasticism in the Latin West* (Cambridge: Cambridge University Press, 2020), 450–464.
13. Bernard Hamilton, *The Latin Church in the Crusader States: The Secular Church* (New York: Routledge, 2016), 14–17.

14. Frank McArdle, *Altopascio: A Study in Tuscan Rural Society, 1587–1784* (Cambridge: Cambridge University Press, 2005), 2–6.

Chapter 4

1. On the use of the banner, see Alasdair C. Grant, "Pisan Perspectives: The Carmen in victoriam and Holy War, c. 1000–1150," *English Historical Review* 131 (2016): 983–1009.
2. "Patrologia Latina," vol. 143, coll. 727–731; Anatole-Joseph Toulotte, *L'Afrique chrétienne* (Paris: E. Leroux, 1912), 2–19.
3. Muḥammad Idrīsī, *Ṣifat Al-Maghrib Wa-Arḍ Al-Sūdān Wa-Miṣr Wa-Al-Andalus: Ma'khūdhah Min Kitāb Nuzhat Al-Mushtāq Fī Ikhtirāq Al-Āfāq*, eds. Reinhart Dozy and Michael J. Goeje (Leiden: Brill, 1866), 104–105.
4. J. E. Merdinger, *Rome and the African Church in the Time of Augustine* (New Haven, CT: Yale University Press, 1997), 3–27.
5. Matt King, "Reframing the Fall of the Zirid Dynasty, 1112–35 CE," *Mediterranean Studies* 26 (2018): 1–25.
6. Uta-Renate Blumenthal, *The Investiture Controversy: Church and Monarchy from the Ninth to the Twelfth Century* (Philadelphia: University of Pennsylvania Press, 1998), 113–126.
7. I. S. Robinson, *Henry IV of Germany 1056–1106* (Cambridge: Cambridge University Press, 1999), 294–318.
8. Eleanor A. Congdon, *Latin Expansion in the Medieval Western Mediterranean* (London: Routledge, 2016), 24–25.
9. Joshua C. Birk, *Baptized Sultans: Norman Kings of Sicily and the Rise of the Anti-Islamic Critique* (London: Palgrave, 2017), 48–50.
10. M. Stroll, *Symbols as Power: The Papacy Following the Investiture Contest* (Leiden: Brill, 1991), 60–62.
11. Silvia Orvietani Busch, Medieval Mediterranean Ports: The Catalan and Tuscan Coasts, 1100–1235 (Leiden: Brill, 2001), 168–171.
12. Jeremy Johns, *Arabic Administration in Norman Sicily: The Royal Diwan* (Cambridge: Cambridge University Press, 2002), 91–114.
13. David Abulafia, "The Crown and the Economy under Roger II and His Successors," *Dumbarton Oaks Papers* 37 (1983): 1–14, 5.
14. Alex Metcalfe, *Muslims of Medieval Italy* (Edinburgh: Edinburgh University Press, 2009), 162–163.
15. Abu Abbas Ahmad al-Qalqashandi, *Subh al-a'sha fi sina'at al-insha'*, 14 vols. (Cairo: Dār al-Kutub al-Miṣrīyah, 1913), 6:459–460.

16. Seda B. Dadoyean, The Fatimid Armenians: Cultural and Political Interaction in the Near East (Leiden: Brill, 1997), 90–106.
17. William of Tyre's commentary offers one of the key foundations for the perspectives of historians Johns and Canard, who linked Roger's interest in Bahram's career with the Norman succession crisis in Antioch. William of Tyre, *A History of Deeds Done Beyond the Sea*, 2 vols., ed. and trans. Emily Atwater Krey and August Babcock Charles (New York: Columbia University Press, 1943), 2:77–78, 113–116; Johns, *Arabic Administration in Norman Sicily: The Royal Diwan*, 263–264.
18. al-Qalqashandi, Subh al-a'sha fi sina'at al-insha', 6:458–463.

Chapter 5

1. *Liber maiolichinus de Gestis Pisanorum Illustribus*, Storia d'Italia 29 (Rome: Forzani, 1904), 17–18; Joseph F. O'Callaghan, *A History of Medieval Spain* (Ithaca, NY: Cornell University Press, 1994), 217–220.
2. Silvia Orvietani Busch, Medieval Mediterranean Ports: The Catalan and Tuscan Coasts: 1100–1235 (Leiden: Brill, 2001), 50–52.
3. Ottavio Banti, "I rapporti di Pisa con gli stati islamici dell'Africa settentrionale tra l'XI e il XIV secolo," in G. Piancastelli Politi (ed.), *Le ceramiche medievali delle chiese di Pisa: Contributo per una migliore comprensione delle loro caratteristiche e del loro significato quale documento di storia* (Pisa: Pacini Editore, 1983), 9–26, 13.
4. *Rasa'il Muwahhidiyya*, ed. Ahmed Azzaoui (Kénitra: Université Ibn Tufayl, 1996), 1:174–175.
5. For an overview of this chronology, see the section "Almoravids and Almohads" in Nehemia Levtzion, "The Western Maghrib and Sudan," in Roland Oliver (ed.), *The Cambridge History of Africa, Volume 3: c. 1050–1600* (Cambridge: Cambridge University Press, 1977), 331–462, 347–348.
6. Michele Amari, *Diploma arabi*, Arabic document No. 1, pp. 1–6, 4; Latin document No. 6, 255–256.
7. David Abulafia, *The Great Sea* (Oxford: Oxford University Press, 2011), 297–299.
8. *Rasa'il Muwahhidiyya*, ed. Ahmed Azzaoui (Kénitra: Université Ibn Tufayl, 1996), 1:17–75.
9. Esther-Miriam Wagner and Magdalen Connolly, "Code-Switching in Judaeo-Arabic Documents from the Cairo Geniza," *Multilingua* 37 (2018): 1–23.
10. Stefan C. Reif, "A Centennial Assessment of Genizah Studies," *The Cambridge Genizah Collections: Their Contents and Significance* (Cambridge: Cambridge University Press, 2002), 2–35.

11. Halper Collection, University of Pennsylvania, 389, 414. A copy of this document can also be found in S. D. Goitein, A Mediterranean Society: The Jewish Communities of the Arab World as Portrayed in the Documents of the Cairo Geniza, Vol. I: Economic Foundations (Berkeley: University of California Press, 1967), 1:39. For further discussion, see Jessica L. Goldberg, Trade and Institutions in the Medieval Mediterranean: The Geniza Merchants and their Business World (Cambridge: Cambridge University Press, 2012), 296–300.
12. Halper Collection, 389.
13. Goitein, *A Mediterranean Society*, 1:40–41.
14. Kelly DeVries and Robert Douglas Smith, *Medieval Military Technology* (Toronto: University of Toronto Press, 2012), 300–301.
15. Lawrence V. Mott, *The Development of the Rudder: A Technological Tale* (College Station: Texas A & M University Press, 1997), 120–123.
16. Abd al-Rahman al-Sufi, *Kitāb Ṣuwar al-Kawākib al-Thamānīyah Wa-Al-'arba'īn* (Beirut: Dār al-Āfāq al-Jadīdah, 1981).
17. Amari, *Diploma arabi*, 241–249.
18. Strickland Matthew, War and Chivalry: The Conduct and Perception of War in England and Normandy, 1066–1217 (Cambridge: Cambridge University Press, 1996), 26–27.
19. Anne Marie Edde, *Saladin*, trans. Jane Marie Todd (Cambridge: Cambridge University Press, 2011), 449.
20. David Jacoby, "Pisa and the Frankish States of the Levant in the Twelfth Century," in Iris Shagrir, Benjamin Kedar and Michel Balard (ds.), *Communicating the Middle Ages: Essays in Honour of Sophia Menache* (London: Routledge, 2018), 91–102.
21. David Jacoby, "Conrad, Marquis of Montferrat, and the Kingdom of Jerusalem (1187–1192)," in Laura Balletto (ed.), *Dai feudi monferrini e dal Piemonte ai nuovi mondi oltre gli Oceani: Atti del Congresso (Alessandria, 2–6 Aprile 1990)* (Alessandria: Società di storia, arte e archeologia, Accademia degli Immobili, 1993), 187–238, 197.
22. Henry IV, "Henry IV's Answer to Gregory VII., Jan. 24, 1076," in *Select Historical Documents of the Middle Ages*, ed. and trans. Ernest F. Henderson (London: George Bell, 1903), 372–373.
23. Patricia Skinner, "From Pisa to the Patriarchate: Chapters in the Life of (Arch)bishop Daibert," in Patricia Skinner (ed.), *The Boundaries of Medieval History: The Legacy of Timothy Reuter* (Turnhout: Brepols, 2009), 158–159.

Chapter 6

1. Marco Tangheroni, "Trade and Navigation," in David Abulafia (ed.), *Italy in the Central Middle Ages 1000–1300* (Oxford: Oxford University Press), 127–146.

2. L. P. Harvey, *Islamic Spain: 1250 to 1500* (Chicago: University of Chicago Press, 1992), 20–40.
3. Constable, Housing the Stranger, 182–184.
4. Giovanni Villani, *Cronica*, ed. F. Dragomanni, 4 vols. (Florence, 1845), II, book VIII, chapter 77, 101.
5. Sean McGrail, *Boats of the World: From the Stone Age to Medieval Times* (Oxford: Oxford University Press, 2004), 242–244.
6. Alwyn A. Ruddock and Peter Rycraft, *Italian Merchants and Shipping in Southampton, 1270–1600* (Southampton: University College, 1951), 20–21.
7. Frederic Chapin Lane, *Venice: A Maritime Republic* (Baltimore, MD: Johns Hopkins University Press, 1973), 125–127.
8. Peter Spufford, "Trade in Fourteenth-Century Europe," in Michael C. E. Jones, David Abulafia, David Edward Luscombe, and C. T. Allmand (eds.), *The New Cambridge Medieval History: Volume 6, c. 1300–c. 1415* (Cambridge: Cambridge University Press, 1995), 155–208, 183–184.
9. Edmond B. Fryde, *Studies in Medieval Trade and Finance* (London: Hambledon, 1983), 296–298.
10. Matteo Salonia, Genoa's Freedom: Entrepreneurship, Republicanism, and the Spanish Atlantic (Lanham, Lexington Books, 2020), 20–21.
11. Ibid., 20
12. An entire monograph was written on this Genoese Londoner. Lawrence Stone, *An Elizabethan: Sir Horatio Palavicino* (Oxford: Clarendon, 1956).
13. David Abulafia, "Cittadino e 'denizen': mercanti mediterranei a Southampton e a Londra," in *Mediterranean Encounters, Economic, Religious, Political, 1100–1550* (London: Routledge, 2000), 281–283; Ruddock and Rycraft, *Italian Merchants and Shipping in Southampton*, 222–224.
14. Adam Anderson, An Historical and Chronological Deduction of the Origin of Commerce, from the Earliest Accounts to the Present Time: Containing, an History of the Great Commercial Interests of the British Empire (London: Millar, 1764), 1:259; Maria Fusaro, Political Economies of Empire in the Early Modern Mediterranean: The Decline of Venice and the Rise of England, 1450–1700 (Cambridge: Cambridge University Press, 2015), 33–34.
15. Constable, *Housing the Stranger*, 126–127.
16. Imperiale di Sant' Angelo (ed.), *Codice diplomatico della repubblica di Genova*, Fonti per la storia d'Italia (Rome: Tipografia del Senato, 1936–1942), 1:247–249.
17. Amari, *Diplomi arabi*, 240.
18. Olivia Remie Constable, "Genoa and Spain in the Twelfth and Thirteenth Centuries," *Journal of European Economic History* 19 (1990): 635–656, 654–655.

19. Amar S. Baadj, Saladin, the Almohads and the Banū Ghāniya: The Contest for North Africa (12th and 13th Centuries) (Leiden: Brill, 2015), 67–69.
20. Michele Amari, *I diplomi arabi del R. Archivio Fiorentino* (Florence: Le Monnier, 1862), pp. 230–236, 273–277; Frédéric Bauden, "Due trattati di pace conclusi nel dodicesimo secolo tra i Banū Ġāniya, signori delle isole Baleari, e il commune di Genova," in Nuria Martínez de Castilla (ed.), *Documentos y manuscritos árabes del Occidente musulmán medieval* (Madrid: Consejo Superior de Investigaciones Científicas, 2010), 33–86.
21. Olivia Remie Constable, Trade and Traders in Muslim Spain: The Commercial Realignment of the Iberian Peninsula, 900–1500 (Cambridge: Cambridge University Press, 1996), 43–44, 129.
22. Constable, *Housing the Stranger*, 130–131.
23. Ibid., 132–133.
24. Conor Kosti, *The Crusades and the Near East: Cultural Histories* (London: Taylor & Francis, 2010), 42–43.
25. Constable, *Housing the Stranger*, 201–202.
26. Andrew Jotischky, *Crusading and the Crusader States* (London: Taylor & Francis, 2017), 163–164.
27. Steven A. Epstein, *Genoa and the Genoese, 958–1528* (Chapel Hill: University of North Carolina Press, 1996), 85–86.
28. Deborah Howard, "Venice as Gateway to the Holy Land: Pilgrims as Agents of Transmission," in Deborah Howard, Wendy Pullan, and Paul Davies (eds), *Architecture and Pilgrimage, 1000–1500: Southern Europe and Beyond* (Farnham: Ashgate, 2013), 87–112, 88–90.
29. Maria Pia Pedani, "The Mamluk Documents of the Venetian State Archives: Historical Survey," *Quaderni di Studi Arabi* (2002–2003), 133–146.
30. Epstein, Genoa and the Genoese, 958–1528, 180–181.
31. Ibid., 179–180.
32. Virgil Ciocîltan, The Mongols and the Black Sea Trade in the Thirteenth and Fourteenth Centuries (Leiden: Brill, 2012), 3–10.
33. Mike Carr, "Trade or Crusade? The Zaccaria of Chios and Crusades against the Turks," in Nikolaos G. Chrissis and Mike Carr (eds.), *Contact and Conflict in Frankish Greece and the Aegean, 1204–1453: Crusade, Religion and Trade between Latins, Greeks and Turks* (London: Routledge, 2016), 115–134, 120–131.
34. Ciocîltan, The Mongols and the Black Sea Trade, 156
35. Maria Georgopoulou, *Venice's Mediterranean Colonies* (Cambridge: Cambridge University Press, 2001), 1–14.

36. Catia Brill demonstrates that Genoa did not fit into a standard colonization model, a point that harmonizes with Gabriella Araldi's analysis of the Genoese republic as a "reticular model which included many centers that were equally important in their own right and acted as parts of a system of which Genoa—the hub where good and capitals were distributed—was the heart, not the mind." Avner Greif, likewise, argues that merchants in the early thirteenth century developed an "individual legal responsibility system" built on limited liability partnerships that allowed them to enforce property rights and establish business ties with non-Genoese partner. Catia Brilli, *Genoese Trade and Migration in the Spanish Atlantic, 1700–1830* (Cambridge: Cambridge University Press, 2016), 6–8.
37. Evgeny Khvalkov, Colonies of Genoa in the Black Sea Region: Evolution and Transformation (New York: Routledge, 2019), 70–72.
38. The most illustrative series of these documents has been published in the following: Ausilia Roccatagliata, "Notai Genovesi in oltremare: Atti rogati a Pera (1453)," *Atti della Società Ligure di Storia Patria* 39 (1999): 101–160; Ausilia Roccatagliata, *Notai Genovesi in oltremare: Atti rogati a Pera e Mitilene, Vol. 1, Pera (1408–1490)* (Genoa: University of Genoa, 1982).
39. Wright offers an analytical picture of the simultaneous rise of Genoese linguistic acculturation in the Greek-speaking Aegean and the rise of Genoese political sovereignty in the region, including in Chios and in greater Constantinople's district of Pera. Christopher Wright, *The Gattilusio Lordships and the Aegean World, 1355–1462* (Leiden: Brill, 2014).
40. Necipoğlu's analysis of the complexities of Byzantine–Latin political alignments contextualizes the changing alliances of the Venetian and Ottoman republics with Byzantium. Nevra Necipoğlu, *Byzantium between the Ottomans and the Latins: Politics and Society in the Late Empire* (Cambridge: Cambridge University Press, 2012), 2–12.
41. Archivio di Stato di Genova, *San Giorgio Manoscritti Membranacei IV*, fol. 304v, published in L. T. Belgrano, "Prima Serie di Documenti riguardanti la colonia di Pera," *Atti della Società Ligure di Storia Patria* 13 (1877–1884), 125–126.
42. Constable, *Housing the Stranger*, 304–305.
43. The agreement took the form of a capitulation charter (*ahidname*) not with the Republic of Genoa, but with the Genoese of Pera, which had been simultaneously part of the republic but independent in practice. The full text of the charter, written in Greek and translated soon afterwards to Turkish and Italian, can be found in the following: Halil Inalcik, "Ottoman Galata 1453–1553," in Edhem Eldem (ed.), *Première Rencontre internationale sur l'Empire Ottoman*

et la Turquie moderne, Institut national des langues et civilisations Orientales, Maison des sciences de l'homme, 18–22 janvier 1985 (Istanbul, 1991), pp. 276ff; L. Mitler, "The Genoese in Galata: 1453–1682," *International Journal of Middle East Studies* 10:1 (1979), 71–91.

44. Constable, *Housing the Stranger*, 107–157.
45. Eric Dursteler, Venetians in Constantinople: Nation, Identity, and Coexistence in the Early Modern Mediterranean (Baltimore, MD: Johns Hopkins University Press, 2008), 130–150.
46. The text of this capitulation charter sent by Mehmed III to King Sigismund III is available in the following: Dariusz Kołodziejczyk, *Ottoman–Polish Diplomatic Relations (15th–18th Century): An Annotated Edition of 'Ahdnames and Other Documents* (Leiden: Brill, 2000), 311–112.
47. Dursteler, Venetians in Constantinople, 111–112.
48. Necipoğlu has traced the final decades of late Byzantine Genoese-held Pera's political and commercial relations with the expanding Ottoman sultanate, highlighting the extent that Pera became partly subsumed into the commercial world of Ottoman trade routes eastward. Necipoğlu, *Byzantium between the Ottomans and the Latins*, 184–233.
49. Inalcik, "Ottoman Galata 1453–1553," 276–277.
50. Ibid., 277.
51. Molly Greene, Catholic Pirates and Greek Merchants: A Maritime History of the Mediterranean (Princeton, NJ: Princeton University Press, 2010), 15–51.
52. On the practice of *berat* issuance more broadly and its connection with debates about sovereignty, see Bruce A. Masters, *Christians and Jews in the Ottoman Arab World: The Roots of Sectarianism* (New York: Cambridge University Press, 2001); Bruce A. Masters, *The Origins of Western Dominance in the Middle East: Mercantilism and the Islamic Economy in Aleppo, 1600–1850* (Cambridge: Cambridge University Press, 1988); Bruce McGowan, *Economic Life in the Ottoman Empire: Taxation, Trade, and the Struggle for Land, 1600–1800* (Cambridge: Cambridge University Press, 1981); Halil Inalcik, "Imtiyazat," in *EI2*. Ottoman administrative concern of Roman Catholic political authority in Ottoman lands was also entangled with this reform of *berat* issuance. Charles A. Frazee, *Catholics and Sultans: The Church and the Ottoman Empire, 1453–1923* (Cambridge: Cambridge University Press, 1983).
53. Eric Dursteler, "Education and Identity in Constantinople's Latin Rite community, c. 1600," *Renaissance Studies* 18 (2004), 287–303.
54. E. Natalie Rothman, *Brokering Empire: Trans-Imperial Subjects between Venice and Istanbul* (New York: Cornell University Press, 2011), 165–187.

55. One example is the case of Orimbei, a Luccan and one-time Venetian dragoman who became Muslim and Ottoman Grand Dragoman and who nonetheless remained on the Venetian payroll for his useful contacts. Bertelè contextualizes Orimbei's career against the backdrop of the Venetians' and Ottoman's overlapping diplomatic networks. Tommaso Bertele, *Il palazzo degli ambasciatori di Venezia a Constantinopoli e le sue antiche memorie ricerche storiche con documenti inediti*. (Bologna: Apollo, 1932), 105–106. Rothman has highlighted the example of Giovanni Piron, an apprentice dragoman from the local Ottoman Catholic elite, who was listed in 1664 as an apprentice and kept on the payroll even at the age of sixty-five. E. Natalie Rothman, "Interpreting Dragomans: Boundaries and Crossings in the Early Modern Mediterranean," *Comparative Studies in Society and History* 51:4 (2009), 771–800, 782–783.

Chapter 7

1. As Georgeopoulou has shown, the question of Catholic–Greek Orthodox tensions was of significant concern to Venetian administrators in their attempts to transfer formerly Byzantine Greek loyalties to expanding Venetian rule. Maria Georgopoulou, *Venice's Mediterranean Colonies: Architecture and Urbanism* (Cambridge: Cambridge University Press, 2001), 165–191.
2. As Necipoğlu has shown, Byzantine Greek perspectives on the prospects of Venetian and Ottoman rule varied especially between the position of political administrative circles and the clergy. Necipoğlu, *Byzantium between the Ottomans and the Latins*, 184–234.
3. On Venice's assimilation of an Alexandrian past and transformation into the city of St. Mark, see Patricia Fortini Brown, *Venetian Narrative Painting in the Age of Carpaccio* (New Haven, CT: Yale University Press, 1988), 193–218.
4. The original text, "The Origins of St. Mark's Library: Cardinal Bessarion's Gift, 1468," is published in Ludwig Mohler, *Kardinal als Theologe, Humanist und Staatsmann* (Paderborn: Schöningh, 1942), 3:541–543. A reproduction is found in *Venice: A Documentary History, 1450–1630*, ed. David Chambers and Brian Pullan (Oxford: Blackwell, 1992), 357–358.
5. From the perspective of the historical construction of civic identity, including the role of political administrators in facilitating in urban visual culture, Howard's analysis suggests that the historicity of the transfer of St. Mark's remains was eclipsed in importance by the historical memory of it. The visual depiction of the event on the façade of St. Mark's Cathedral, which Howard examines, offers an enduring illustration of how the visual and material culture of Venice afforded pilgrims the opportunity to endow the city with sacred meaning. Deborah

Howard, *Venice & the East: The Impact of the Islamic World on Venetian Architecture, 1100–1500* (New Haven, CT: Yale University Press, 2000), 65–111.

6. Martin Lowry, The World of Aldus Manutius: Business and Scholarship in Renaissance Venice (Ithaca, NY: Cornell University Press, 1979), 22–24.

7. Goy's analysis of the intersection of patrons, architects, and builders in the construction of Venice's most important fifteenth-century structures sheds light on the extent to which these various dimensions of Venice's civic past and present were closely intertwined. Richard John Goy, *The Building of Renaissance Venice: Patrons, Architects, and Builders, c. 1430–1500* (London: Yale University Press, 2006).

8. Venice's place as a holy site along the pilgrimage routes was not exclusive to the city and included rural and peripheral regions. Stephen D. Bowd, *Venice's Most Loyal City: Civic Identity in Renaissance Brescia* (Cambridge, MA: Harvard University Press, 2010), 83–104.

9. A look at the commercial activities of Sephardic families in northern Europe, especially Amsterdam, highlights the continued centrality of Mediterranean trade networks in sixteenth-century Sephardic economic life. Renée Levine Melammed, *A Question of Identity: Iberian Conversos in Historical Perspective* (New York: Oxford University Press, 2004), 69–80.

10. A record of the case against Diogo Mendes is preserved in the Antwerp Municipal Archives and has been published in Pierre Génard, "Personen te Antwerpen in de XVIe eeuw voor het 'feit van de religie' gerechterlijk vergold. Lijst en ambtelijke bijhoorige stukken," *Antwerpsch Archievenblad* 9 (n.d.), 205–236.

11. Juan I. Pulido Serrano, "Las negociaciones con los cristianos nuevos en tiempos de Felipe III a la luz de algunos documentos inéditos (1598–1607)," *Sefarad* 66 (2006), 345–375; António Augusto Marques de Almeida, "O Perdão Geral de 1605," *Primeiras Jornadas de História Moderna. Actas*, vol. 2 (Lisbon: Centro de História da Universidade de Lisboa, 1986), 885–898; Ana Isabel López-Salazar Codes, *Inquisición portuguesa y Monarquía Hispánica en tiempos del perdón general de 1605* (Lisbon: Colibri, 2010).

12. A series of eighteen documents preserved in the Portuguese National Archives, Vatican Secret Archives, the National Archives of Brussels, the National Archives of Modena, and the National Archives of Ferrara that detail the circumstances of both cases, including assurances of protection from Rome, have been published in: Herman Prins Salomon and Aron di Leone Leoni, "Mendes, Benveniste, de Luna, Micas, Nasci: The State of the Art (1532–1558)," *Jewish Quarterly Review* 88 (1998), 135–211.

13. Halil İnalcık's classic examination of Ottoman commerce in the eastern Mediterranean contextualizes this importance of Ancona in the Ottoman's expanding control over the silk trade with Iran through Bursa. Halil İnalcık, "Bursa and the Silk Trade," in Halil İnalcık and Donald Quataert (eds.), *An Economic and Social History of the Ottoman Empire, 1300–1914* (Cambridge: Cambridge University Press, 1994), 218–255.
14. Viviana Bonazzoli, "Ebrei italiani, portoghesi, levantini sulla piazza commerciale di Ancona intorno alla metà del Cinquecento," in Gaetano Cozzi (ed.), *Gli Ebrei e Venezia, secoli XIV–XVIII* (Milano: Edizioni Comunità, 1987), 727–770.
15 Deborah Howard examines the development of Venetian urban political theater as a lens for understanding the connections between Venice and Middle Eastern Christianity in the Mamluk and Ottoman eras. Howard, *Venice and the East: The Impact of the Islamic World on Venetian Architecture, 1100–1500* (New Haven: Yale University Press, 2000), 189– 216.
16. Bonazzoli, "Ebrei italiani, portoghesi, levantini," 727–770.
17. Louisa S. Hoberman offers several illustrative examples of *converso* merchant houses that connected Mexican production of cochineal with Spanish silk commerce. Louisa S. Hoberman, *Mexico's Merchant Elite, 1590–1660: Silver, State, and Society* (Durham, NC: Duke University Press, 1991), 94–146.
18. The enforcement of sumptuary laws governing Venetian public space had a long history of uneven enforcement. Kovesi Killerby, "Practical Problems in the Enforcement of Italian Sumptuary Law, 1200–1500," in Trevor Dean and K. J. P. Lowe (eds.), *Crime, Society and the Law in Renaissance Italy* (Cambridge: Cambridge University Press, 1994), 99–120. Rothman has offered an overview of the way Jewish participation in the Rialto commercial activities were contested by Venetian guilds, particularly against the backdrop of the guilds' declining profits from Levantine trade in Rothman, *Brokering Empire*, 29–60.
19. In their respective studies of the early modern history of Ottoman subjecthood, Julia Philips Cohen and Michelle Campos offer a comparative overview of the history of Sephardic Jews, Ottoman Greeks, and Ottoman Armenians in eastern Mediterranean commerce. Julia Philips Cohen, *Becoming Ottomans: Sephardi Jews and Imperial Citizenship in the Modern Era* (Oxford: Oxford University Press, 2014); Michelle Campos, *Ottoman Brothers: Muslims, Christians, and Jews in Early Twentieth-Century Palestine* (Stanford: Stanford University Press, 2011).
20. Aryeh Shmuelevitz, The Jews of the Ottoman Empire in the Late Fifteenth and the Sixteenth Centuries: Administrative, Economic, Legal and Social Relations as Reflected in the Responsa (Leiden: Brill, 1984).

21. Hoberman, Mexico's Merchant Elite, 1590–1660, 94–146.
22. Emrah Safa Gürkan, "Mediating Boundaries: Mediterranean Go-Betweens and Confessional Diplomacy in Constantinople, 1560–1600," *Journal of Early Modern History* 19 (2015), 107–128; Cecil Roth, *The House of Nasi: The Duke of Naxos* (New York: Greenwood Press, 1948); Norman Rosenblatt, "Joseph Nasi, Friend of Spain," in Izaak A. Langnas and Barton Sholod (eds.), *Studies in Honor of M. J. Benardete: Essays in Hispanic and Sephardic Culture* (New York: Las Americas, 1965), 323–332. Gürkan offers an analytical comparison of how the diplomatic networks of Nasi and Passi operated across Ottoman, Venetian, and Habsburg boundaries.
23. In what reflects Sinan's fame among world powers at the time, the Portuguese governor in India in 1528 thought he was sent by the Ottomans to fight the Portuguese, and he was referred to shortly after as "the famous Jewish pirate" by Henry VIII's ambassador in Rome in a letter to the king in 1533. John Sherron Brewer, Robert Henry Brodie, and James Gairdner (eds.), *Letters and Papers, Foreign and Domestic, of the Reign of Henry VIII: Preserved in the Public Record Office, the British Museum, and Elsewhere* (London: Longman, Brown, Green, Longmans & Roberts, 1862–1933), 6:426–428; Samuel Tolkowsky, *They Took to the Sea: A Historical Survey of Jewish Maritime Activities* (New York: Thomas Yoseloff, 1964), 174–175; Benjamin Arbel, *Trading Nations: Jews and Venetians in the Early Modern Eastern Mediterranean* (Leiden: Brill, 1995), 180–182; Emrah Safa Gürkan, "Espionage in the 16th-Century Mediterranean: Secret Diplomacy, Mediterranean Go-Betweens and the Ottoman Habsburg Rivalry," PhD dissertation, Georgetown University, 2012, 394–395; José María del Moral, *El Virrey de Nápoles: Don Pedro de Toledo y la guerra contra el turco* (Madrid: Consejo Superior de Investigaciones Científicas, 1966).
24. Benjamin Ravid, "The Socioeconomic Background of the Expulsion and Readmission of the Venetian Jews, 1571–1573," in Phyllis Cohen Albert and Frances Malino (eds.), *Essays in Modern Jewish History: A Tribute to Ben Halpern* (Rutherford, NJ: Fairleigh Dickinson University Press, 1982), 27–55.
25. Killerby, "Practical Problems in the Enforcement of Italian Sumptuary Laws, 1200–1500," 99–120.
26. Rothman, *Brokering Empire*, 29–60.
27. Arbel, *Trading Nations*, 95–168.
28. Mark Mazower has provided an analytical overview of the arrival of Sephardic merchants in the Ottoman Aegean in his discussion of the premodern history of Greece. Mark Mazower, *Salonica, City of Ghosts: Christians, Muslims and Jews, 1430–1950* (New York: Knopf, 2005), 46–63.

29. The archival Lettere e scritture turchesche collection in the Venetian Archives is an important source for documents such as the Judaeo-Spanish contractual agreement between Ḥayyim Saruq and Joseph Segura in 1566/67. Archivio di Stato di Venezia (ASV), Lettere e scritture turchesche, filza 2, fol. 192. An inventory of the collection, which includes this agreement, was recently published in Maria Pia Pedani (ed.), based on the materials compiled by Alessio Bombaci, *Inventory of the Lettere e Scritture Turchesche in the Venetian State Archives* (Leiden: Brill, 2010).
30. Arbel, *Trading Nations*, 95–168.
31. The original source used by Arbel was examined previously by Benayahu, who quotes key portions of the text, and is also available in an edited collection of Rabbi Samuel de Medina's responsa. M. Benayahu, "Further Evidence on Ḥayyim ben Saruq in Venice" (in Hebrew), *Ozar Yehudei Sefarad* (*Tesoros de los Judíos Sefardíes*) 8 (1965), 135–136; Shmuel de Medina, *She'elot u-teshuvot Maharashdam* (New York: ha-Aḥim Polaḳ, 1958), 3:99; Arbel, *Trading Nations*, 95–97.
32. Gürkan, "Mediating Boundaries," 107–128.
33. Ottomans contemplated and took steps, with Venetian support, to establish a political alliance with the Southeast Asian Sultanate of Aceh in competition with the Portuguese in Melacca. Giancarlo Casale, *The Ottoman Age of Exploration* (Oxford: Oxford University Press, 2010), 123–125.

Chapter 8

1. Halil İnalcik, "Bursa and the Silk Trade," in Suraiya Faroqhi, Halil Inalcik, and Donald Quataert (eds.), *An Economic and Social History of the Ottoman Empire, Volume I* (Cambridge: Cambridge University Press, 1997), 234–235.
2. Doris Behrens-Abouseif, Practising Diplomacy in the Mamluk Sultanate: Gifts and Material Culture in the Medieval Islamic World (London: I. B. Tauris, 2014), 114–115.
3. Stefano Dall'Aglio, *The Duke's Assassin: Exile and Death of Lorenzino De' Medici* (New Haven, CT: Yale University Press, 2015), 12–24.
4. Andras Kubinyi, "The Battle of Szavaszentdemeter—Nagyolaszi (1523): Ottoman Advance and Hungarian Defence on the Eve of Mohacs," in Géza Dávid and Pál Fodor (eds.), *Ottomans, Hungarians, and Habsburgs in Central Europe: The Military Confines in the Era of Ottoman Conquest* (Leiden: Brill, 2000), 71–116, 80–87.
5. Benjamin Arbel, "Roman-Catholics and Greek-Orthodox in the Early-Modern Venetian State (Mid-Fifteenth to Mid-Seventeenth Century," in Katsumi Fukasawa, Benjamin J. Kaplan, and Pierre-Yves Beaurepaire (eds.), *Religious Interactions in Europe and the Mediterranean World: Coexistence and Dialogue from the 12th to the 20th Centuries* (New York: Routledge, 2017), 245–260, 250–251.

6. C. Scott Dixon, *The Reformation in Germany* (Oxford: Blackwell, 2008), 24–26.
7. Murat Iyigun, War, Peace, and Prosperity in the Name of God: The Ottoman Role in Europe's Socioeconomic Evolution (Chicago: University of Chicago Press, 2012), 90–98.
8. Carlos M. N. Eire, *Reformations: The Early Modern World, 1450–1650* (New Haven, CT: Yale University Press, 2016), 214–217.
9. James Davison Hunter, To Change the World: The Irony, Tragedy, and Possibility of Christianity in the Late Modern World (New York: Oxford University Press, 2010), 300 n. 79.
10. Christopher Ocker, Luther, Conflict, and Christendom: Reformation Europe and Christianity in the West (Cambridge: Cambridge University Press, 2018), 167–171.
11. Greene, *Catholic Pirates and Greek Merchants*, 89–91.
12. Necipoğlu, *Byzantium between the Ottomans and the Latins*, 191–192.
13. Ibid., 228.
14. Ibid., 192.
15. İnalcik, "Bursa and the Silk Trade," 231.
16. Ibid., 231–232.
17. Ibid.
18. Franz Babinger, *Mehmed the Conquerer and His Time*, trans. Ralph Manheim (Princeton, NJ: Princeton University Press, 1978), 255–257.
19. Stefano U. Baldassarri and Arielle Saiber, *Images of Quattrocento Florence: Selected Writings in Literature, History, and Art* (New Haven, CT: Yale University Press, 2000), 82–84.
20. Kate Fleet, European and Islamic Trade in the Early Ottoman State: The Merchants of Genoa and Turkey (Cambridge: Cambridge University Press, 2006), 102–104.
21. Kalman Bland, "Elijah del Medigo's Averroist Response to the Kabbalahs of Fifteenth-century Jewry and Pico della Mirandola," *Journal of Jewish Thought and Philosophy* (1991), 23–53.
22. *Lorenzo De' Medici at Home: The Inventory of the Palazzo Medici in 1492*, ed. and trans. Richard Stapleford (University Park, PA: Penn State University Press, 2014), 7–8.
23. Rosamond E. Mack, *Bazaar to Piazza: Islamic Trade and Italian Art, 1300–1600* (Berkeley: University of California Press, 2002).
24. *The Inventory of the Palazzo Medici*, 89–90.
25. Ibid., 172–173.
26. Ibid., 33–34.
27. Ibid., 114–115.

28. Ibid., 161–162.
29. Catherine Hess (ed.), *The Arts of Fire: Islamic Influences on Glass and Ceramics of the Italian Renaissance* (Los Angeles, CA: J. Paul Getty Museum, 2004), 20–21.
30. Ibid., 20
31. Ibid., 110
32. Ibid., 20
33. Ibid., 110
34. Ibid., 113
35. Ibid., 19–20.

Chapter 9

1. Corey Tazzara, The Free Port of Livorno and the Transformation of the Mediterranean World (Oxford: Oxford University Press, 2017), 198–199.
2. Hendrik Thijs van Veen, *Cosimo I De' Medici and His Self-Representation in Florentine Art and Culture* (Cambridge: Cambridge University Press, 2006), 4–5.
3. Francis Haskell and Nicholas Penny, *Taste and the Antique: The Lure of Classical Sculpture 1500–1900* (New Haven, CT: Yale University Press, 1981), 25–27.
4. Sidney H. Griffith, The Church in the Shadow of the Mosque: Christians and Muslims in the World of Islam (Princeton, NJ: Princeton University Press, 2012), 45–74.
5. Timothy Mitchell, *Colonising Egypt* (Berkeley: University of California Press, 1991), 133–137.
6. Hafez Chehab, "Reconstructing the Medici Portrait of Fakhr al-Din al-Ma'ani," in Gulru Necipoğlu (ed.), *Muqarnas: An Annual on Islamic Art and Architecture* (Leiden: Brill, 1994), 117–119.
7. Corey Tazzara, The Free Port of Livorno and the Transformation of the Mediterranean World, 1574–1790 (Oxford: Oxford University Press, 2017), 24–26.
8. L. P. Harvey, *Muslims in Spain, 1500 to 1614* (Chicago: University of Chicago Press, 2008), 354–356.
9. These occupations go back partly to the downward social mobility of Moriscos after the Alhambra Decree. Mary Elizabeth Perry, *The Handless Maiden: Moriscos and the Politics of Religion in Early Modern Spain* (Princeton, NJ: Princeton University Press, 2007), 173–174 (also an original source in it).
10. Houssem Eddine Chachia, "Moment of Choice: The Moriscos on the Border of Christianity and Islam," in Claire Norton (ed.), *Conversion and Islam in the Early Modern Mediterranean: The Lure of the Other* (London: Routledge, 2016), 129–154, 135.

11. Donald Frederick Lach and Edwin J. Van Kley (eds.), *Asia in the Making of Europe, Volume 3: A Century of Advance, Book 4: East Asia* (London: University of Chicago Press, 1993), 164–170.
12. Olatz Villanueva Zubizarreta, "The Moriscos in Tunisia," in Mercedes Garcia-Arenal and Gerard Wiegers (eds.), *The Expulsion of the Moriscos from Spain: A Mediterranean Diaspora* (Leiden: Brill, 2017), 357–387, 375–376.
13. Ibid., 375–376.
14. Jessica Roitman, The Same but Different?: Inter-cultural Trade and the Sephardim, 1595–1640 (Leiden: Brill, 2011), 63–110, 92.
15. Luca Molà, *The Silk Industry of Renaissance Venice* (Baltimore, MD: Johns Hopkins University Press, 2000), 64–68.
16. Roitman, The Same but Different?, 92
17. John Efron, Steven Weitzman, and Matthias Lehmann, *The Jews: A History* (London: Routledge, 2018), 249–250.
18. Asher Salah, "An Attempted Morisco Settlement in Early Seventeenth-Century Tuscany," in Kevin Ingram and Juan Ignacio Pulido Serrano (eds.), *The Conversos and Moriscos of Late Medieval Spain and Beyond, Volume 3: Displaced Persons* (Leiden: Brill, 2009), 164–197, 194–195.
19. This document, found in ACEL Filza de Minutas 3 (1740–1746), August 2, 1745, is examined in Matthias B. Lehman, "*La Puerta de la Franquia*: Livorno and Pan-Jewish Networks of Beneficence in the Eighteenth Century," in Francesca Bregoli, Carlotta Ferrara degli Uberti, and Guri Schwarz (eds.), *Italian Jewish Networks from the Seventeenth to the Twentieth Century* (Basingstoke: Palgrave Macmillan, 2012), 39–58, 54
20. Lehman, "*La Puerta de la Franquia*," 53; ACEL Filza de Minutas 4 (1747–1751), October 26, 1747.
21. Lehman, "*La Puerta de la Franquia*," 53; ACEL Filza de Minutas 10 (1782–1788), November 26, 1782 and April 13, 1783.
22. Lehman, "*La Puerta de la Franquia*," 44
23. Stephanie Nadalo, "Populating a 'Nest of Pirates, Murtherers, etc.': Tuscan Immigration Policy and *Ragion di Stato* in the Free Port of Livorno," in Timothy G. Fehler, Greta Grace Kroeker, Charles H. Parker, and Jonathan Ray (eds.), *Religious Diaspora in Early Modern Europe: Strategies of Exile* (London: Routledge, 2016), 31–46, 38.
24. Greene, Catholic Pirates and Greek Merchants, 92–94.
25. Ibid., 94 n. 61
26. Nadalo, "Populating a 'Nest of Pirates, Murtherers, etc.,'", 31–46.

27. Ibid., 41–42.
28. Katerina Galani, British Shipping in the Mediterranean during the Napoleonic Wars (Leiden: Brill, 2017), 95–97.
29. N. Brooke, *Observations on the Manners and Customs of Italy with Remarks on the Vast Importance of British Commerce on that Continent* (London: Bath, R. Crutwell, 1798), 212–213; Galani, British Shipping in the Mediterranean during the Napoleonic Wars, 95–100, 97.
30. Daniel Schroeter, *The Sultan's Jew: Morocco and the Sephardi World* (Stanford: Stanford University Press, 2002), 40–45.
31. Samuel Romanelli, *Travail in an Arab Land* (London: University of Alabama Press, 2004), 123–124.
32. Ibid., 124.
33. Alessandro Guetta, Philosophy and Kabbalah: Elijah Benamozegh and the Reconciliation of Western Thought and Jewish Esotericism, trans. Helena Kahan (Albany: SUNY Press, 2009), 67–68.
34. Francesca Fauri, "A Provincial Level Analysis of Italian Emigration to African in Mass Migration Years: Who Left and Why," in Elena Ambrosetti, Donatella Strangio, and Catherine Wihtol de Wenden (eds.), *Migration in the Mediterranean: Socio-economic Perspectives* (London: Routledge, 2016), 15–31.
35. Daniel J. Schroeter, *The Sultan's Jew: Morocco and the Sephardi World* (Stanford: Stanford University Press, 2002), 41–42.
36. Keith Walter, "Education for Jewish Girls in Late Nineteenth- and Early Twentieth-Century Tunis and the Spread of French in Tunisia," in Emily Benichou Gottreich and Daniel J. Schroeter (eds.), *Jewish Culture and Society in North Africa* (Bloomington: Indiana University Press), 257–281, 261.

Chapter 10

1. Michael V. Leggere, Napoleon and the Struggle for Germany: The Franco-Prussian War of 1813, Volume 1, The War of Liberation Spring 1813 (Cambridge: Cambridge University Press, 2015), 21–32.
2. Francesca Bregoli, Mediterranean Enlightenment: Livornese Jews, Tuscan Culture, and Eighteenth-Century Reform (Stanford: Stanford University Press, 2014), 35–38.
3. Konstantina Zanou, Transnational Patriotism in the Mediterranean, 1800–1850: Stammering the Nation (Oxford: Oxford University Press, 2018), 137–140; Maurizio Isabella, Risorgimento in Exile: Italian Émigrés and the Liberal International in the Post-Napoleonic Era (Oxford: Oxford University Press, 2009), 69–73.

4. Harry Hearder, *Italy in the Age of the Risorgimento 1790–1870* (London: Routledge, 1983), 82–84.
5. Arnold Anthony Schmidt, *Byron and the Rhetoric of Italian Nationalism* (Palgrave: New York, 2010), 29–30.
6. Alyssa Reiman, "Claiming Livorno: Commercial Networks, Foreign Status, and Culture in the Italian Jewish Diaspora, 1815–1914," PhD dissertation, University of Michigan, 2017, 53–54.
7. Ibid., 53–54.
8. Sarah A. Curtis, *Civilizing Habits: Women Missionaries and the Revival of French Empire* (Oxford: Oxford University Press, 2010), 131–150.
9. Leon Carl Brown, *The Tunisia of Ahmad Bey, 1837–1855* (Princeton, NJ: Princeton University Press, 1974), 323–325.
10. Curtis, *Civilizing Habits*, 101–130.
11. Ibid., 131–135.
12. Keith Walters, "Education for Jewish Girls in Late Nineteenth- and Early Twentieth-Century Tunis and the Spread of French in Tunisia," in Emily Benichou Gottreich and Daniel J. Schroeter (eds.), *Jewish Culture and Society in North Africa* (Bloomington: Indiana University Press, 2011), 257–281.
13. Julia A. Clancy-Smith, *Mediterraneans: North Africa and Europe in an Age of Migration, c. 1800–1900* (Berkeley: University of California Press, 2012), 268–270.
14. Sarah Taieb-Carlen, *The Jews of North Africa: From Dido to De Gaulle* (Lanham, MD: Rowman & Littlefield, 2010), 125–127.
15. Ibid., 125–126.
16. Clancy-Smith, *Mediterraneans*, 278–279.

Chapter 11

1. Rudolf Agstner, "Palazzo Venezia in the mid-19th Century: Contributions by Gaspare Fossati and Domenico Pulgher" in Paolo Girardelli and Ezio Godoli (eds.), *Italian Architects and Builders in the Ottoman Empire and Modern Turkey: Design Across Borders* (Newcastle upon Tyne: Cambridge Scholars, 2017), 29–44, 31–32.
2. The document is found in the Austrian State Archives' House, Court, and State Archives (Haus-Hof und Staatsarchiv, HHStA), which was founded in 1749 as a central repository in Vienna of legal and imperial documents of the House of Habsburg. Submission Buol 5150 / A of May 6, 1855, imperial resolution of May 12, 1855, box 15, Dept. 6, AR, HHStA. Agstner, "Palazzo Venezia in the mid-19th Century," 31.

3. Thomas Row, *Economic Nationalism in Italy: The Ansaldo Company, 1882–1921* (Baltimore, MD: Johns Hopkins University Press, 1988), 76–77.
4. Timothy Winston Childs, *Italo-Turkish Diplomacy and the War Over Libya: 1911–1912* (Leiden: Brill, 1990), 84–86.
5. Reiman, "Claiming Livorno," 253–254.
6. Tamara Van Kessel, *Foreign Cultural Policy in the Interbellum: The Italian Dante Alighieri Society and the British Council Contesting the Mediterranean* (Amsterdam: Amsterdam University Press, 2016), 35–47.
7. Reiman, "Claiming Livorno," 234–246.
8. Ibid., 234–235; Luigi Balboni, *Gli Italiani nella civiltà egiziana del secolo XIX* (Alexandria: Società Dante Alighieri, 1906), 3:480–481.
9. Wizārat al-Māliyah, *The Census of Egypt Taken in 1907* (Reprinted: UC Southern Regional Library Facility), 29; Lanver Mak, *The British in Egypt: Community, Crime and Crises, 1822–1922* (New York: I. B. Tauris, 2012), 23–24.
10. Rosetta Giuliani Caponetto, *Fascist Hybridities: Representations of Racial Mixing and Diaspora Cultures under Mussolini* (New York: Palgrave, 2016), 57–92.
11. Lucia Re, "Alexandria Revisited Colonialism and the Egyptian Works of Enrico Pea and Giuseppe Ungaretti," in Patrizia Palumbo (ed.), *A Place in the Sun: Africa in Italian Colonial Culture from Post-Unification to the Present* (Berkeley: University of California Press, 2003), 163–196.

ACKNOWLEDGMENTS

This book was completed while conducting research and teaching at several institutions. They include, most importantly, the Ottoman archives, Venetian archives, Florentine archives, Genoese archives, Portuguese archives, Spanish archives, the University of Wisconsin-Madison, New York University, Princeton University, Koç University in Istanbul, the American School of Classical Studies in Athens, the Università Ca' Foscari in Venice, Ewha Womans University in Seoul, the University of Tokyo, the National University of Singapore, Bates College, Bowdoin College, AUI: Al Akhawayn University in Ifrane (Morocco), and the Hillary Clinton Center for Women's Empowerment (Morocco).

At UW-Madison, where I was Robert Kingdon Fellow at the Institute for Research in the Humanities, I thank Director Dr. Susan Friedman for her leadership. I also thank Dr. Csanád Ziklos at the Institute for Regional and International Studies for hosting me as a Visiting Scholar. At NYU and Princeton, I thank the faculty and library staff for access to the universities' special collections.

At Koç University in Istanbul, I thank Dr. Scott Redford (SOAS, University of London) for recommending new directions in the study of the Republic of Venice. At the American School of Classical Studies in Athens, I thank Dr. Maria Georgeopolou for insights on Greek cultural networks across global history. At Università Ca' Foscari in Venice, I thank Dr. Maria Pia Pedani for guiding my expertise in the use of the Venetian and Ottoman archives.

At Ewha Womans University, I thank Dr. Harris Kim for inviting me to teach a course exploring the intersections of history and sociology. At the University of Tokyo, I thank Dr. Nagasawa Eiji and Dr. Soto Emi for introducing me to new dimensions of global history from non-Western perspectives. At the National University of Singapore, I thank Dr. Peter Borschberg and Dr. Wang Gungwu for offering new insights and directions in my global history research.

At Al Akhawayn University in Ifrane (AUI) and the Hillary Clinton Center for Women's Empowerment, I thank Dr. Chris Taylor and Dr. Asma Abbas for their support of my continued research and pedagogy. I also thank the faculty of both Bates College and the wider NESCAC liberal arts consortium, including Dr. Russell Hopley and Dr. Robert Morrison of Bowdoin, for encouraging my interdisciplinarity in research and pedagogy.

I thank the staff of the archival libraries, university libraries, and museums who welcomed me throughout the course of this book's completion, including Middle East and Islamic Studies Librarian Peter Magierski of Columbia University.

At Edinburgh University Press, I thank Nicola Ramsey and Rachel Bridgewater for taking on this project and offering invaluable insights on its content and direction. I also thank editorial assistant Isobel Birks and managing desk editor Eddie Clark for shepherding it through production. I thank Professor Carole Hillenbrand and the anonymous peer reviewers for feedback and insights on an earlier version of the manuscript.

Most importantly, I would like to express a heartfelt thanks to my family, friends, and students for their great company, conversation, community, and inspiration.

INDEX

Aachen, 3, 42, 45, 59
Abbasid, 20, 25, 27, 41, 55, 84, 86–8, 99, 116, 157, 165, 172
Abbey, 49, 58
abbots, 38, 40–1, 46, 48–51, 58–9, 91–2
Achaemenid, 8, 24–5
Adriatic, 3, 9–11, 20, 34, 37, 64, 82–3, 99, 124, 130–2, 134, 139, 144–5, 148, 154, 176, 189, 205
Aegean, 6, 9, 11, 16, 20, 24, 26, 69, 82–3, 93, 97–9, 101, 112–16, 118, 122–4, 126, 128–9, 131, 134–5, 140, 146, 149–50, 152, 156, 172, 205, 207, 213, 217
Aleppo, 20, 54, 70, 184, 205
Alexandria, 2–3, 11–12, 14–17, 23, 40, 44, 68, 70, 83, 85–6, 88–9, 108, 110, 117, 124–5, 127, 138, 147, 150, 154–5, 170, 184, 190, 192, 194, 196, 198, 202, 204, 207–20
Algeria, 13, 52, 55, 70, 187, 189, 196–7, 200, 206, 209
Alhambra, 127–8, 169, 172
Almohads, 7, 71, 74–7, 83–5, 98, 106–7, 184
Almoravids, 75–6, 106

Amalfi, 6, 58, 108
ambassador, 14, 83, 110, 122, 142, 153, 219
Americas, 95, 107, 130, 173, 190
Amsterdam, 20, 169, 173–4, 183, 198
Anatolia, 4, 24, 27, 29–30, 82, 86–7, 146, 154, 205, 207
Ancona, 3, 9–10, 34, 72, 130–2, 135, 139, 145–6, 149, 154, 164, 168, 174, 178
Andalusi, 116, 159, 164, 170
Annaba, 55, 77, 102
Antioch, 40, 67, 69–70, 89, 94, 147
Arabia, 3, 20, 22–3, 25–6, 28, 30–2
Arabia Petraea, 3, 23, 26, 28, 31–2
Aragonese, 75, 127–8, 144, 163
Aramaic, 23, 25, 29, 79–80, 164
archbishop, 40, 47, 60–1, 72–3, 77, 90, 92–4
Armenian, 68–70, 80, 82, 116, 123, 164, 168, 172, 175–6, 179, 217, 220
Arsenale, 8, 57, 85
Ashkenazi, 171, 173
Asia, 4, 18, 20–2, 24, 86, 95, 98, 112, 123, 158, 169–70, 179
Athens, 3, 23–4, 156

Atlantic, 7–8, 20–1, 54, 76, 95, 101, 107, 123, 129, 132
Augustus, 24, 26, 29, 45
Aurelius, 24, 30, 32
Austria, 24, 190, 192, 204
Awrantis, 23, 27
Ayyubid, 5, 80, 86–7, 99, 108, 110

Babylon, 24–5
Baghdad, 3, 19–20, 25, 54–5, 84–8, 99, 110
Baldwin, 89, 94, 109
Balearics, 62, 74–5, 77, 104–6
Balkans, 28, 32, 82, 118, 132, 135, 141, 153, 171, 206
banking, 98, 140, 154, 204
Barcelona, 7, 75, 102, 105–6
Bedouin, 23, 81
Beirut, 2, 89, 109, 165–6, 205
Belgium, 42
Berber, 42, 52–3, 55, 65, 80
Beyazid, 132, 141
beys, 87, 118, 192, 196
bilingual, 33, 80, 116, 217–18, 220
bishop, 9, 25, 31, 34–5, 38–40, 45, 47, 50, 58, 60–1, 63, 70, 93–4
Boccara, 198
Braudel, 20–2
Britain, 15–16, 188, 190, 205–6
Byzantines, 1, 33–4, 63, 99, 108, 113, 115–16, 150
Byzantion, 26–7, 32
Byzantium, 74, 108, 125

Caesar, 2–3, 23–30, 33, 45, 50–1, 73
Caffa, 111–15
Cairo, 2–6, 9–10, 13–17, 20, 41, 52–3, 55, 57, 65, 68–71, 73–4, 77–81, 83–8, 99, 108, 110, 116–17, 130, 132, 140–2, 145, 153–4, 157–8, 170, 184, 190, 194, 198, 204, 207, 212, 214–17, 220

caliph, 35, 57, 67–70, 77, 83, 88, 107
caliphate, 4, 7, 20, 25, 27, 33, 41–2, 44, 52–3, 55, 65, 87, 98
carracks, 21, 79
Carthage, 3, 22–3, 25, 35, 37–42, 44, 47, 50, 52–6, 74
Castile, 7, 98, 107, 169
Castilian, 5, 105, 107, 127–8, 144, 163, 213
Catalan, 75, 105–7, 112
Catholicism, 43, 95, 167, 172, 178–9, 190, 193–4, 199–200
Chalcedonian, 34–5, 43, 51, 66
Charlemagne, 3, 42, 44–5, 47–9, 60–1, 64–5, 88
China, 7, 18–20, 82, 85, 95, 104, 124, 169
Chios, 112–14, 117, 153
Christianity, 2, 23, 25, 31, 34–5, 43, 51, 53
chronicler, 31, 62, 67, 82, 100
Church, 9, 25, 34–5, 44, 61–3, 66, 73, 94–5, 110–11, 117, 124, 129, 147, 156, 176–8
Cialente, Fausta, 12, 208, 215
Clement, 61, 93, 129–30, 145–6, 168
Cleopatra, 3, 23, 25, 28
cleric, 39, 62, 90, 93, 198
cog, 8, 21, 100–1, 104
Constantinople, 1, 3–4, 8, 24, 26–8, 30, 32–5, 37–41, 43–9, 51, 54–5, 59, 65–6, 69, 89, 99, 107–9, 112, 115–16, 123–5, 127, 138, 140, 147, 150–2, 156
consul, 41, 89, 96, 103, 107, 109, 111, 113, 115, 150, 152–3, 178–80, 195, 197, 212
consulate, 15, 111, 116, 204, 216
conversos, 9, 123, 128–30, 169, 172–3, 178
Copenhagen, 20, 147
Coptic, 16, 40, 82, 116, 147, 207, 217
Cordoba, 3–4, 52, 79
corsairs, 118–20

Crete, 114, 123
Crimean, 20, 99, 112–13
Crusaders, 1, 57, 84–5, 88, 99, 109, 112, 115
Crusades, 34, 38, 46–7, 49, 51, 53, 55–61, 63, 84, 86–7, 89, 94, 108, 165
Cyprus, 123, 133, 206–7

Dagobert, 47, 50, 60–1, 72, 90
Dalida (Iolanda Gigliotti), 15, 190, 198, 214, 216, 218
Danube, 24, 26–7, 30, 33
decentralized, 97, 100, 106, 163
democratic, 13, 189–90
Denia, 75, 106
diaspora, 11, 13–14, 100, 105, 114, 190, 192, 194, 201, 212–13
dinars, 65, 67
diocese, 34, 39, 41, 44, 47, 50, 52, 56, 60–1
diplomacy, 44, 58, 65, 68, 70–1, 73–4, 76, 84–6, 97–8, 106–7, 132–3, 135–6, 142–3, 197, 213
Djem, 141–2, 156
doge, 11, 41, 95, 113, 125–6, 157, 175, 185
Doria, 111–12
dragomans, 2, 121, 137
Dubrovnik, 9–10, 126
ducats, 128–9, 142
Duchy, 6, 9–11, 13, 39, 44, 139, 141, 143, 149, 156, 162, 172, 187–8, 191, 194
Duke, 10, 39, 142, 144, 148, 161–3, 190–1
Dutch, 8, 10, 18–19, 95, 128, 130–1, 136–7, 154, 159, 170, 178–9, 188
ecclesiastical, 34–5, 37–42, 47, 52, 57, 59–61, 63–4, 124, 146, 165, 167

Edirne, 123–4, 140
Egyptian, 3, 16–17, 27, 67, 70, 83, 87–8, 109–11, 142, 158, 160, 193, 207–12, 214–20
Elagabalus, 32, 55

embargoes, 53, 72
Emessa, 23, 27–8, 31–2, 55–6
emir, 80–1, 86, 107
emirates, 51, 57, 60, 62–6, 74, 83, 127
emperor, 23–4, 26–8, 30–3, 38, 40, 44–5, 55, 60–1, 93, 112, 124
empress, 27, 30, 32, 89
England, 17, 98, 100–3, 166, 174, 178
espionage, 120, 133–4, 153
evangelism, 45, 95
Exarchate, 37–39, 41–4, 55
excommunicated, 40, 61, 93, 147
expulsion, 15, 77, 127–8, 203, 207
extraterritorial, 15, 98, 121, 204, 207, 216
Ezra, 79–80

Fascism, 12, 16, 208, 215–16
Fatimid, 20, 52–3, 55, 57, 65, 67–70, 77, 79, 83–4, 86–8, 108, 111, 157, 172
Fener, 122
Ferdinando, 10, 143, 149–50, 159, 161, 163–7, 173, 177–8
Ferrara, 135, 174
Fez, 11, 54–5, 138, 181–2, 186
Florence, 4–7, 9–13, 46–8, 53, 59–60, 73, 98, 101, 130, 138–40, 142–4, 148–51, 153–8, 160, 162, 164–5, 167–8, 172, 176–7, 182
Fokaia, 101, 112–13
fondaco, 21, 83, 85, 105, 107–9, 115, 117, 168, 172
Francia, 3, 17, 25, 27, 35
Francophile, 193, 206
Francophone, 11, 13, 196, 198, 200–1, 212, 216
Frankish, 3, 17, 19, 25, 34–5, 38, 41–9, 64, 81, 83–4, 86, 116–17
Franks, 3, 25, 33–4, 36, 38, 41–4, 47, 50, 56, 59, 88
Frederick, 5, 66, 106, 108

Gabès, 55, 57, 68, 70
Galata, 1, 111, 119–20, 152
galley, 8, 101–2, 104
Genghis, 69
Genizah, 78
Genoa, 1, 3, 6–8, 10–12, 34, 42, 46, 53–4, 91, 98, 100–1, 103–6, 108, 110–15, 182
Genoese, 1, 3–4, 6–9, 11, 14, 21, 52–3, 57, 62, 65, 67, 69, 74–9, 81–6, 88–91, 94–121, 123–4, 130, 134, 138, 140, 143, 150, 156, 159–60, 162, 168, 188, 190–1, 209, 213, 216
Germanic, 24, 26, 34, 38–9, 42–3, 45, 59, 61
Germany, 42, 44, 49, 93, 95, 147–8, 153, 206
Ghassanids, 23, 28, 33
Gibraltar, 183–4
Gigliotti, Iolanda (Dalida), 15, 190, 198, 214, 216, 218
giraffe, 142, 155
Giuliano, 129, 140, 143–4, 147–8, 168
Goths, 24, 28, 30, 32–4, 36–8, 43
government, 8, 18, 87, 92, 107, 113, 129–31, 136, 138, 143, 152, 176, 188, 193, 195–6, 199–202, 206, 211–12
Granada, 7, 55, 78, 98, 107, 127
Greece, 134, 152, 205, 213
Greek, 1, 3–6, 8, 11, 15, 17, 19–21, 24, 29, 33, 35, 38–41, 44–5, 62, 64, 80, 86–90, 92, 95, 108, 113–14, 116, 120, 122–6, 131, 134, 138, 144, 146, 148, 151–2, 156–7, 164–5, 167, 172, 175–8, 189, 193–4, 204, 207, 213–14, 216–18, 220
Gucci, 1–2, 4
Guiscard, 64–5, 69, 93, 108
gunpowder, 19–20

Habsburg, 5–6, 76, 95, 98–100, 104–5, 108, 128–9, 133–4, 144–5, 148–9, 163, 188, 213

Hanseatic, 9, 20–1, 82, 96, 100–2
haraç, 117, 119–20
Hawran, 23, 27, 30
Hebrew, 78–80, 145, 157, 175–6, 185
Hellenistic, 23, 26, 40–1, 45, 51, 95, 123, 126, 156
Heraclius, 33
heresies, 129–30
heretics, 178
Hijaz, 23
Hippo, 55
historians, 19–22, 200
Hohenstaufen, 5, 66
Homs, 23, 27–8, 32, 55–6
Horde, 99, 113, 115
Hormuz, 82
Hospitaller, 50, 141, 152
hospitals, 196–7
Hungarian, 141–2, 204, 206, 213

Iberia, 7, 9–10, 20, 35, 41, 47, 50, 55–6, 74–5, 99, 103–7, 121, 127–8, 130, 158, 161, 167–9, 172, 183
iconography, 43
Idrisi, 52, 54, 66
Ifriqiya, 52, 54–5, 57, 67, 70, 81
ilkhanate, 69, 86
immigrants, 193–4, 196, 198, 204
Imperator, 29–30, 44–5, 60, 64
imported, 18–19, 58, 88, 175
imports, 18, 21, 84, 103, 110, 166
independence, 28, 34, 36, 40–2, 46–50, 57, 59–60, 63–5, 92, 95, 114, 177, 191, 196, 210
India, 8, 18–19, 153, 173, 179, 188
Indian, 7, 18, 21, 33, 54, 82–3, 95, 118, 123, 129, 137, 152–4, 157
Indies, 6, 21, 181
Indonesia, 7, 82
indulgences, 147

industrialization, 14, 17, 192, 205, 208
Inquisition, 11, 127–30, 145, 162, 173, 177–8, 184
invaded, 19, 65, 93, 206–7
Iran, 9, 24, 31, 86
Iraq, 24–9, 31, 82, 86, 109
Ireland, 179
Irish, 2
Isfahan, 8, 114
Islam, 5, 88, 147
Islamic, 4, 23, 25, 27, 35–7, 55, 57–8, 60, 76, 78, 81, 88, 98, 105, 107–8, 111, 116–17, 128, 130, 132, 147, 155, 169, 173
Istanbul, 1, 4, 7–10, 13–15, 72, 78, 89–90, 95, 100, 105, 111, 120–2, 124, 127, 130–2, 135–6, 139–40, 142–3, 145–6, 148, 150, 152–4, 159, 162, 168, 170–1, 175, 178, 187, 190, 192, 194, 202–5, 216, 218, 220
Italianization, 201, 213
Izmir, 15, 174, 194, 204, 207, 217
Iznik, 158–9

Japan, 18, 20, 95
Japanese, 18–19
Jerusalem, 2, 5, 40, 48, 50, 53, 56–7, 60–1, 66–7, 69, 71–2, 74, 85, 87, 89–91, 93–4, 110, 153, 205
Jesuits, 50, 95, 165, 169
Jesus, 50, 64–5
Jewish, 9, 11, 34, 57, 78–82, 121, 123, 127–7, 139, 144–6, 161, 164, 168, 170–5, 177–8, 181–6, 192–6, 198–202, 208–13, 217
Jordan, 23, 25, 27–8, 31
Judaism, 128, 172–3, 178, 199
Julia, 23, 26–7, 30–2, 55–6
Julius, 2–3, 23–6, 28, 33, 50, 73, 143
Justinian, Emperor 33, 37–9

Kamil, 5, 66
khanates, 4, 8, 113, 115
khedivate, 15, 204, 207, 212, 217
khedives, 15–16, 193, 210
Khurasan, 76
Khurasanid, 77
kingdom, 1, 3, 6, 11–13, 23–5, 41, 43–4, 48, 51, 56, 59, 61, 63, 81, 162, 173, 182, 188–90, 192–3, 204–5, 212–13
Knights, 2, 50, 141, 148, 152
Konya, 86, 154
Kurdish, 80

landlords, 49, 113
Latin, 1, 3–5, 19, 21, 29, 32–3, 35, 38–9, 42–5, 47, 50, 52, 54–6, 60–2, 65–6, 69, 72–3, 75–7, 79, 81–2, 84, 86–95, 99, 106, 108, 116–17, 119–21, 124, 132, 136, 146, 148, 151, 157, 165, 176–8
League, 9, 20–1, 96, 100, 145
Lebanon, 3, 16, 31, 165–6
Leo, 33, 44, 54, 113, 129, 139, 143–7
Levantines, 12, 14, 193, 204
Levantini, 13–14, 190, 193, 203, 205
Libya, 15, 27, 32, 52, 70, 203, 205–7, 213
lighthouse, 155, 166
Ligurian, 104, 159, 213
liturgical, 146, 165, 177
livornans, 163, 165, 167, 169, 171, 173, 175, 177, 179, 181, 183, 185
Livornese, 11–14, 174–6, 178, 181–6, 189, 191–9, 201–2, 208, 210–13
Livorno, 9–11, 92, 98, 126, 131, 138–9, 143, 148–50, 153–4, 156, 161–84, 186–8, 190–1, 193–5, 210
Lombards, 3, 13, 34, 42–4
London, 17–18, 20, 96, 100–3, 112, 173–4, 191, 197
Lucca, 130–1, 191
Luchetto, 113, 115
Lutheran, 147–8

INDEX | 249

Maghrib, 35, 54–5, 72, 74, 76–7, 79, 83–4, 98, 104, 106, 159
Mahdia, 52–7, 60–3, 65–7, 69, 71–2, 74–7, 81, 105
Maimonides, 79–80, 157
Majorca, 75, 101, 105–6
Majorcan, 62, 73, 75, 106
Malta, 68
Maltese, 196
Mamluk, 2, 10, 20, 87, 98, 108, 115–18, 128–9, 132, 140–2, 145, 150, 153, 155, 157–8, 160
Manila, 7–8, 95, 124, 163
Marinetti, Tommaso 12, 208–12, 215
maritime, 3, 5–8, 20, 22, 34, 54, 56, 69, 76, 78–9, 89, 91, 95–6, 98, 114, 118, 138, 176
markgraf, 46–9, 59, 74
Marmara, 20, 99, 112
Maronite, 165–6
Marrakesh, 7, 71, 75, 77, 79, 84, 169
Martel, 41–2
Mary, 110, 160
Mashriq, 35, 54–7, 66, 71–2, 74, 79, 84, 98
Matilda of Tuscany, 3, 46–50, 59–61, 74, 90–1, 93–4, 162
matriarchs, 23, 28, 31–2
Medici family, 4, 9–11, 72, 90, 98, 129–31, 139–40, 142–50, 152, 156–64, 166–70, 178, 187–8
Mediterranean, 2–3, 7–8, 13, 17, 20, 24, 26, 28–9, 34, 38, 41, 46, 48, 51, 57–60, 62, 64–6, 73–4, 76, 78–9, 81–7, 89–90, 95, 98–101, 103–8, 110, 112, 115, 121, 123–4, 126, 128–30, 132–5, 138, 143–5, 149, 153–7, 162, 164–7, 170, 173–5, 179–80, 182–7, 189, 195–6, 205–7, 209, 212, 218
Mehmed II, The Conqueror, 117, 140–1, 143, 153
Melkite, 67, 95, 165

menagerie, 142, 155, 157
mercantile, 123, 125, 127, 133–4, 137, 143, 158, 164, 170, 172, 211, 213
Mexico, 9, 98, 130, 132, 145
Michaelangelo, 164
military, 6–8, 15, 18–19, 24, 26–8, 32, 50, 57, 60, 62, 65, 69, 73, 84–7, 90–1, 99, 101, 105–6, 108–9, 143, 148, 165, 188, 204, 209
monarchy, 7, 15, 92–3, 216–17
monasteries, 35, 48–9, 91–2
Mongol, 69, 86, 99, 113, 115
Moriscos, 168–71, 173, 178
Morocco, 169, 182–3, 186, 198
multiconfessional, 15, 175, 194, 198, 200–1, 215
multilingual, 68, 181, 202
Muslims, 2, 5, 8, 10, 95, 110, 117, 127, 162, 164, 166–8, 170, 172, 175, 196–7, 200, 209, 217
Mussolini, 12, 15, 25, 192, 194, 208–9, 212, 215–16

Naples, 64–5, 133, 143–4
Napoleon, 6–8, 11, 13, 180, 185, 187–8
Nasrid, 78, 98, 107
Nasser, Gamal Abdel 16, 210–11, 218
nationalism, 16, 122, 126, 189, 193–4, 215–17
naval, 6–7, 46, 53, 57, 59–60, 64, 68, 71, 73, 89, 97, 105–6, 108–9, 112, 163, 165, 205
Nestorian, 25, 165
nineteenth, 12, 14, 122, 182, 185–6, 190, 193, 195–6, 198, 201–2, 205, 210, 213
Norman, 5, 54, 57, 59–60, 63–71, 77, 80–1, 83, 90, 93, 108, 155, 185
Norway, 100, 147
notarial, 110, 115, 135, 170

Odoacer, 24, 27, 33–6, 38–40, 45, 54
Orient, 156, 179, 204
Orthodox, 5–6, 11, 35, 40, 66, 68, 82, 92, 95, 116–17, 120, 123–4, 126, 131, 146–8, 156, 165, 177, 179, 189, 217
Ostrogoths, 3, 24, 26, 33–4, 43
Ottoman, 4–6, 8–11, 14–16, 20, 34, 78, 85, 87, 89–91, 94–5, 98–100, 104–5, 108, 111–12, 115–56, 158–9, 161, 164–8, 171–2, 174–80, 184, 187, 190, 192, 196–7, 203–7, 210–13, 216–17, 220

Padua, 111, 159
painters, 124, 155
Palaiologos, 1, 112–13, 151
Palermo, 5, 19, 52, 54, 57–60, 63–6, 69–71, 81, 155
Palmyrene, 3, 27–30, 51
papacy, 34, 38–61, 63–6, 71–2, 74, 90–3, 113, 126, 141, 143–4, 146, 148, 167
patriarch, 39, 47, 50, 56, 61, 64, 66, 70, 72, 90, 94, 108, 124
patrons, 5, 49, 65, 123, 156, 164
Pera, 1, 4, 6, 89, 110–12, 115–17, 119–20, 123, 140, 150, 152–3, 162, 204
Persian, 2, 4, 24, 26, 54, 80, 82, 84, 131, 157, 159–60, 169
Petra, 23, 28, 30–1
Petraea (Arabia Petraea), 3, 23, 26, 28, 31–2
Philip the Arab, 23, 27–8, 30–2,
Phoenician, 3, 26, 32, 50–2, 54–6
physicians, 79–80, 146, 174, 185
Pisa, 6, 10, 12, 46–8, 50–1, 53–4, 58–64, 69, 72–7, 84, 89–94, 98, 105–6, 109–10, 149, 153, 159, 161–2, 165–6
Pisanorum, 62, 73, 75, 89
podestà, 111, 115–17
Poland, 118
Pope, 40, 43–4, 54, 61, 73, 92–4, 129, 139, 142–6, 163, 168
porcelain, 7, 18–19, 82, 157–60

Portugal, 7–8, 108, 128–31, 145
Portuguese, 6–8, 79–80, 95, 104, 123, 128–31, 134, 137, 171–3, 179, 185
privatization, 103
Protestant, 95, 144, 147–8, 178, 180
Ptolemaic, 25, 51, 157

Qaitbay, Sultan 141–2, 157–8
Qalawun, Sultan 110–11
qermez, 130–1
quarter, 67, 77, 89, 151
queens, 3, 23, 25, 51, 128, 179

Ragusa, 9, 72, 118, 130, 132, 139, 146, 154, 168, 178
Ravenna, 34, 36–44, 61
Reformation, 163
refugees, 166, 194, 217, 220
Renaissance, 4–5, 8, 17–20, 34, 44, 73, 123, 126, 157, 160, 164
renegades, 2, 5
revolution, 15–16, 23, 79, 193, 215, 217–18
Rex, 24, 64
Risorgimento, 12–14, 91, 111, 162, 191, 202, 204
Roger I and II, 54, 57, 63–71, 77, 80–1, 83, 89–90, 93–4, 108
Romanesco, 149
Romaniote, 134
Romans, 3, 8, 23, 25, 28, 30–1, 33–34, 44–5, 53, 60, 63–4, 66
rudders, 21, 82–3

Safavid, 8–9, 123, 168, 172, 176, 179
saint, 44, 29, 91, 110
Saladin, 57, 59, 66, 71, 80, 84–90, 99, 109–10
Samarqand, 160
Sanu, Yaqub Rafel, 193, 208, 210–12
Sardinia, 68, 191
Sassanians, 8, 25–6, 28, 30–3
Saxon, 92–3

Scandinavia, 20, 147
schism, 35, 40, 44, 51, 124, 146
Senate, 26, 123–6, 130–1, 135, 172
Sephardic, 9, 11, 121, 123, 127–38, 145–6, 164, 168, 170–4, 177, 184, 189, 195, 202, 210–11, 213
Severus, Septimius 27, 32, 55
Seville, 7, 48, 54–5, 74, 98, 100, 105–7
Sfax, 80–1, 153
ships, 11, 21, 68, 77, 80, 82, 89–90, 97, 100, 146, 166, 180, 209
Sicilian, 20, 35, 52, 55, 57, 64–8, 70, 74, 76, 78, 80, 90
Sicily, 39, 47, 56, 60, 62–5, 67–70, 80–1, 93–4, 102, 105, 108, 185
Spain, 7–8, 41, 75–6, 98, 108, 129, 131, 144–5, 149, 166
Spalato, 9–10, 72, 126, 130, 132, 139, 146, 154, 168
Split, 9, 126
sultans, 86, 110, 116, 129, 141–2, 157–8
sumptuary, 131, 133
Syria, 3, 16, 24–32, 48, 55, 67–71, 86–7, 93, 99, 117–18, 128–9, 135, 154, 220
Syriac, 147, 164

Theodora, Empress, 37
Theodoric, 24, 33, 39
Thessaloníki, 133, 135–6
Trieste, 189, 213
Tunisia, 3, 13, 52–6, 65, 68, 70, 74, 80–1, 85, 184, 187, 189, 196–201, 206, 209, 213, 220
Tuscany, 1, 3, 6, 9–11, 40, 43, 47, 49, 60–1, 63, 90–1, 129, 138–9, 142–3, 149, 153–6, 158–9, 161–3, 165–7, 172, 177–8, 180, 182, 184–5, 187–96, 202, 211

Ukraine, 112, 118
Umayyads, 3, 20, 28, 33, 41, 52, 54–6, 66, 116
unionism in Christian theology, 124–5, 151
urban, 76, 79–80, 102, 131–2, 204
urbanization, 48
usurped, 25, 87

Vaballathus, 29–30
Valencia, 102, 106–7
Valencian, 157, 159
Vandals, 3, 34, 37–8, 43, 53–4
vassals, 33, 51, 53, 56–7, 69, 87, 113
velvet, 9, 95, 123, 130–1, 145
Venice, 1, 6–12, 18, 21, 39–41, 44, 46, 53, 72, 85, 91, 95, 98, 100–5, 107–9, 114, 118–21, 123–8, 130–7, 139–40, 143, 145–6, 152–4, 159–60, 162, 164–8, 171–6, 179, 182, 191
vernacular, 4, 21, 52, 54–6, 73, 81, 193, 208, 214
Vienna, 190–1, 207
Vietnam, 13
Vikings, 20
Visigoths, 3, 24, 26, 33–4, 43
vizier, 67–70, 83, 87

Wallachia, 122
warehouse, 21, 77, 83, 85
wool, 100–3, 153

Zaccaria, 110–13
Zeno, 24, 38, 58
Zenobia, 3, 23, 27–32, 51
Zirid, 52, 55–6, 65, 67, 71, 76, 81
zoo, 142